Technological Evolution, Variety and the Economy

Technological Evolution, Variety and the Economy

Pier Paolo Saviotti

INRA-SERD, University of Grenoble, France

Edward Elgar

Cheltenham, UK • Brookfield, US

Published by
Edward Elgar Publishing Limited
8 Lansdown Place
Cheltenham
Glos GL50 2HU
UK

Edward Elgar Publishing Company
Old Post Road
Brookfield
Vermont 05036
US

British Library Cataloguing in Publication Data
Saviotti, Pier Paolo.
   Technological Evolution, Variety and the
   Economy
   I. Title
   330.01

Library of Congress Cataloguing in Publication Data
Saviotti, Paolo
      Technological evolution, variety, and the economy / Pier Paolo
   Saviotti.
         p.   cm.
      Includes bibliographical references and index.
      1. Evolutionary economics. 2. Technological innovations—Economic
   aspects. 3. Diffusion of innovations—Mathematical models.
   4. Economics, Mathematical. I. Title.
   HB97.3.S28   1996
   338'.064—dc20   95–32858
                                                                          CIP

ISBN 1 85278 774 0

Printed and bound in Great Britain by
Hartnolls Limited, Bodmin, Cornwall

Contents

1. Introduction

QUALITATIVE CHANGE

Technological change seems to have acquired an important place in debates about economic policy. While many people may be aware of its importance, our understanding of the phenomenon of technological change is still very limited. The limitations of our knowledge in this area are not only due to a lack of information. The study of technological change poses some fundamental challenges to the theoretical analysis of socioeconomic reality. First and foremost, technological innovations lead to qualitative change, that is to the emergence of new entities, qualitatively different from those that preceded them, and, therefore, to a change in the composition of the economic system. New outputs, new activities and new actors are amongst the results of technological change. Other categories of innovation (social, legal, organizational) contribute to qualitative change, but perhaps technological innovations are the most fundamental of them. In this sense it is possible that some of the analyses and of the conclusions reached in studies of technological innovation are generalizable to an economics of innovation or of qualitative change.

Such an analysis of qualitative change presents some important difficulties. It could be argued that it is impossible to study it, since the features of entities that are qualitatively different from those that existed before cannot be predicted. Although there is some truth in this criticism, this applies only to the case in which the new entities have nothing in common with pre-existing ones. In fact, very often new entities have something in common with previous ones and the birth of a new entity may be predicted on the basis of inducements created by the development of the previous ones. The study of patterns and regularities in economic evolution can give us some insights which are very useful both at the theoretical and at the policy level. This is not to deny that the study of qualitative change is both more problematic and more challenging than the study of a system that undergoes only quantitative changes. It is perhaps due to these difficulties that in the past economics has confined itself to the study of a system characterized by a constant set of activities. Accordingly, in neoclassical economics technological change leads to productivity growth in this constant set of activities, which in turn lowers prices and causes economic growth. Of course, neoclassical economics is not blind and can see the new outputs, activities and actors, but it can only register their presence ex-post. This would not create any problems if qualitative change were only an accidental by-product of economic development. However, it is argued in this book, and it was one of Schumpeter's central contributions, qualitative change is an essential ingredient of long-term economic development. If this is the case, theories of economic development and growth which do not incorporate qualitative change are likely to incur serious limitations. For this reason the analysis of qualitative change is one of the central concepts in this book.

The importance of qualitative change had been clearly realized by Schumpeter. One of the main tasks of economic theory today consists of giving an analytical structure to the basic Schumpeterian intuitions. A number of generalizations, emerging largely from studies of technological change, are making an important contribution in this sense. Perhaps it is not an accident that so far evolutionary theories, in which qualitative change plays a central role, are largely the result of studies of technological change. In fact in two recent reviews (Nelson, 1995; Dosi and Nelson, 1994) evolutionary theories are distinguished from neo-classical ones for their more explicitly dynamic character. This is true in general, but it is possible to find neoclassical studies which have a dynamics, for example in terms of equations representing the time development of some economic system. However, what is systematically absent from neoclassical treatments is the dynamics of qualitative change.

If we now assume that the study of qualitative change is an important task for economics, we have to pose ourselves the question of how to go about it. In order to try and answer this question we can go back to the way in which technological change was studied in neoclassical economics. There it was expected to lead to productivity growth, to lower prices, to affect rates of outptut growth and international trade. Only the consequences for known economic variables, and not technological change *per se*, were analysed. We can call this an *implicit* approach to the analysis of technological change. By technological change *per se* we mean the actors, activities and objects which create it, such as the institutions, the research laboratories, the types of knowledge, the processes and products, etc. Only by introducing *explicitly* these missing characters into models of technological change can we achieve a full under-standing of qualitative change. Two sets of missing characters, changes in product technology (Chapters 4 to 6) and new forms of knowledge (Chapters 7 to 9) occupy a large portion of this book. The analysis contained in these chapters is an example of an explicit approach to the study of technological change. The use of an explicit approach amounts to an extension of the observation space of economics. Here it is not argued that the simplification that can be achieved in an implicit approach is useless, but that it is limited. For example, an implicit approach rules out ex-ante structural change, the formation of product strategies at firm level, and the dynamics of scientific and technological knowledge.

Therefore, an explicit approach is at least required to complement an implicit approach and to fill the gaps left by it.

As it has already been pointed out, the study of qualitative change creates some very difficult problems. Essentially we are trying to understand why and how a given economic system, characterized by a set of components and interactions is transformed into another system, with different components and interactions. The study of these discontinuous transitions can be carried out much more easily on the basis of relatively recent theoretical developments than on the conceptual foundations of neoclassical economics. For example, transitions leading to qualitative change in their structure are predicted for open systems out of equilibrium. Also, biological models provide us with analogies which can be used to ask important questions and to create models of technological populations. Without pre-empting the discussions that follow, we can make the point that the analysis of qualitative change not only requires an explicit approach to the study of technological change, but must be based on theoretical foundations and methods different from those underlying neoclassical economics. Accordingly, Chapters 2 and 3 of this book are devoted to a discussion of the theoretical and methodological problems involved in the study of technological change.

Summarizing the previous considerations, we could say that qualitative change is the central concern of this book, that an explicit approach is required for the full understanding of the role of technological change, and that new theoretical foundations are required for the study of qualitative change. Technological change is one of the most important ingredients leading to qualitative change. Unsurprisingly, evolutionary theories, which give a central role to qualitative change, have emerged largely from studies of technological innovation. A review of the historical development of studies of innovation and of technological change follows. Such studies fall into three categories. First, there are several studies of the sources of economic growth, in which technological change played an important role; second, there are a number of empirical innovation studies conceived outside orthodox economic theories; third, studies of the diffusion of technological innovation.

Since the classical economists, investment had been considered the main determinant of economic growth. The importance of technological change was taken for granted, as it was self-evident and there was no need to study it. During the 19th century a few authors, such as Marx and Babbage, attempted to analyse the processes and mechanisms of technological change. Within the neoclassical tradition the first author who tried to measure the contribution of technological change and that of investment was Solow (1957). His pathbreaking work inspired a number of studies. For the purposes of this chapter it is useful to remember some features of Solow's work. In his papers, technological change was defined as 'anything that shifts the production function', and it was measured by computing the contribution of investment to economic growth and by deducing it from the total observed growth. That is, technological change was calculated as a residual (Coombs *et al.*, 1987). One could say how much there was of it, but not what it was. This study was a prototype of an implicit approach: technological change increased productivity by shifting the production function, and allowed it to produce a greater output. The actors and processes of technological change remained outside the picture.

The previous criticisms do not attempt to devalue Solow's contribution and the following growth literature. Their aim is only to point out that although an implicit approach, stressing the economic effects of technological change, is useful for some purposes, it is incomplete. Thus an implicit approach could not provide any guidance for the formulation of technology policies aiming at creating or diffusing particular technologies. This limitation of Solow's studies was recognized relatively early, for example by Denison (1962).

EMPIRICAL STUDIES OF INNOVATION

The Second World War, with the success of programmes like the Manhattan (A bomb) and radar, gave a decisive impulse to R&D and to innovation. Although the initial motivation was predominantly military, R&D and innovation expenses increased sharply also in the civilian sector in the main industrialized countries. By the late 1950s the first studies aimed at evaluating the effects of all this increased funding were carried out. Such studies had to understand the mechanisms by which particular innovations were created and adopted. They had to be explicitly concerned with the internal features of innovative processes. They could not use an implicit approach and found very limited guidance in orthodox theories.

Studies such as Hindsight, Traces, Sappho, *Wealth from Knowledge* (Langrish *et al.*, 1972), etc. (see Freeman (1982) and Coombs *et al.* (1987) for a summary of several of these studies) developed empirical, somewhat *ad hoc* approaches to study the determinants of successful technological innovations. Thus they could incorporate findings and phenomena which were completely outside the scope of orthodox studies. In so doing, they created a rich observation base and constituted a sort of natural history of innovation. However, like all empirical studies, they were very limited in their comparability and generalizability. These studies gave rise to the need/demand pull, technology push dichotomy, consisting solely in asking whether need/demand or technology was the most important determinant of successful technological innovations. Such dichotomy quickly turned out to be an oversimplification. Also, the conclusion generally drawn from these studies in the 1970s, that need/demand pull was the most important, turned out not to be warranted by the methodological criteria used in the studies themselves (Mowery and Rosenberg, 1979; Walsh, 1984).

DIFFUSION STUDIES

Diffusion studies were amongst the earliest studies of technological innovation (Griliches, 1957; Mansfield, 1963, 1969). They occupy a particular place amongst general innovation studies. On the one hand, diffusion studies had from the very beginning an analytical framework and, on the other, this analytical framework, which had been borrowed from other disciplines (epidemiology), remained completely separate from the main body of economic theory. It is possible to see the development of diffusion studies as the critical evaluation of the early studies and the attempt to gradually integrate them better within economic theory.

The analytical framework adopted in the early diffusion studies was based on the analogy between the spread of technological innovation and that of contagious diseases. The so called epidemics model (Griliches, 1957; Mansfield, 1963, 1969) gave rise to an expected logistic shape of the diffusion curve. This model provided a good fit of empirical data and until the late 1970s was the dominant model in diffusion studies.

During the 1970s a number of scholars started to point out some deficiencies in the epidemics model. Adopting firms were not identical and it was not equally convenient for them to adopt a given innovation at the same time (David, 1975; Davies, 1979). In order for an innovation to be adopted it had to be produced and the supply side was as important as the demand side (Metcalfe, 1981; Stoneman, 1983). Different innovations could have different shapes of the diffusion curves (Davies, 1979) and post-innovation improvements could change very considerably the scope for the diffusion of an innovation (Metcalfe, 1981). Some attempts to better articulate diffusion models and to integrate them with economic theories were made in an evolutionary direction by Silverberg, Dosi and Orsenigo (1988) and in a neoclassical direction by Stoneman (1983). A recent review of diffusion studies can be found in Antonelli, Petit and Tahar (1992).

The diffusion studies so far referred to generate a diffusion curve of a particular shape (e.g. logistic). More recently, other studies which were not classified as diffusion by their authors are contributing to our understanding of diffusion. Examples are studies of standards and of compatibility, and of competing technologies under increasing returns. Such studies will be described in a later section (see pp. 108, 172).

FROM INNOVATION STUDIES TO EVOLUTIONARY THEORIES

At the stage of development which innovation studies had achieved in the late 1970s it was necessary to retain the explicit approach required to underpin technology policies, but to develop some general concepts and frameworks which could overcome the limitations of purely empirical studies.

A number of generalizations started emerging in the 1970s and 1980s. Rosenberg (1976) spoke of technological imperatives. Abernathy and Utterback (1975, 1978) introduced the idea of a technology life cycle, ending up with a dominant design. Nelson and Winter (1977) introduced the somewhat similar concepts of technological regimes and of natural trajectories. Sahal (1981a and b) talked of technological guideposts and Dosi (1982) of technological paradigms. Such concepts are somewhat different, but they have a common core. First, they imply the existence of patterns of development sufficiently general to be applicable to many if not to all technologies. Second, they imply the presence of discontinuities, during which dramatic qualitative changes take place, followed by generally longer periods of incremental development, during which most participants converge upon common solutions and approaches. Also, such generalizations could be considered the result of opening up the black box of technology (Rosenberg, 1982). A further example of this process of opening up the black box of technology is given by the adoption of a twin characteristics approach to represent product technologies (Saviotti and Metcalfe, 1984; Saviotti, 1991b). This approach has the advantage of allowing an explicit but sufficiently general representation of technologies while being related to some current economic theories.

The seminal work of Nelson and Winter, *An Evolutionary Theory of Economic Change* (1982), proved to be the catalyst and threshold for the development of evolutionary theories. This book combined in a novel way a Schumpeterian approach to economic development and innovation with the behavioural theory of the firm, with the results of innovation and of industrial economics studies, and made a moderate use of biological metaphors. Nelson and Winter's book did not produce a fully-fledged framework for evolutionary theories, but it contained the fundamental ingredients which allowed the development of these theories to begin. Particularly fruitful and well worked out concepts were those of the routines of firms and organizations, and of search activities.

A number of developments followed Nelson and Winter's book. Some analytical models of diffusion and competition (Silverberg, 1987; Silverberg, Dosi and Orsenigo, 1988; Metcalfe and Gibbons, 1987, 1989) started to appear. In 1988 a book (Dosi *et al.*, 1988) brought together a large number of chapters broadly related to an evolutionary metaphor. These chapters had in common a critical position with respect to orthodox theories, the desire to incorporate the results of many studies of technical change, and contained some interesting departures. Thus, for example, the concept of a national system of innovation made its first appearance here (Lundvall, 1988; Freeman, 1988; Nelson, 1988). Also, an important paper by Arthur (1988) proved that path dependence and irreversibility occur in the diffusion of technologies in the presence of increasing returns to adoption. An interesting historical analysis of the development of technology along evolutionary lines has been made by Mokyr (1990a and b, 1991).

At this point we have a twofold problem: (a) why does technological change as a problem/subject of study need evolutionary theories; and (b) what are evolutionary theories; what are their main assumptions/foundations?

A unified framework for evolutionary theories is still to come and cannot be expected to appear overnight. Evolutionary theories are developing by the convergence of a number of research traditions, the most important of which are: the Schumpeterian approach to economic development; the biological research tradition; irreversible thermodynamics; and systems theory and organization theories (Saviotti and Metcalfe, 1991).

EVOLUTIONARY THEORIES

Technological innovation/change gives rise to qualitative change, the emergence of new entities, qualitatively different from those that existed before. All types of innovation, and not only technological (e.g. also organizational) can create qualitative change. This book is mostly concerned with technological innovation, but some of the generalizations about it may be applicable to other types of innovation. A theory emerging from a generalization of technical change must include qualitative/structural change as one of its fundamental problems. Orthodox theory excludes the study of the reasons for which qualitative/structural change emerges and the mechanisms by means of which it contributes to economic development. An evolutionary theory can provide a better generalization of the phenomenon of technological innovation or, more in general, of any type of innovation leading to qualitative change in the economic system.

The previous paragraph begins to define qualitative change as one of the fundamental aspects of evolutionary theories, differentiating them from orthodox ones. The nature of evolutionary theories as they are developing now is identified by many other assumptions and approaches which will be discussed in greater detail in Chapter 3. However, some of their main aspects deserve to be briefly mentioned here. Economic systems in most cases are likely to be open systems. The transitions in such systems are likely to be irreversible and path dependent. The point can be made in general (Prigogine and Stengers, 1984; Nicolis and Prigogine, 1989) and has been given an application to economic and technological phenomena by Arthur (1983, 1988, 1989a) in situations characterized by increasing returns to adoption. Furthermore, transitions in open systems can give rise to multistability. This has the interesting implication that different institutional configurations can be equally stable and produce equivalent outcomes. Thus the imitation of the institutional configurations which gave rise to successful technological innovations in country A is not necessary in order for country B to be able to reproduce the same innovations.

In a similar way to what innovation studies had done for technologies, a number of organization theories had attempted to open up the black box of the firm. The term organization theories is used here to include post neoclassical theories of the firm (Cyert and March, 1963), business history studies (Chandler, 1962, 1977), transaction cost analysis (Williamson, 1975, 1985), and a number of other organizational studies (e.g. McKelvey, 1982; Lawrence and Lorsch, 1967; Emery and Trist, 1965). As opposed to the neoclassical structureless and conflictless profit-maximizing unit, these theories stress the boundaries of the firm, its internal structures, its conflicts, and its limited rationality.

Biology with its description of the evolution of species provides a powerful metaphor which can be used to ask questions in economics. Technologies and organizational forms can be conceptualized as species and the problem of qualitative change finds a much more natural home in a biologically inspired vision than in orthodox economics. Also, a population approach, which is generally absent in economics, is currently used in biology. Naturally it would be very dangerous to translate to economics any conclusions reached in biology. The usefulness of the biological research tradition consists in formulating problems and hypotheses, not in providing answers.

Thus evolutionary theories start from the Schumpeterian tradition, but integrate within it other research traditions. A recent book by Hodgson (1993) places evolutionary economics in the context of economic thought.

Another problem which represents one of the most important challenges for economic theory, and which has been particularly stressed by studies of technological change, is that of the creation and utilization of knowledge. If we start defining technology as a means by which mankind adapts to its external environment, we can then distinguish between artefacts or exosomatic instruments (Georgescu Roegen, 1971) and knowledge. Both represent means of adaptation, but exosomatic instruments provide adaptation to a given environment, while knowledge allows, in principle, adaptation to different and changing environments. The two are related in the sense that artefacts can be considered embodied knowledge. To the extent that economic theories have been concerned with technological change, they have been concerned with artefacts, usually in the form of capital equipment. Recent developments in studies of technological change and of organizations have started analysing the collective knowledge which is created in organizations by means of concepts such as knowledge base and corporate capabilities. Such developments will be analysed in Chapter 8.

OUTLINE OF THE BOOK

In the previous section it was argued that an explicit approach to the study of technological change which takes qualitative change into account can be more adequately developed on an evolutionary basis than on that of neoclassical economics. The main purpose of this book is not to make claims for a particular theory, but to contribute to our understanding of technological change. However, given the discussion in the previous sections of this chapter, a more adequate definition of what is meant by evolutionary theories and some methodological criteria needed to compare theories are required. Accordingly, Chapter 2 develops these methodological criteria and Chapter 3 provides a more extended discussion of the nature of evolutionary theories.

An explicit representation of technological change must take into account the characters that create and use it, such as products, processes and their characteristics, individuals with their qualifications, experience and their modes of interaction in organizations. This book cannot claim to have taken into account all the possible characters and mechanisms of technological change, only some of them. In this sense it constitutes more an example of an explicit approach than its complete application to the economic analysis of technological change. The particular characters that are given greater prominence at the beginning of the book are product technologies. Chapter 4 provides a generalized representation of product technologies, which relies on a twin characteristics approach, similar to that developed by Lancaster (1966) for quite different purposes, and on a population approach. Such an approach allows us to incorporate a considerable number of concepts and results of innovation studies, and to do it in a systematic, generalizable way, avoiding the *ad hoc* character of many early innovation studies. In Chapter 5 such general representation of product technology is applied to a number of examples and allows us to perform technology mapping, that is to follow the evolution of real technological populations in characteristics space.

The twin characteristics representation and its application to a number of examples are based on a partly inductive approach. Their derivation relies partly on the observations made in a number of empirical innovation studies. This does not imply an undue confidence in induction as a method for theory formulation but simply the assumption that theories have a limited power. Using a terminology which will be more fully developed in Chapter 2 we can say that theories have a *local* character, that is, their effectiveness in explaining phenomena falls as we move away from the phenomena for which the theories were initially created. Thus theories which were created to correlate economic variables will be less effective or ineffective when applied to variables representing technological artefacts or scientific theories. Such considerations imply that a certain degree of realism is necessary in the construction of theories, especially if they are intended to have policy implications. In fact, the explicit approach to technological change advocated at the beginning of this chapter represents a realistic approach to the problem.

At this point the next logical steps are, on the one hand, to use the results of the twin characteristics representation to formulate an analytical model of technological evolution and, on the other, to link technological evolution to economic development.

Qualitative change is an extremely important part of economic development, to which technological change makes a fundamental contribution. Economic theory has generally taken the composition of the economic system as given. Structural change, as the change in the composition of the economic system is more often changed, has been analysed only in less orthodox and more historically oriented economic literature (see, for example, Tylecote, 1993; Freeman, Clark and Soete, 1982). One of the few analytical attempts to deal with the problem of structural change has been that of Pasinetti (1981, 1993). However, even in his case, technological change has been treated in a largely implicit way. One of the goals of this book is to link an explicit analysis of technological change to the qualitative or structural change which takes place in the course of economic development. The problem is to find an analytical approach which links the analysis of technological change to that of economic development. It will be done here by following two axes: first, changes in artefacts and activities will be linked to the concept of variety, as a means of representing qualitative change; and, second, examining changes in knowledge and in institutions.

The outcome of qualitative change is the emergence of new entities and, sometimes, the disappearance of old ones. The diversity or variety of the economic system, defined as the number of distinguishable entities constituting the system, is consequently affected. The entities which are required to define the system are actors, activities and artefacts. It is fairly obvious, even by casual observation, that the variety of the economic system has increased enormously in the course of economic development. Evidence in favour of this statement will be provided later in the book. The question which is posed in Chapter 6 is whether growth in variety is an accidental consequence of economic development or whether it is a fundamental component of it. The answer which is given to this question is that growth in variety is a necessary requirement for the continuation of long-term economic development and that growing variety and growing efficiency in pre-existing activities are complementary tendencies.

Variety is, therefore, an extremely important component of economic development and technological change makes a fundamental contribution to it. As a variable to represent qualitative change, variety has the disadvantage of presenting some measurement problems, but it can provide the basis for an analytical treatment of Schumpeterian dynamics. In Schumpeter's models (1912, 1942) economic development is inextricably linked to qualitative change. Radical innovations, introduced either by entrepreneurs or by large corporations, provide renewed stimulus for the economy and allow the continuation of long-term economic development. Such innovations then change the variety of the system.

The twin characteristics representation (Chapter 4) allows us to map trends in technological evolution. Together with the previous considerations about variety this allows us to formulate a number of hypotheses, which are used in Chapter 7 to establish a model of technological evolution based on replicator dynamics. The model is based on two sets of replicator equations – a more aggregate one of the Lotka Volterra type, and a more micro type. Such replicator equations are of biological origin, but they are suitably modified to represent technological evolution. This model allows us to reach interesting conclusions about: the conditions required for variety growth; the relationship between competition and variety; the role of search activities; and the presence of chaos in technological evolution.

The characters of technological change which have been emphasized up to this point are product technologies. As previously pointed out, knowledge and institutions are equally important characters of technological change. Chapter 8 represents a move towards the analysis of the consequences of technological change for organizational structures. Using the concept of information entropy it is demonstrated that different organizational structures can constitute information saving devices by means of which firms can produce a constant or increasing output variety without raising correspondingly their information costs. In particular, it is demonstrated that division of labour and hierarchical organizations are, among other things, information-saving devices, and that an M-form organization is more information efficient than a U-form organization in producing a given output variety.

The analysis in Chapter 8 runs parallel to and confirms a number of findings in industrial organization, such as the stability of hierarchical organizations. This analyis in its present form does not allow us to explain the emergence of IICAs (inter institutional collaborative agreements). This problem is discussed in Chapter 8, where it is argued that the relative stability of IICAs and of other forms of industrial organization (markets, hierarchies, etc.) can be explained by the balance of division of labour and of coordination in the presence of an external environment of variable complexity and rate of change. In this context, transactions would be a form of coordination. Markets, hierarchies or IICAs would predominate depending on coordination difficulties, which in turn would depend on the external environment. The analysis of Chapter 7 addresses the problem of impact of the information on organizational structures in the absence of coordination problems. Chapter 8, on the other hand, introduces coordination problems and thus justifies the presence, under certain conditions, of IICAs.

Knowledge is a very important component of the external environment of enterprises. Very rapid changes in the nature of knowledge can make existing firms' knowledge bases redundant (see Tushman and Anderson (1986, 1990)).

Radically new knowledge created in universities and research laboratories can present enormous opportunities which cannot be exploited by existing firms, given their knowledge bases. In these conditions either the entry of new high-technology firms established by science-based entrepreneurs or IICAs can overcome the limitations of existing firms' knowledge bases. The growing knowledge intensity of economies (Mytelka, 1991a) seems to be accompanied by a growing degree of interaction of firms and of other organizations. IICAs are an example of this. The fact that not only firms, but also universities, government laboratories, etc., are members of these networks is emphasized by the concept of technoeconomic networks (TEN) (Laredo and Mustar, 1993). Inter-institutional interactions constitute one of the main aspects of the concept of national system of innovation (NSI). This concept, which has been introduced and emphasized recently in the literature on technological change (see, for example, Lundvall, 1985, 1988, 1992; Freeman, 1987, 1988; Nelson, 1988, 1990; Chesnais, 1988; Niosi *et al.*, 1992, 1993), is intended to capture the high degree of specificity which national systems have had up to the present time in generating and adopting technological innovations. The concept is receiving growing attention amongst economists and policy makers, but it is still in need of a complete theoretical explanation. In Chapter 9 it is argued that the main features of the NSI are not explicable in an orthodox economic framework, but that they can be given a logical foundation in terms of evolutionary theories.

Furthermore, the question of the permanence of the NSI is posed. Is the growing trend towards globalization going to make the concept of the NSI redundant? Even leaving aside the time dimension of the problem, that is the slowness of the adjustment towards the hypothetical world economy without any local features, the problem can be formulated as the balance between convergence and divergence in economic systems. Diffusive forces (technology diffusion, technology transfer, international trade, etc.) lead to an international homogenization of practices, while innovation (including organizational and institutional innovation) arises locally and increases heterogeneity. This line of reasoning, combined with the hysteresis and slow adjustment of existing institutional configurations, leads to the conclusion that national and local (e.g. regional) specificity will be around for a while and that globalization will not necessarily make the concept of the NSI redundant.

Summarizing briefly, this book starts from methodological and theoretical considerations underlying evolutionary theories, proceeds to formulate a model of technological evolution in which qualitative change and variety play a prominent role, and examines the relationship of variety to economic development, and of changes in technological knowledge and variety to institutional and organizational structures. The book does not claim to have solved these problems which have occupied a prominent place in the economic analysis of technological change. However, it is hoped that it has made some progress towards a more general and coherent treatment of the previously mentioned aspects of technological change, which are of growing policy relevance, but which have generally been neglected by orthodox economic theories. Finally, a brief observation must be made about the espousal of evolutionary theories. This is not done in the spirit of opposing different research traditions as if they were armies. Trench warfare is rarely, if ever, productive. The main thrust of this book comes from the acknowledgement that technological change, like a number of other economically relevant phenomena, is quite intractable with the concepts traditionally used in economics. As some of the most intellectually sensitive and open minded exponents of the orthodoxy recognize (see Hahn, 1991; Mitchell Waldrop, 1992), progress on these critical fronts might require courageous departures that will lead us, for a while at least, into unknown territories. In this situation a considerable theoretical pluralism is desirable, even if we hope, in the end, to achieve a more general and encompassing theoretical framework. Whether such a theoretical framework will be achieved, whether it will be an extension of neoclassical economics or more evolutionary, no one can tell. An attitude which is both open to experimentation and aiming towards generality and coherence is required. Such has been the underlying attitude in writing this book.

PART 1

The Nature of Evolutionary Theories and their
Relationship to Neoclassical Economics

2. Some methodological considerations about the local character of knowledge and about the comparability of theories

INTRODUCTION

The discussion in Chapter 1 pointed out that the phenomena of technological innovation and technological change tend to escape the boundaries of orthodox economic theory and that there is a need to extend the scope of economics by taking into account explicitly the characters and mechanisms of technological change. In particular it was pointed out that qualitative change, one of the main effects of technological innovation, is an extremely important aspect of economic development and that it is systematically absent from economic theory. It was also argued that the incorporation of these new aspects would be easier into an evolutionary rather than an orthodox theory. In order to develop this theme further in this chapter some considerations about the scope and comparability of theories are developed. In such considerations, concepts developed for the analysis of scientific theories (e.g. paradigm, core, protective belt, etc.) will be applied to the analysis of technological change, and concepts developed for the analysis of economics and of technological change (e.g. competition, life cycles, local character of knowledge, etc.) will be applied to scientific theories. This mixing of conceptual backgrounds has already a precedent in the extension of the concept of paradigm to technology (Dosi, 1982). The possibility of mixing concepts created for different disciplines/research traditions gives rise to some interesting intrepretations in the present chapter. However, it might have some more fundamental and deeper meaning. For example, it has been suggested that the discontinuity in the transition between different technological paradigms might be due to the self-regulating properties of complex technological systems (Saviotti, 1986; Saviotti and Mani, 1994). It would then be possible for some underlying similarity to exist between complex technological systems and the complex systems constituted by scientific theories. Furthermore, since technology and the economy are becoming more knowledge intensive the underlying similarity between technological systems and scientific theories might be increasing. Such similarities and some of the generalizations introduced here will be used in Chapter 8 for the analysis of the knowledge used by firms and productive organizations.

CAN THEORIES BE COMPARED?

Observation Spaces and the Span of Theories

Neoclassical or evolutionary economics are more than individual theories. They could be described as schools of economic thought or research traditions in economics. For the purpose of this chapter, research traditions can be considered to be sets of models of different parts of the real world, plus a set of assumptions, tools and methods which are common to all models and underlying them. Models themselves are subsets of the real world (Casti, 1989). In each model, theorems about observables and linkages/relations between observables are established. In the present context it is relevant that different models may contain different observables. A theory can then be considered a set of models. Different theories can similarly contain different observables. For simplicity of expression, the set of observables of a given theory will from now on be called its *observation space*. Using a different terminology this will be called the *span* of a theory, or more in general of a piece of knowledge (Chapter 8).

From this initial set up a number of very interesting implications follow. First, different theories will in general have different observation spaces. Thus a theory of biological evolution will have a different observation space with respect to a theory of international trade. However, it is conceivable that two or more theories have the same observation space. Such observation spaces will differ for the type and number of variables described, and for the extent of correlation provided (range over which the correlation is effective and accuracy of the correlation). These considerations imply that both theories and more practical pieces of knowledge are *correlational structures*, a feature which will be analysed in greater depth in Chapter 8. Theories/pieces of knowledge differ for the span of their observation space.

The situation described previously can be useful in comparing different theories. In general, one can imagine that when comparing theories pair by pair there will be some which have observation spaces exactly the same, some completely different, and some partly overlapping. It is possible to formulate this situation in a slightly more formal way by means of set theory. Thus the intersection of the observation space of two different theories can be anything from equal to each of the the two observation spaces on the one hand to an empty set on the other(Saviotti, 1986).

One or more variables can be used to describe each of the observables of the theory. As previously pointed out, one of the most important goals of theories is to correlate variables. The formulas and theorems which are the result of formalized theories represent relationships between variables. This is also the case for qualitative theories, except that the relationships are established less accurately. In this sense, theories can be more or less successful depending on the extent of relationships/correlations that they find amongst the variables describing their observation space. Both explanations and predictions can be conceived in terms of relationships between the variables of the observation space of given theories. In principle we can have two (or more) theories competing for correlations/explanations of their observation space. The explanatory power of theories increases with the extent of correlation that they find amongst the group of variables.

It is possible to derive some interesting consequences from the previous considerations by means of the concept of competition. In a biological sense, two species compete for a resource or a set of resources. In economics, firms compete for customers. In a similar way it could be said that theories having the same observation space compete for the best correlations amongst the variables which describe their observation space. However, if one compares theories which have different or only partly overlapping observation spaces the situation becomes more similar to one in which firms differentiate their products. If one imagines to start with firms producing identical products and then differentiating them gradually, the firms become less and less comparable. Similarly, theories will become less and less comparable as their observation spaces become gradually more and more different. To compare two theories with only slightly overlapping observation spaces is very different from comparing two theories with the same observation space.

In this sense it is possible to stretch the analogy between theories and firms and say that two theories having exactly the same observation space are substitutes or competitors for the explanation/correlation of the variables describing their observables. On the other hand, when theories have completely different observation spaces, they are either independent or complementary.

The situation described above would be true both in the case in which theories were developed inductively from observations and in the case in which observations are theory guided. In the former case, involving a random sampling of the environment prior to the construction of a theory, the probability of two different theories having the same observation space would be very low. In the latter case, observation spaces would be constructed differently because the sampling would already be guided by at least pre-theoretical assumptions.

A further property of observation spaces is their span. The observation space of a theory can be based on the sampling of a restricted number of phenomena and therefore require a limited number of variables. Other theories can be based on the sampling of a very large number of phenomena and therefore require a very large number of variables. The greater the number of variables the greater the span of the theory. Furthermore, some theories can give reliable predictions only within selected ranges of the variables characterizing their observation spaces and become ineffective outside those ranges. Both the number of underlying variables and the range over which the theory can give reliable predictions contribute to the span of the theory. To measure the span of different theories is likely to prove a difficult or impossible task. However, the concept is useful because it leads to other interesting implications. Thus it is possible for a theory to originate with observations on a given set of variables and to establish correlations amongst those variables. In this process a number of conceptual tools, including the correlations themselves, are established for the initial set of variables. If subsequently the theory proceeds to incorporate a set of other variables, it is natural to extend the same conceptual tools to the new variables. It is as if the theory had an in-built bias due to the initial set of variables contained in its observation space. Theory development would then display path dependence. In other words, the span of the observation space grows during the development of theories, but the relationships established amongst the variables are not made anew when new variables are incorporated. On the contrary, the tools established for the first variables are extended to the analysis of the new variables (Saviotti, 1986). This situation is very similar to that described by Nelson and Winter (1974, 1982) for what concerns the knowledge of firms. They consider that this knowledge is *local* and that firms are likely to progress more by searching and by developing new products/output types in the vicinity of their existing knowledge. Given the existence of heuristics, decision rules, routines, etc., it is likely that in the absence of a paradigm change the vicinity is going to be searched and modified by using the existing heuristics, decision rules, etc., until this is possible, which means until it does not give rise to any anomalies. Moreover, concepts such as localized learning (Atkinson and Stiglitz, 1969; Stiglitz, 1987) and the degree of specificity of technologies (Patel and Pavitt, 1994) bear a close resemblance to the local character of knowledge.

The concept of tools could be given a more concrete interpretation by means of an example. Classical physics has been remarkably successful in describing and correlating a selected subset of the natural environment. This portion is constituted by particularly simple phenomena, which gave classical physics the possibility of constructing a very sophisticated theoretical structure. At the heart of the substance of classical physics and of its success lie the mathematical tools which have been used by it. Thus the development of calculus coincided with that of classical physics and it would be impossible to imagine the success of classical physics without calculus. Calculus is a branch of mathematics which is particularly suited to the analysis of a world which is deterministic, reversible and continuous. At the transition of the 19th and the 20th centuries the discovery of anomalies in classical physics induced a transition to quantum mechanics. This new branch of physics, among other things, required new mathematical tools more suited to describe a world characterized by uncertainty and probabilistic outcomes.

In a similar way neoclassical economics was developed when both classical physics and calculus were already relatively mature disciplines or subsets of disciplines. There is evidence that neoclassical economics borrowed from classical mechanics more than some marginal inspiration and that it was explicitly set up to emulate its formal structure (Clark and Juma, 1987, 1988). Thus while classical physics needed calculus for its development, neoclassical economics found it ready-made. It is legitimate to suspect that the structure of neoclassical economics has at least partly been determined by the previous existence of calculus. In this case a pre-existent intellectual tool would have contributed to shape the field of enquiry and above all the world view of neo-classical economists. Since calculus is particularly appropriate to describe a world which is continuous, differentiable and deterministic these features were at the core of neoclassical economics.

A theory can be characterized by its span (number of variables that it describes and it intends to correlate) and by the effectiveness with which it establishes correlations between the variables of its observation space (explanatory power). It is in principle possible to imagine the case of a theory having a very large span but not being very successful at establishing correlations between variables.

Two problems then follow: first, there will be theories studying phenomena and variables at different levels of aggregation; second, theories develop in the course of time and may increase both their span and their explanatory power.

In an extreme reductionist approach, at the beginning of the 20th century, everything could be considered constituted by electrons, protons and neutrons. Explanations of any phenomenon could be given in terms of these elementary constituents and of interactions between them. Very few people would share such a view today. However, it is generally true that there are theories which study variables at different levels of aggregation and that sometimes the variables of two such theories are related. Moreover, explanations tend in general to be given in terms of entities at a lower level than the explanandum (Elster, 1983). While in a purely reductionist approach the theory at the higher level of aggregation is deductively derivable from that at a lower level of aggregation, in practice theories have often developed independently and formed separate and not necessarily compatible conceptual tools. There is, in other words, path dependency in the development of theories. When developments in one theory have potential implications for another at a higher level of aggregation, such developments may be partly incorporated but without necessarily displacing the pre-existing conceptual tools of the theory at a higher level of aggregation.

Theories are extended in the course of time. They begin with an observation space and a span, and may increase either the extent of correlation of the variables describing their observation space (explanatory power) or their span or both. In this sense it is quite likely that, as already mentioned above, the conceptual tools developed in the early generalizations are extended to the analysis of further variables. Theories will then have a life cycle in which their span and explanatory power will increase in the course of time, at least until they encounter significant crises and bottlenecks.

THE LIFE CYCLE OF THEORIES

There is considerable evidence that theories do not emerge complete and perfect, but that they are gradually established around a core of few fundamental concepts and intellectual tools. The concept of paradigm captures this essential idea. In the course of time a paradigm is gradually articulated by being extended in a period of normal science (Kuhn, 1962). In terms of the concepts introduced in the previous section, theories increase their span and explanatory power. The paradigm becomes more extensive and able to deal with a greater range of phenomena. Phenomena here do not have to be interpreted as purely physical. They could also be social or biological for example, depending on the observation space of the theory which is being considered. By a gradual accumulation of applications to new phenomena (or ranges of) the theory becomes more versatile and more robust. Therefore the theory emerges in a form which may be intuitively appealing and able to deal with observations which defied the previous theory, but is altogether formally poorly articulated and has a limited span. During the course of its development the theory increases its versatility and robustness and acquires a growing number of supporters. In this sense evolutionary economics is not different from any other theory. At the moment it is still in a rather immature and initial state.

An additional way of interpreting the evolution of theories or research traditions is in terms of Lakatos (1974), (cited in Blaug, 1980) research programmes. Thus the hard core of the theory could be created first and the development of the protective belt could follow. One could then interpret the present stage of development of evolutionary economics as one at which the hard core is being constituted. The following chapter about the research traditions converging into it and about key points in evolutionary economics deals precisely with the nature of its hard core. One can then imagine that if the research programme of evolutionary economics is to remain a progressive one, a protective belt of supplementary assumptions, methodological tools, etc. will have to be constructed.

It must be realized that the previous considerations are somewhat limited. One cannot necessarily expect concepts such as paradigm, hard core and protective belt, which have been developed from the study of the physical sciences, to apply without any modifications to the social sciences in general and to economics in particular (Blaug, 1980). Furthermore, economics is not just a science but has some features similar to those of philosophy or religion

(Foster, 1985). Theoretical changes implying a redefinition of the hard core could be even more difficult to achieve than in the physical sciences.

The limitations in the applicability of the previous concepts to economics are not very serious for this discussion. The main aim of the considerations here is simply to establish to what extent evolutionary and neoclassical economics are equivalent descriptions of the same observables or whether they have at least partly non-overlapping observation spaces.

From the previous considerations it seems very likely that different approaches to economics, such as neoclassical, classical, Marxist, evolutionary, etc. economics have different, although largely overlapping, observation spaces and that these approaches are not entirely comparable. Furthermore, at least neoclassical and evolutionary economics have very different degrees of development, the former being very mature while the latter is still in its infancy. It is, therefore, logical that neoclassical economics has a sophisticated formal structure that evolutionary economics lacks. An evaluation of evolutionary economics, which, as previously pointed out, involves necessarily a comparison with neoclassical economics, has to take these considerations into account. In order to evaluate evolutionary economics then its observation space and state of development relative to that of neoclassical economics will have to be analysed.

Before passing to this type of analysis, however, it is important to introduce some more general considerations. From the previous discussion it follows that the development of theories can be loosely interpreted according to a life-cycle hypothesis. Thus theories emerge in a rather simple and poorly articulated state, from which they develop by being extended, further articulated and becoming more robust. A paradigm represents a particular type of life cycle, in which the maturity begins with the transition from revolutionary to normal science. The obsolescence of the theory comes when anomalies which cannot be accommodated by it are encountered or when the research programme becomes degenerating (Lakatos, 1974). If this were correct, one could say that there are similarities between the development of theories and the development of technologies. Some such similarities have already been found in the opposite sense, by introducing the concept of technological paradigm (Dosi, 1982). Discontinuities in technological evolution have been compared to paradigm shifts, while the pattern of incremental improvement which occurs within a given technology has been compared to normal science. As with science, the stabilization of a paradigm is based not only on features of the technology *per se* but also on social configurations which interact with this same technology. The knowledge base of engineers, technicians and managers may be designed around an existing technology and they may be reluctant to change it in order to introduce a new one. Thus the evolution of technologies seems to follow patterns which are not entirely dissimilar from those encountered in the evolution of scientific theories. Naturally one cannot exaggerate the extent of these simi-

larities which exist only at a very high level of generality. Differences and speci-
ficities exist between the development of scientific theories and those of
technologies (Dosi, 1982; Clark and Juma, 1987). However, and always at a
high level of generality, one could stretch these similarities a bit further and
notice that there could be an evolutionary theory of theories themselves. In this
perspective the maturation, the appearance of anomalies and the degeneration
of research programmes could act as inducements for the emergence of new
paradigms. Furthermore, once a theory had accepted a new paradigm it would
tend to exclude competing theories in a way that resembles the situation characterized by increasing returns to adoption described by Arthur (1983, 1988,
1989a) for the development of technologies.

It seems that concepts developed for the analysis of scientific theories can
be adapted to the evolution of technologies and that concepts developed for the
analysis of technologies can be adapted to the evolution of scientific theories.
This transfer with adaptation of concepts from one research tradition to others
should not seem strange here. It will be shown later that evolutionary economics
itself in its present stage is deriving inspiration from a number of other research
traditions, although this inspiration can never imply a mechanical transfer of
concepts. Here some concepts currently used in economics will be applied to
the analysis of theories. This same approach will be followed later (Chapter 8)
in analysing the role played by knowledge generation and adoption in firms and
productive organizations. As we have already seen, theories having the same
observation spaces could be considered as substitutes and competitors for the
explanation of the same phenomena. On the other hand, theories having
completely different and non-overlapping observation spaces could not be
considered as competitors but would more likely be complements. These two
represent extreme cases and a number of theories could be in a position in which
they have only partly overlapping observation spaces. In this case the theories
would be competitors for the explanation of some phenomena and would be
complementary for what concerns the explanation of other phenomena which
are contained only in the observation space of one of the two theories. Alternatively, one could say that theories specialize in particular observation spaces,
which constitute the equivalent of niches while simultaneously competing in
other parts of their observation space. This is likely to be the situation of neoclassical and evolutionary economics.

In this context one could also ask if the very limited reliance placed by neoclassical economics on empirical studies as a basis for the development of theories
was the only possible and the best approach. Furthermore, one could ask if this
same approach is the most appropriate for evolutionary economics. An approach
to the problem consists of dividing the operations to be performed to create a
theory into (a) observation + data gathering, (b) data elaboration, and, (c)
inference and theory building. We can also assume that the 'resources' that can

be used in theory development are limited and that they will be allocated in the most rational way (this does not necessarily imply an optimizing perspective but is compatible with a satisficing one). Naturally, the kind of resources that can be used in this particular task are predominantly human resources, although at present information technologies can make a substantial contribution to it. To gather large amounts of data requires large quantities of skilled labour. Also, sometimes information about economic activities is not easily accessible when the secrecy of that information is a competitive weapon for firms. Hence to use information other than what is easily available, such as government statistics, may even now involve the commitment of very large amounts of resources. In other words, the costs of (a) above could be very high. Data elaboration as well can require large amounts of resources, although this has become relatively much easier after the advent of information technology. However, if we think of the time at which neoclassical economics was first created, a commitment to data gathering and elaboration on a large scale might not have been the most 'rational' choice. If paradoxically one had to wait to gather the data first in order to create inductively theories later, very little would have been achieved, given the high initial costs of (a) and (b). It was probably more rational to rely on casual observations of the 'world' and to build theories from them. This situation has been described as the performance of 'mental experiments' (Binmore and Dasgupta, 1989). Mental experiments are present in the physical sciences as well, although they are not as dominant as in economics.

This initial preference for theoretical work developed from few casual observations might be interpreted as a form of procedural rationality (Simon, 1981). In other words, whether or not to begin by gathering data and elaborating them was the most substantively rational solution, the computational cost of it would have been so high with respect to other solutions as to make it procedurally inferior. This habit once it had been acquired by the profession would then have been 'embodied' in its routines and stabilized by normal self-regulating mechanisms. Such a routine would in the course of time have led to a preference for theoretical-deductive procedures as opposed to a combination of interacting empirical studies and theories. Assuming that the relative scarcity of resources at the time neoclassical economics was built was a sufficient justification for the previous routine we should ask whether the situation has changed and whether the same routine is still justified now, especially for what concerns evolutionary economics. A change in the situation has been the already mentioned availability of information technologies, which allow a much faster elaboration of data.

Different knowledge strategies are in principle possible for economics now. To begin with, an exclusively deductive approach is not appropriate. Deduction implies that the generalizations/relations derived from a particular set of variables will be extended to another set of variables. If the knowledge contained in theories is local, then deduction will become less and less effective the further removed the phenomena studied are from those which gave rise to the initial generalizations. It is, therefore, essential to keep referring to empirical analysis in the process of extending the theory. In other words, it follows from the local character of knowledge that a mixture of induction and deduction has to be used. An interesting suggestion also is that neither induction nor deduction, but abduction, the creative process of forming an explanatory hypothesis (Hodgson, 1993, pp. 16–17), is used in scientific development. In any case, the hyper-deductive syndrome which has affected economics in the recent past, might have reached its limits.

After having developed these general considerations, let us analyse some of the possible differences between the observation spaces of neoclassical and evolutionary economics. First, neoclassical economics deals with an economic system in which there is a constant set of activities and products. New products and activities can be introduced into the system ex-post, after they have been invented or innovated. The process of the emergence of new products, services and activities is completely exogenous to a neoclassical economic system. Thus, for example, the production function contains only variables describing the inputs used (Salter, 1962). The outputs are generally considered to be homogeneous. On the other hand, Schumpeter (1912, 1942) understood the role played by new products and new processes in economic development. Although evolutionary economics is not purely neo-Schumpeterian and different research traditions are converging into it, Schumpeter is still one of the main influences on its development, and the innovations constituted by new products and new processes were considered by him to be amongst the most important components of the process of economic development. Thus evolutionary economics takes innovations in the form of new products, processes, materials, markets and organizational forms as extremely central elements in its representation of the process of economic development. Perhaps it is an exaggeration to say that such elements are not part of neoclassical economics, but it is certainly true that innovations are more naturally at home in evolutionary rather than neoclassical economics. More fundamentally, neoclassical economics accepts innovations as coming from outside the economic system with the limited exception of the induced innovation theory (Hicks, 1932; Kennedy, 1964; Ahmad, 1966; Binswanger and Ruttan, 1978). However, even in these cases, innovation is almost always treated as if it could affect only the factor proportions used in production processes. Problems of the internal structures of technologies are not faced by neoclassical economics while they are becoming central to a modern evolutionary approach. This is true even if Schumpeter was not himself very interested in the internal structure of technologies (Hertjee, 1977; Hagedoorn, 1989). Such an interest was instead found in Marx (Rosenberg, 1976; Hagedoorn, 1989). Whether it is a matter of emphasis or of presence/absence, innovations play a much more central role ex-ante in evolutionary rather than neoclassical economics. The observation spaces of the two research traditions are then different, at least for what concerns this aspect. In this sense neoclassical and evolutionary economics are not necessarily competitors but have at least partly complementary roles.

A further contribution to a difference in observation spaces can come from the nature of the organizations that appear in either evolutionary or neoclassical economics. In a capitalist economic system the main organization responsible for production is the firm. In neoclassical economics the firm is characterized by a number of assumptions: it is a price taker, a profit maximizer, it is owner managed, it produces a homogeneous product, and demand and supply are in equilibrium in all relevant markets (Coombs, Saviotti and Walsh, 1987, p. 24). Such a theory of the firm is therefore very unrealistic because it does not take into account internal aspects of the structure and performance of firms as they have been gradually developing from the end of the 19th century. These new firm features have been analysed by some alternative theories which have remained outside the main body of neoclassical economics. Thus the ownership-control debate (Berle and Means, 1932) and the behavioural theory of the firm (Cyert and March, 1963) emphasize conflicts within firms. Marris (1964), Penrose (1980) and Cyert and March (1963) have analysed the complexity of managerial motivation far beyond the profit maximizing hypothesis. Williamson (1975, 1979, 1981) and Chandler (1962, 1977) studied the organizational structures which have emerged in modern firms and the reasons for their existence. These very brief notes about modern firm theories can in no way be an adequate treatment of them. A slightly more detailed discussion of these issues and of their importance in the context of evolutionary theories will take place later in this chapter. Their purpose here is only to point out that the observation space of evolutionary theories contains elements of the internal structure of firms while that of neoclassical economics does not. This is one more difference between the observation spaces of the two theories. A possible reason for the exclusion of these more realistic features from the neoclassical theory of the firm has been suggested by Machlup (1967). According to him (but see also Moss, 1981; Rosseger, 1980) the neoclassical theory of the firm is first and foremost a theory of markets and the assumptions made about the firm in the theory are those found to be logically required as axioms to support this theory of markets. It is, therefore, not unthinkable that some elements of the potential observation space of neoclassical economics have been suppressed in order to defend what could be considered as more fundamental components of the neoclassical picture. This situation bears some similarity to that of a theory defending its hard core by changing its protective belt (Lakatos, 1974).

The previous considerations imply that when attempting to compare two theories we have to take into account both their observation spaces and their relative position in the respective life cycles. Only theories which have the same observation space and are at an equivalent position in their life cycle are strictly comparable. In this situation theories are substitutes, competing to explain the same set of events/phenomena. Two theories having very different observation spaces are not competing to explain the same events/phenomena and may well be in a complementary position. However, the implicit assumption which is made in comparing theories are that they are potential substitutes.

Neoclassical and evolutionary economics, as we have seen, have largely overlapping but not identical observation spaces, and are at very different positions in their life cycles. Therefore, they cannot be perfect substitutes. It is even conceivable that there are some relationships of complementarity between the two approaches. We can certainly expect that each of the two approaches will be more appropriate to deal with different sets of events. Thus neoclassical economics can be expected to be very effective in dealing with a static economic system characterized by a constant set of activities and by limited uncertainty. On the other hand, evolutionary economics is likely to be more appropriate to deal with a world characterized by increasing uncertainty and the emergence of new products/activities/markets/organizational structures, etc. This situation would in some way be equivalent to a partial specialization, in which the two theoretical approaches select different subsets of their potential observation spaces and develop theoretical structures which are particularly appropriate for those subsets. Given the earlier phase in its life cycle, evolutionary economics is unlikely to have reached its 'best practice' in terms of explanatory power of the events in its chosen subset. Whatever evidence we are going to consider in favour of evolutionary economics these things will have to be taken into account. These considerations are going to be placed in a more specific context in the next chapter, which analyses the present state and possible developments of evolutionary theories.

3. What is evolutionary economics now?

INTRODUCTION

In Chapters 1 and 2 the need for an evolutionary approach in economics was proposed on the basis of a number of failures in neoclassical economics, including the failures to take into account the internal features of technological change and to address the problem of qualitative change in economic development. However, very little was said about the nature of evolutionary theories. In this chapter the nature of evolutionary theories, their intellectual background and their present state of development will be examined.

Attempts to interpret economics according to an evolutionary metaphor are not new (Clark and Juma, 1987, 1988; Boulding, 1981). An excellent survey of the work of economists who in the past have been inspired by an evolutionary metaphor has recently been done by Hodgson (1993). Extensive reference to his work will be made in this chapter, although the interpretations adopted here differ in a number of cases.

To begin with, it is necessary to mention that the term 'evolutionary' has been given several considerably different interpretations. Examples of two such interpretations are: 'development according to a pre-established pattern, of which the actual evolution is only the realization', and 'Darwinian evolution, in which random mutations are selected by the environment in which they exist'. A classification of different interpretations of evolution in economics has been given by Hodgson (1993).

Hodgson maintains that a biological metaphor is more useful than the mechanical one which has been adopted in orthodox economics, and proceeds to find traces and influences of a biological metaphor in past economists. Also, in two recent surveys of evolutionary economics (Nelson, 1993; Dosi and Nelson, 1994), biology is recognized as the main non-economic influence on evolutionary theories. The position adopted in this book is slightly different. Although it is recognized that the biological research tradition is one of the most important in defining modern evolutionary economics, it is maintained that today's evolutionary economics is arising from the convergence of a number of research traditions. These research traditions were in the past separate and are now converging in the sense that they complement one another in the explanation of given phenomena and events. Some of these research traditions provide concepts which are more fundamental or underlie those of the others. In the following analysis the fundamental concepts of the different research traditions and their mutual relationships will be discussed. The presentation will begin with systems theory and out of equilibrium thermodynamics, because they provide a theoretical justification for several of the concepts and theories which can be used in biology, organization theory and economics. Biology will be presented next because it has dealt much more explicitly with qualitative change and because it has used a population approach. Finally, organization theories and heterodox approaches in economics will be presented, pointing out their relationships to the other research traditions.

At the end of this chapter we should be in a position to point out the main distinguishing features of evolutionary economics. However, before proceeding to the following analysis it is necessary to state that past evolutionary attempts in economics did not lead to a change in the orthodox economic approach at the time at which they were proposed, but they remained isolated and incomplete 'experiments'. However, interest in evolutionary economics has recently undergone a revival of interest, probably due to the way in which orthodox economics deals with processes of technological change in particular and with any type of change which transforms in a fundamental way the economic system. In the time which has passed since these first 'experiments' the evolutionary approach has changed very substantially. As discussed previously, it is still far from being a complete theoretical system. One could say that the evolutionary metaphor or paradigm is just emerging and that it will require an extended period of 'normal science' (Kuhn, 1962) to articulate it adequately.

THE DIFFERENT TRADITIONS CONTRIBUTING TO EVOLUTIONARY ECONOMICS

Non-equilibrium Thermodynamics and Systems Theory

These two research traditions are presented jointly because they have a number of concepts in common. Also, as already pointed out, they provide a theoretical justification for a number of the concepts used by the following research traditions. They were developed for separate purposes but there are elements of convergence between them. Attempts to formulate a theory of complex systems date back to the 1920s (Lotka, 1956; von Bertalanffy, 1950). The underlying motivation was the need to develop a series of overarching concepts and theoretical structures which could be common to large numbers of complex systems (Emery, 1969). Any such system would have a very high degree of specificity but also some more aggregate features which were common to other systems. Without trying to assess the state of development or the degree of success of this attempt one can point out that it has produced a number of concepts which are generally accepted and used in several disciplines and subdisciplines, including non-equilibrium thermodynamics. A fundamental distinction can be made between open and closed systems. Open systems are those which can exchange matter, energy and information with their environment. Closed systems cannot exchange anything with their environment. The two types of systems behave in completely different ways. Closed systems when left to themselves tend to move towards an equilibrium state, corresponding to the maximum possible disorder and randomness. The degree of disorder is measured by entropy. Open systems, on the other hand, do not have equilibria but steady states, in which the time invariance of at least a number of variables characterizing the system can be maintained in the presence of continuous exchanges of matter and energy with their environment (von Bertalanffy, 1956). Economic systems are open (Boulding, 1978; Silverberg, 1988) and behave accordingly.

Non-equilibrium thermodynamics applies to open systems. It was developed from the work of Lars Onsager in the 1930s (Prigogine, 1976, 1987; Prigogine and Stengers, 1984; Nicolis and Prigogine, 1989). In order to understand better the differences between these types of systems one can imagine taking a closed system and submitting it to gradually stronger and stronger interactions with its environment, thus imposing new constraints on the behaviour of the system. The extent of interactions determines the degree of openness of the system. Systems submitted to weak external constraints give linear responses to changes emanating from the environment. Even the presence of weak interactions makes the behaviour of the system become irreversible and this irreversibility corresponds both to dissipation and to the formation of order. Irreversibility exists because the system cannot recover its previous state without some further change in the environment.

This situation can be understood by imagining initially a closed system, subsequently opening it up and gradually increasing its interactions with the environment. As these interactions are increased the system is subjected to stronger and stronger constraints. One can then use a control parameter to measure the 'distance' of the system from equilibrium. At small distances from equilibrium the behaviour of the system is linear, which means that flows (e.g. movements of matter or heat flows) are a linear function of the forces (e.g. concentration or temperature gradients) which cause them (Prigogine and Stengers, 1984). In this region the behaviour of the system becomes irreversible but does not yet lead to qualitative changes to different structures, or, in other words, to evolution.

As the constraints acting on the system, and, therefore, the distance from equilibrium, are increased the system begins to behave in a qualitatively different way. Beyond a given distance from equilibrium, at what is called a bifurcation point (Prigogine and Stengers, 1984; Nicolis and Prigogine, 1989; Allen, 1988), the system undergoes a transition to a greater number of states, each characterized by a high degree of order and by a different structure. This process can be represented by plotting a variable X, describing the behaviour of the system, against some control parameter describing the conditions of the external environment (see Figure 3.1). A number of points are worth noting here. First, in the vicinity of a bifurcation point the behaviour of the system is not predictable and fluctuations can lead to transitions to any of the states possible after the bifurcation point. There is an essential indeterminacy in its behaviour in this neighbourhood. Alternatively, one can describe this change as a transition from one attractor to two (or more) different attractors. Non-equilibrium can become a source of order: new, more complicated types of attractors may appear, and give the system remarkable new spacetime properties. This can be understood in terms of total entropy changes (see Figure 3.2). In an open system the total entropy change (dS_T) is equal to the sum of the entropy changes of the system (dS_S) and of the environment (dS_E).

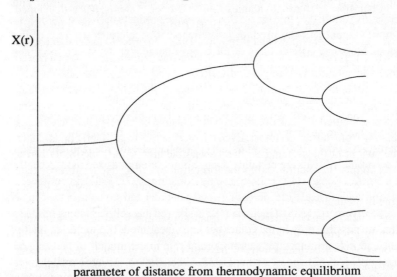

X(r)

parameter of distance from thermodynamic equilibrium

Figure 3.1   Bifurcation diagram representing the stationary states which are possible for a dissipative structure

It is quite possible for dS_S to be negative, therefore leading to a greater order, if dS_E is positive and sufficiently large to ensure that $dS_T < 0$. In other words, in moving to states which are increasingly further away from equilibrium the system would be 'exporting' entropy to the environment and becoming internally more ordered and structured. In this region the behaviour of the system is extremely specific and few generalizations are possible (Prigogine and Stengers, 1984; Nicolis and Prigogine, 1989).

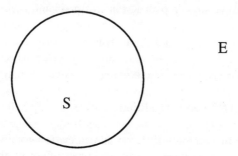

Figure. 3.2   Entropy changes of a system and of its environment: $dS_T = dS_E + dS_S$

Another important feature of these processes is that their autocatalytic nature seems to be a necessary condition for them to lead to a greater order and complexity. Intuitively this means that one of the products of the process is also an input/reagent. As the product is produced it accelerates the rate of the process. For some critical value of the control parameter the system becomes unstable and new solutions emerge. This is a bifurcation point and here the system has a choice between the different branches of the bifurcation diagram (Allen, 1988). Mathematically, autocatalysis involves non-linearity.

These concepts were developed for the analysis of physical and chemical systems, but are sufficiently general to be adapted to biological and social systems. As Lotka (1956) and Marshall (1949) had already realized, biological and economic systems are certainly open, a point re-emphasized more recently by Georgescu Roegen (1971, 1976) and by Boulding (1978, 1981). In both cases, evolution tends to lead to an increasing degree of order and structure in the course of time (Silverberg, 1988). Goodwin (1951) showed that self-sustaining business cycles are possible only in the context of non-linear models. Stochastic fluctuations and indeterminacy play an important role in the models of Nelson and Winter (1974, 1982) and of Arthur (1983, 1988, 1989a). Arthur's model gives rise to irreversibility and path dependency in the evolution of technology when there are increasing returns to adoption. Some or all of these aspects are contained in models based on catastrophe theory, on game theory and on replicator dynamics, the last one being based on Fisher's mathematical formulation of natural selection (Silverberg, 1988). Some recent ecological theories of organizational change (McKelvey, 1982; Hannan and Freeman, 1977, 1989) seem to have been conceived along similar lines.

A number of important concepts which will be applicable to biology and to economics have emerged from systems theory and from out of equilibrium thermodynamics. The formation of order and structure, and the discontinuous transitions leading to qualitative change occur as open systems move away from equilibrium. Irreversibility, path dependence and multistability follow from the basic features of open systems. Non-linearity and the autocatalytic nature of processes are required in order for changes of structure to occur. All these properties and types of behaviour predicted by systems theory and from out of equilibrium thermodynamics are common to biological and to economic systems.

The Biological Research Tradition

It is mainly in this research tradition that an evolutionary approach has been adopted (Mokyr, 1991). Such an approach has, therefore, reached in this tradition its greatest degree of articulation and refinement. In particular, the biological research tradition has placed much greater emphasis on qualitative change and it is a powerful source of inspiration at the conceptual, the modelling, and the empirical level for evolutionary economics. Of course, we cannot expect to transfer biological models unchanged to economics. There is always a need for adaptation, whatever the two research traditions involved in the transfer. We can say that between biology and evolutionary economics there is a relationship of structural and of goal similarity, in the sense that we can find a correspondence between the entities observed by the two disciplines (e.g. animal species vs. institutions or technologies) and between their knowledge goals (explain long-run behaviour in terms of qualitative change). This similarity entitles us to use biological analogies to ask new and interesting questions and to construct models, but not to transfer biological answers to economic problems.

If there are structural and goal similarities between biology and economics, both disciplines derive their theoretical justification from the research traditions previously described, that is system theory and non-equilibrium thermo-dynamics. Both biological and economic systems are open, they possess order and structure, and the degree of such order and structure does not fall in the course of evolution. The two types of systems undergo both incremental and discontinuous changes. Such changes are irreversible and often characterized by path dependence and by multistability. In other words, the existence of the main properties of biological and of economic systems is predicted by systems theory and by non-equilibrium thermodynamics. We can then establish a hier-archical order amongst the various disciplines/research traditions: systems theory and non-equilibrium thermodynamics are in a more fundamental position than biology, economics and organization theories. At the moment the theoretical justification provided by systems theory and non-equilibrium thermodynam-ics does not allow us to deduce the specific properties and detailed models of biological and economic systems. It is then perfectly justified to use biological metaphors and models in studying economic systems, although with the limi-tations already described.

The biological research tradition has now acquired a richness and complexity that is far beyond the boundaries of this chapter to elaborate. The role of the discussion in this section is not to give a comprehensive review but to point out some of the main ideas generated within the biological research tradition that can be used, although sometimes in a modified form, in economics and in the social sciences. A more detailed analysis of the main ideas and controversies in biology can be found, for example, in Mani (1991).

In its modern form, the theory of biological evolution is generally associated with the name of Charles Darwin. Two of his main aims in studying evolution were to establish that all existing organisms are descendants of one or a few simple ancestral forms, and to show that evolutionary change was due to natural selection operating on the variations within the population. Qualitative change was produced by the slow and gradual emergence of new species, or speciation, related to the pre-existing species. This is due to the process of variation, which in the biological world occurs mainly by means of mutations. Not all new species survive but some of them are eliminated through natural selection. As a result the number of surviving species had changed in the course of time with new species appearing and others becoming extinct. Thus two fundamental components of biological evolution are variation and selection.

The thread of continuity existing in this process of qualitative change is due to the fact that members of each generation pass on their genetic make-up. Central to the modern evolutionary synthesis are the concepts of phenotype and genotype. The phenotype is identified by the external appearance of an organism (its characteristics and morphological structure) while the genotype is constituted by its genetic make-up, as embodied in the DNA structure. The third fundamental component of evolution is inheritance. Here differences are likely to exist between the biological and socio-economic sphere.

Species having different genetic make-up have different morphological and behavioural characters and as a consequence differ in the degree to which they are suited to their environment. The poorly adapted ones 'perish' through natural selection, whereas the well-adapted ones 'survive' and pass on their beneficial genetic underpinning to their offspring. It is important to stress that in Darwinian evolution adaptation takes place in an unintentional way. Mutations which alter the genetic make-up of species appear at random. Those that can adapt better to their environment are subsequently selected. However, in Darwinian evolution there is no relationship between the generation of mutations (and therefore of variety) and the subsequent process of selection. The environment can only influence the phenotype but such changes are not passed on to the offspring. This mechanism of natural selection constitutes one of the fundamental differences between a Darwinian and a Lamarckian model of evolution. According to the latter, organisms had an intrinsic tendency to improve themselves and therefore would try to develop the characteristics which allowed them to adapt better to their environment. Very little evidence seems to have been found for a Lamarckian type of biological evolution. However, the situation is likely to be quite different in the social sciences, where, for example, economic entities often display a purposeful behaviour (Hodgson, 1991; Faber and Proops, 1991). Firm strategy and search activities imply a degree of intentional behaviour in the presence of uncertainty. While it is true that the outcomes achieved differ, sometimes considerably, from the goals pursued, it is also true that ex-ante adaptation of firms to their external environment and adaptation of the environment to firm requirements are essential components of firm behaviour.

The ideas described previously are the most important in biological evolution. Other concepts which can be relevant for economics are used in ecology. For example, the concept of species, environment, habitat and niche can be transferred and adapted to economics. Similarly relevant are the different types of species' interactions, such as competition, commensalism and predation (Maynard Smith, 1974, p. 5). Some of these concepts will be analysed to a greater extent in Chapters 4 to 6 and 8.

Firm and Organization Theories

As already mentioned, the observation spaces of evolutionary and neoclassical economics differ, among other things, for the extent to which they analyse the internal structure of firms and organizations. In the standard neoclassical theory the firm has no internal structure and no conflicts. On the other hand, work by Simon (1947, 1957), Cyert and March (1963), Penrose (1980), Coase (1937) and Berle and Means (1932) started to open up the black box of the firm. Their work has become part of the intellectual background of evolutionary economics, while it has not been properly integrated into neoclassical economics. Some of the fundamental aspects that these theories stress are imperfect knowledge, satisficing (rather than optimizing), behaviour, and conflict and bargaining in organizations. Furthermore, organization theorists have developed a relatively more detailed characterization of the external environment of firms (see, for example, Emery and Trist, 1965; McKelvey, 1982). The fundamental contributions contained in the work of the above-mentioned authors have been incorporated by Nelson and Winter into their evolutionary theory (Nelson and Winter 1974, 1982). For them, firms possess *local* knowledge, which means that it rapidly becomes less effective as the firm moves away from its established area of operation (Nelson and Winter, 1974). Firms behave according to *routines* and *decision rules* as long as they reach or exceed their targets and switch to new routines and decision rules when such targets are not achieved. New routines/decision rules emerge from the firm's *search activities*.

A different kind of imperfect knowledge is used by David (1975; see also Elster, 1983). According to David, firms at any time have immediate and free access to a small number of practices and to any linear combination thereof. Firms change their technological practices both in response to changes in factor price ratios and by means of local, neutral technical change based on learning by doing. When factor price ratios change, firms switch to different production techniques but subsequently improve these new techniques by means of learning by doing. The new techniques can become absolutely superior to any of those existing before, which means at whatever factor price ratio. Even if the previous factor price ratio could be reestablished, the new and improved technique would still be superior to the old one. Thus imperfect knowledge and local neutral technical progress lead to irreversibility, a narrowing of substitution possibilities and path dependence. Firms' choice of techniques becomes a function of history. It is to be stressed that the concepts that David uses (production functions, etc.) are distinctly neoclassical and that the non-neoclassical outcomes of irreversibility and path dependence are introduced by imperfect knowledge and by neutral technical progress.

The imperfection of the knowledge used by firms can be interpreted in two quite different ways. First, it could be assumed that firm knowledge ought to be perfect and that firms will perform better the closer to perfection their knowledge is. In this approach, knowledge imperfections would be interpreted as frictions, leading to a sub-optimal firm behaviour. In this sense the real world would be interpreted as a deviation from an ideal frictionless world. This ideal world is the one underlying equilibrium theories of competition. Second, perfect knowledge would not be considered as a reference, but knowledge would simply be considered as dynamic and continuously evolving. Firms would occupy different areas of a knowledge landscape that expands continuously. In their respective areas they would try to be as close as possible to the local best practice. In this sense their position in terms of best practice knowledge would determine their performance. However, no two firms would have the same knowledge: due to the phenomena of differential creativity and of localized learning each firm would end up knowing different things. The specific combination of knowledge elements 'owned' by each firm is encapsulated by the concept of the *knowledge base*, the collective knowledge used by a firm/organization to underpin its production activity (Metcalfe and Gibbons, 1987, 1989).

Another important contribution of organization theories has been the study of the external environment of organizations. Both systems theory and organization theories stress the difference between the system/organization and its environment. In order to be able to study their interactions it is important to have an adequate characterization of the external environment. In economics the external environment of the firm is extremely oversimplified. In perfect competition the external environment is constituted by a structure of product and factor prices over which the firm has no influence. A far more complex concept of environment has been developed by organization theorists (Jurkovitch, 1969;

Terreberry, 1968). In principle the environment of an organization is everything outside its boundaries. This concept is not very useful since many components of the external environment do not have any effect on the behaviour of organizations. A useful distinction can be introduced between the climate and the texture of an environment (McKelvey, 1982, p. 120). The climate has a general effect on the organization(s) considered. Adaptation to the climate is likely to involve generic competences which are common to all the organizations with the same climate. Organizations are also embedded in a texture of causal relations composed of other (myopically) purposeful organizations and of their interrelations. Actions by one organization affect mainly other organizations having an equivalent structure of output.

In this section we only begin to analyse the role of firms and organization theories in an evolutionary approach. The main aim is to point out that the black box of the firm has been opened and that knowledge, however imperfect, is one of its important components. The knowledge possessed by an organization determines its performance. A more detailed discussion of the features of technological knowledge, leading to the concept of the knowledge base of the firm, will be given in Chapter 8.

Evolutionary Intepretations in Economics

The following discussion of evolutionary ideas in economics is not intended to be exhaustive. For a survey of this type the reader is referred to Hodgson (1993). The following emphasizes some ideas relating to the construction of evolutionary theories.

Herbert Spencer   The social scientist and philosopher Herbert Spencer was amongst the first to develop an evolutionary approach to social development. He was deeply influenced by Darwin and contributed to the popularization of his ideas. It is in fact Spencer and not Darwin who coined the expression 'the survival of the fittest' (Hodgson, 1993, p. 81). Spencer's early and complete espousal of an evolutionary metaphor may have contributed to the subsequent rejection of such a metaphor by most economists and social scientists. Spencer's advocacy of *laissez-faire* was less extreme than it is usually held. The most openly pro-aristocratic, racist and sexist overtones of his ideas were often added by his admirers and followers (Hodgson, 1993). However, such *laissez-faire* implications do not necessarily follow from today's evolutionary theories.

Some of Spencer's ideas are quite relevant for modern evolutionary developments. Spencer (1892, p. 10) defined evolution as 'a change from an indefinite, incoherent, homogeneity, to a definite, coherent heterogeneity through differentiations'. Spencer thought that evolution necessarily involves progress, and that complexity is generally associated with fitter and more adaptable forms.

These two elements of Spencer's thought are not necessarily linked. We do not have to share the inevitability of progress in evolution to admit that there is a growing tendency towards differentiation. In turn, this tendency towards differentiation would give rise to a growing variety of the system. While such a tendency may not be applicable to all biological (Mani, 1991), or other, systems, historical trends in economic development seem to point towards a growing variety (see Chapters 5 and 6). Spencer also thought that together with the tendency towards homogenization there is a simultaneous tendency towards integration. The first tendency contributed to variation while the second to selection. However, the inevitability of progress in the form of increasing differentiation meant that selection had a rather limited role. Spencer evolution was more ontogenic than phylogenic (Hodgson, 1993).

Marshall   Marshall's attraction for a biological metaphor is often documented by the citation that 'the mecca of the economist lies in economic biology rather than in economic dynamics' (Marshall, 1949). Marshall clearly recognized that 'economics, like biology, deals with a matter, of which the inner nature and constitution, as well as the outer form, are constantly changing' (1949, p. 637), a relatively clear reference to qualitative and structural change in economics. While it is undoubtedly true that he was deeply influenced by Spencer (Hodgson, 1993, p. 100), most of his work dealt with economic statics and with a mechanical analogy. He certainly realized the value of a biological metaphor much more than he used it.

Veblen   Veblen made explicit use of Darwin's ideas in his attempt to construct a biologically founded economics (Veblen, 1898; Hodgson, 1993). A central role in Veblen's analysis was played by institutions. According to Veblen, institutions owe their origin to habits of thought, which in turn come from instincts. What Veblen called 'idle curiosity' became for him the source of variety or mutation in the evolutionary process. The institution became the unit of selection, but also in the meantime the replicator. Institutions were characterized by a relative stability and continuity through time. They could thus transmit variety from one period to the next ensuring that selection had relatively stable units on which to operate. Variation, selection and inheritance were thus present in Veblen's analysis. Furthermore, Veblen realized that institutions were themselves the effect of cumulative change, which caused their stability and also forms of hysteresis which limited the adaptation of institutions to their external environment. In summary, Veblen made an explicit attempt to use a biological metaphor in economics and had a number of interesting intuitions. He deserves to be considered one of the precursors of modern evolutionary theories. However, he was not a system builder and his contribution has not been adequately recognized.

Schumpeter   Schumpeter is probably the economist who has had the greatest influence on recent attempts to construct evolutionary theories (see, for example, Nelson and Winter, 1982; Dosi *et al.*, 1988). Schumpeter anticipated a great number of concepts and intuitions that are now incorporated in evolutionary approaches. To begin with economic development is defined by the carrying out of new combinations of productive means by entrepreneurs (Schumpeter, 1912, p. 66). These new combinations are broadly defined as products, processes, markets, sources of raw materials and organizational forms. All these new combinations give rise to products, processes, etc. which are qualitatively different from those that preceded them. In more modern terms one would say that Schumpeter attached great importance to radical innovations as ingredients of economic development. As he emphasized, no amount of improvement in the horse-drawn carriage would have resulted in a transport system competitive with the railroad. The qualitative differences between the two technologies were schismatic. Different knowledge bases, different organizational structures and different working practices were required to exploit the railroad. Thus in his view qualitative change and the generation of economic variety are central to long-term economic development. Furthermore, Schumpeter stresses the non-equilibrium aspects of capitalist development. The creative destruction which 'incessantly revolutionizes the economic structure from within, incessantly destroying the old one, incessantly creating a new one' is one of the fundamental mechanisms of capitalist economic development (Schumpeter, 1942). According to Hodgson (1993) Schumpeter was less evolutionary than his followers have taken him to be. Schumpeter's admiration for Walras is well documented. It is also true that Schumpeter explicitly rejected the use of any biological analogy in economics (Hodgson, 1993, p. 146) and that he was always much closer to a mechanical analogy. However, in spite of these and of other contradictions, Schumpeter provided a broad description of the process of capitalist development based on a number of novel concepts which, although they were not derived from a biological metaphor, can be incorporated in it. This is precisely what some recent evolutionary models of economic and technological change have done.

It is therefore understandable that theories of economic and social change concerned with long-term developments are more likely to emphasize qualitative change, discontinuities and transitions between different forms than are theories concerned with short-term movements and the establishment of equilibrium. The latter would instead emphasize temporary displacements with respect to stable positions. By contrast, Schumpeter and evolutionary economists are concerned with long-term developments which entail qualitative and quantitative change in economic structures. The concept of balanced growth in which all economic activities expand at the same rate is quite foreign to this approach. Of course, the classical economists, including Marx, were also mainly concerned with long-term developments in the economy and society and, even if they did not classify their theories as evolutionary, their relevance to modern evolutionary thinking is considerable. As Clark and Juma (1987) point out, the difference between neoclassical and evolutionary economics is, therefore, one of fundamental goals or more explicitly the analysis of processes of change as distinct from the characterization of states of equilibrium. While neoclassical economics is mostly concerned with what makes the world coherent and ordered, the emphasis in evolutionary theory is upon what makes the world change. This of course does not imply that evolutionary analysis can proceed without some theory of system coherence. As Dosi (1988) has rightly pointed out, there is a conflict between understanding order and understanding development, a conflict which evolutionary theory must address.

Hayek Hayek's thought underwent some changes during his career. In particular, while his emphasis on individual liberties and his opposition to central planning remained, his approach became more consciously evolutionary. An important element of Hayek's evolutionary ideas is the role of rules. Hayek speaks of the 'genetic primacy of rules of conduct' (1982, vol. 3, p. 199; cited in Hodgson, 1993, p. 164). A rule is defined by Hayek as a regularity of conduct of individuals. The durability of rules is due to replication through imitation. This mechanism accounts for the much faster rate of cultural evolution compared to the sluggish biotic process of genetic change and selection (Hodgson, 1993, p. 165). The selection procedure for rules, however, is quite interesting. Rules are selected on the basis of their human survival value, that is, they are indirectly selected through association with a particular group. The groups that follow certain rules are able to procreate more successfully and include outsiders, and are thus going to be imitated more frequently. Therefore, the transmission of rules occurs from individual to individual while selection occurs on a group basis (Hodgson, 1993, p. 170).

Hayek attaches great importance to the idea of spontaneous order. He compares it to the concepts of autopoiesis, cybernetics, homoeostasis, self-organization, synergetics (Hayek, 1988, p. 9; in Hodgson, 1993, p. 177). In support of spontaneous order he also quotes Prigogine and his school (Hayek, 1982, vol. 3, p. 200; cited in Hodgson, 1993, p. 177). Autopoietic or self-organizing systems are defined by the emergence of order from apparent chaos in a far from equilibrium state. However, the stability of self-organizing systems is limited, and drastic fluctuations in the environment can lead to bifurcations and to structural change (Laszlo, 1987, p. 46).

Hayek does not believe that there is such a thing as a perfect society, but he considers some rules superior to others. In particular, he considers collective values atavistic and individualistic values superior to them. The rules which support a liberal society should be superior to those underpinning collectivist societies. A number of tensions and possible contradictions arise in Hayek's thought between his methodological individualism and the presence of rules and of group selection; between the denial of the existence of a perfect society and the belief in superior rules that will lead to spontaneous order; and between the market as selection environment and the market as the object of selection. These tensions do not in any sense diminish the greatness of his work. In fact, a number of his ideas are used by people who do not share his political beliefs but are interested in developing an evolutionary theory.

KEY CONCEPTS IN AN EVOLUTIONARY APPROACH

Evolutionary economics is now being generated by the convergence of the research traditions previously analysed. The new body of knowledge which is being and will continue to be generated by this synthesis is obviously complex and highly differentiated. It is precisely at this stage that one can expect a proliferation of concepts and ideas and that the need to start focusing on the fundamental concepts of the approach arises. This is the purpose of the present section.

The Generation of Variety (Variation)

Economic development consists of the addition to the economic system of new products, processes, markets, organizational forms, etc. which are different from those that composed the system before. One can make here some interesting analogies with what exists in the biological world. Innovations, especially those of a radical nature, are equivalent to mutations. Innovations/mutations continuously generate new forms, products, etc. and therefore lead to a continuously increasing variety. In modern economies innovations are generated mostly by search activities. In the absence of any force limiting it, variety would increase at a pace as high as the generation of new forms. However, there are forces limiting variety, such as selection, which will be analysed in the next section. More positively, not all the new products, processes, etc. which are attempted succeed. Moreover, some older products become extinct due to their complete replacement by new products. The balance between the creation of variety by mutation/innovation and its limitation by selection leads to a surviving net variety of the system.

At variance from what happens in the biological world, innovations/mutations are not produced completely at random. Firms deliberately seek to differentiate themselves from rivals through a multitude of types of product and process innovations. This process contains random elements but it is also shaped by the environment in which firms operate. Firms deliberately design their innovations to adapt to their external environment and sometimes to adapt the environment to themselves. The purposefulness of this adaptation is limited and both bounded rationality and serendipity play a role in innovations. However, there is an anticipatory component within them which is quite foreign to evolution in nature. In this sense socio-economic evolution has a Lamarckian character.

An attempt to relate innovation to the environment in which it was developed took place within neoclassical economics in the form of the induced innovation theory (Hicks, 1932; Kennedy, 1964; Ahmad, 1966; Binswanger and Ruttan, 1978). However, in such theories the only effect innovations had was to change the shape, and therefore the factor requirements, of the production function and could not deal with the generation of new products. This is due to the fact that neoclassical explanations proceed within an optimization framework, generally focus on improvements in process technology for a given set of commodities and have a very low institutional content. On the other hand, evolutionary theory seeks to include an explanation of the processes which generate economic variety through product and process speciation. The processes by which the products, technologies and institutions which surround us today have emerged and become part of the economic system are a central concern of evolutionary economists.

The simplified picture presented above can be refined to take into account the degree of radicalness of an innovation or the gradual/sudden character of evolution. An example of the former is represented by the different attitudes of Schumpeter, who believed that economic development occurred by discrete changes, and Marshall, who was a gradualist. The latter difference has recently been reproposed in biology. Darwin thought that evolution was slow and gradual but more recently some biologists have challenged this concept and proposed the concept of punctuated equilibria (Eldredge and Gould, 1972; Mani, 1991). Naturally, it is not possible to transfer mechanically these concepts to economics. Considerable differences can exist. For example, economic and technological evolution seem to be remarkably faster than their biological analogue (Faber and Proops, 1991).

Selection

Variety generating mechanisms act together with selection mechanisms. The outcome of this combination is the pattern of survival of species/products/technologies/firms that one can observe. In biology, natural selection is determined by the differential adaptation of different species to their environment. Similarly in economic evolution firms are selected on the basis of their adaptation to the environment in which they operate. Firms design products to satisfy consumers and to increase their market share. They prosper and gain economic weight to the extent that customers or users of their products select them. Although there are in this sense similarities between economic and biological evolution there are also differences.

The nature of selection mechanisms was at the root of the differences between Darwin and Lamarck. For Darwin there was no relationship between the generation of mutations and the process of selection. Mutations were produced randomly but only the best adapted ones would survive. For Lamarck, on the other hand, organisms tried to improve their characteristics and therefore mutations were generated with the purpose of achieving the best possible adaptation to their external environment.

No evidence seems to have been found for Lamarckian evolution in biology (Mani, 1991) and Darwinian natural selection is usually considered to be valid by most biologists. The situation is different in economics. Firms' behaviour is boundedly rational and their environment is subject to considerable uncertainty (Simon, 1981). However, conscious processes of planning and strategy-making imply that innovative activities are deliberately designed to improve the firm's adaptation to the environment. A Lamarckian selection mechanism has therefore a much greater plausibility in economics than in biology.

It would, however, be inappropriate to draw from the previous considerations the conclusion that as soon as a change in the environment takes place firms immediately adapt, and those that do not perish. In reality, environmental changes put pressure on firms to adapt but there are significant delays. First, it takes time to design and implement the search activities required to introduce the new productive processes needed for a better adaptation. Second, in addition to the objective difficulties mentioned before, firms may be reluctant to change their managerial culture and their knowledge base and therefore delay the introduction of new practices. To learn new things may mean to 'unlearn' old elements of knowledge (Duncan andWeiss, 1979). This is relevant in the sense that it applies not only to the worst 'adaptors', who in the course of time are eliminated by selection, but to the best performers in the economic system as well. The observation that radical innovations have often to wait for new firms to be introduced is quite common. Established firms having a large share of existing markets may be too committed to their present practices. There are many examples of such situations in the development of the electronics and the biotechnology industries.

The generation of mutations and selection would have a very limited impact on the pattern of survival of species were it not for the fact that information about adaptation is transmitted to subsequent generations. The next two key points are derived from the two distinct and related problems of reproduction and inheritance.

Reproduction and Inheritance

One of the fundamental processes in biological evolution is reproduction. In biology, species reproduce, generally sexually, and can transmit their genetic make-up to their offspring. There is thus some continuity between different generations, which allows the identification of species. The phenotype can instead change depending on the external environment, but phenotypic modifications are not passed on to subsequent generations. Analogues of the phenotype and of the genotype can be defined in the social sciences (Faber and Proops, 1991) but some differences are likely to exist.

The meaning of reproduction is clearly different in economics. Particular artefacts or outputs can be replicated by producing organizations. In a strict sense the replicator should be the combination of the firm and of its output. However, in the meantime within the firm routines and decision rules are passed on to subsequent generations of employees. Continuity in output structure is linked to some continuity in the internal structure of the organization, at the level of routines and decision rules.

An exact analogue of the phenotype does not exist in economics. One can point to some continuities in the course of time in the way in which organizations 'do things'. Habits of thought, institutions (Veblen, 1919), rules of conduct (Hayek, in Hodgson, 1993, ch. 11), routines, decision rules (Nelson and Winter, 1974, 1982), etc. may be maintained for considerable periods of time, or have short-term stability. This is necessary if the organization is to be recognizable in the course of time. What can be generalized is the difference between some components of, for example, a firm which interact directly and continuously with the environment and are modified by those interactions, and other components which are shielded by these interactions and maintain relatively constant values for relatively long periods of time. However, the impossibility that the genotype is modified by environmental interactions need not apply to social systems. In social systems, such as firms and organizations, the difference between genotype and phenotype might be more one of degree than of presence/absence. Environmental interactions might affect the phenotype to a much greater extent and with much faster response times than the genotype. However, selected environmental interactions might affect the genotype as well, and their effect might be transmitted to subsequent generations.

Examples of economic and organizational genotypes have been given by: Boulding (1978, 1981), who considers know-how to be the equivalent of the genetic make-up of human societies; Nelson and Winter (1982), who consider routines and decision rules as the equivalent of the genetic make-up in firms; McKelvey (1982), who sees the pool of dominant competences of an organization as its genotype. Know-how, routines, decision rules and dominant competences are relatively invariant with respect to many types of environmental changes thus giving rise to dominant designs, technological regimes and paradigms. Thus engineering know-how, routines and competences are not affected by short-term fluctuations in demand. However, important environmental changes requiring, for example, substantial modifications of the technologies used by a firm, are likely to induce changes in routines, know-how and competences which are then transmitted to subsequent generations.

A greater similarity can be expected between the concept of phenotype in biology and in economics. In economics output characteristics will be modified to adapt them better to the external environment. Such adaptation will rarely lead to a change in the internal structure of the output or in the routines leading to its production. Here the already mentioned difference between the units of observation in biology and in economics becomes relevant. The analogue of the DNA cannot be found only in the output (see also Chapter 4) but in the knowledge base, routines and decision rules of firms producing the given output. One can expect that environmental changes of a limited and somewhat predictable nature will be 'filtered' by a constant knowledge base and routines and will lead to incremental innovations in the products of the firm. More dramatic, qualitative changes in the environment are likely to require a modification of the current knowledge base and routines. These, after having been changed, will remain constant for a relatively long period of time. The previous observations do not exclude that dramatic changes in the knowledge base and routines may be generated by developments internal to the firm. Paradigm shifts can be induced by the emergence of a new and vastly superior technology, by other (non-technological) drastic types of environmental changes, which first lead to a search and then to the emergence of a new technology, and by the internal searches of a particular firm. Naturally the last mechanism applies only to the inventing firm. All the other imitating firms will follow the first mechanism.

The situation becomes more complicated if one considers a multiproduct firm. Here the genotype is more complex both because it needs to contain more competences and because these competences may be interacting. The knowledge base may be different from the sum of the competences corresponding to each individual product, especially if there are significant synergisms. In this case, environmental changes affecting a given part of the knowledge base may have an effect on apparently unrelated technologies. Moreover, the firm has a set of financial competences which are located in a different part of the knowledge base. The firm's reaction to environmental changes in financial markets may allow it to partly shield itself from competition in product markets. Therefore, in the case of a multiproduct firm with a substantial involvement in financial markets, both the constitution of the genotype and its interactions with the environment become far more complicated. However, the basic principles remain the same.

Fitness and Adaptation

A very important role was played in Darwinian evolution by fitness, to the extent that the expression 'the survival of the fittest' came to epitomize evolution. The definition of fitness poses some problems. In principle, fitness refers to the capacity of a species to adapt to a given environment. However, it can acquire a tauto-logical meaning if it is judged ex-post by the capacity to survive. We need a definition of fitness separate from that of evolutionary success. In other words, fitness refers to the propensity of a unit to be successful in a given environment (Hodgson, 1993, p. 49). Furthermore, it is now clear that it is not the absolute fittest, but only the tolerably fit that survives (ibid., p. 94). Survival is determined both by adaptation of a species to its external environment and by its fertility (ibid., p. 95). A discussion of the concept of fitness in the analysis of techno-logical evolution will take place in Chapter 6.

Population Perspective

The concept of population is one of the fundamental concepts in biology. In the social sciences, however, a population perspective has been overshadowed (Hannan and Freeman, 1977, 1989) by a typological perspective. According to the latter, entities are regarded as identifiable in terms of a few distinct char-acteristics which represent their essential qualities. In a population perspective, on the other hand, the variations internal to a species are extremely important. Then it becomes relevant to consider not only average values but also variances and their relation to the evolutionary process. In other words, whereas in typo-logical thinking variation is seen as a classificatory nuisance, in population thinking variation is an essential component of an evolutionary process.

Elementary Interactions

It would be useful to be able to classify all the possible types of interactions between firms, organizations and economic agents in terms of a few elementary interactions. In biology all the possible interactions between pairs of species can be classified into three types (Maynard Smith, 1974, p. 5):

(a) *Competition* – each species has an inhibiting effect on the other.
(b) *Commensalism* – each species has an accelerating effect on the growth of the other.
(c) *Predation* – one species, the 'predator', has an inhibiting effect on the growth of the other, the 'prey'; the prey has an accelerating effect on the growth of the predator.

Naturally one cannot expect to be able to transfer the same types of elementary interactions to economics. In economics, competition is virtually the only type of interaction studied. In biology, where competition is for a common resource in short supply, it is not the only process contributing to natural selection (Sober, 1984, p. 100; cited in Hodgson, 1993, p. 30). In economics, as well, collaboration is an important if unrecognized type of interaction, as recent trends in industrial organization have shown (see Chapter 8). Furthermore, competition has been conceptualized in a rather narrow way, with an excessive emphasis on perfect competition. Perfect competition is that most commonly encountered in textbooks. It describes a situation in which firms are price takers, there is free entry which establishes a position of normal profitability, and all firms produce a homogeneous and equal product. Perfect competition is, however, more a state of affairs to be attained after all competitive forces have been eliminated rather than a force leading to change (McNulty, 1968). A different type of competition called innovation competition is described by Metcalfe and Gibbons (Metcalfe, 1984; Metcalfe and Gibbons, 1987, 1989). This type of competition is driven by 'technological differences between firms which has as its outcome continuous changes in the relative economic performance of firms'. Clearly the latter type of competition is much more reminiscent of the Schumpeterian introduction of 'new combinations' by entrepreneurs (Schumpeter, 1912, pp. 65–6).

One of the important differences between these types of competition consists in the nature of firms' output. In perfect competition all firms are equal and therefore they cannot generate any qualitative change in their output or method of production. In innovation competition firms deliberately differentiate their products . Therefore innovation competition is compatible with evolution while perfect competition on its own is not.

In Chapters 4 and 6 competition will be analysed in characteristics space, thus allowing us to place real life competitive situations in a range of which perfect and innovation competition are the extremes. As perfect competition is approached the products of different competitors become progressively more similar; as one moves towards innovation competition the products become progressively more different. Examples of both these trends have been found in the evolution of motor car and aircraft technologies (Saviotti, 1985, 1988a) (see Chapters 4 to 6).

External Environments

Here we can only point out that the concept of external environment is a key element in evolutionary economics. Further and more detailed examination of this concept will take place in Chapter 8.

UNRESOLVED ISSUES AND DIRECTIONS FOR FURTHER DEVELOPMENTS

As previously pointed out, evolutionary economics is at a fairly early stage in its development. This stage can be characterized as one of formation of fundamental assumptions and basic concepts. Remembering also that there is at present a convergence of different research traditions into evolutionary economics one can understand that this could lead to two classes of problems. On the one hand, given the different goals for which these fundamental assumptions and basic concepts had been developed, one cannot expect them to be coherent and compatible from the beginning. On the other hand, there is the problem of avoiding coarse forms of reductionism. It can, therefore, be expected that an initial proliferation of concepts will be followed by a gradual selection and adaptation of them to the new research tradition.

Naturally, at this early stage, evolutionary economics does not yet have a formal structure of sophistication comparable to that of neoclassical economics. It can be expected that the construction of such a formal structure will be one of the next and most important tasks of evolutionary economics and one which will determine its success or failure. The predominance of a Keynesian with respect to a Schumpeterian approach was due at least in part to the greater ease with which Keynes's ideas could be put in mathematical form (Hanusch, 1988, p. 5).

Problems related to the choice of fundamental assumptions, to the development of formal methods and to the construction of conceptual tools are now discussed.

Some Basic Assumptions

As previously mentioned, the different research traditions which are converging in forming modern evolutionary economics are not simply added up, but are related in a hierarchically structured complementarity. Some of them provide theoretical justification for others, and it is in principle possible to transfer concepts and methods between different research traditions, although with some modifications. In this context it is important to understand the limitations to the transferability of concepts and ideas between different disciplines. According to Elster (1983) the physical, biological and social sciences differ for the mode of explanation that they use. Thus physics uses a causal, biology a functional and the social sciences an intentional mode of explanation. In a causal mode of explanation events are explained by means of a regular conjunction with certain causes. On the other hand, a feature of an organism is functionally explained if it can be proved to be part of a local individual maximum with respect to reproductive capacity (ibid., p. 53). Finally we explain intentionally an action when we are able to specify the future state it was intended to bring about (ibid., p. 70). Clearly these modes of explanation are related to our basic perception of the subject matter we are studying. Thus we usually attach a certain degree of intentionality to human behaviour but not to animal behaviour. In particular we consider that technical evolution differs from biological evolution in that the changes are far from random but to some extent directed. These changes are also screened by a mechanism in which human intentionality plays a role (ibid., p. 12).

The separation of these modes of explanation as presented above is somewhat excessive. Thus in intentional explanation one needs to relate particular actions to a goal or a set of goals that the actions are aimed at bringing about. However, the existence of a goal does not necessarily imply that it will be achieved. Causal mechanisms will have to be invoked in order to explain how the goal itself has been achieved. Therefore, the different modes of explanation are not entirely incompatible and can to a certain extent be used jointly. There are however incompatibilities, such as the impossibility to use intentional explanation in physics.

These considerations are relevant in the present context because the different research traditions which converge in modern evolutionary economics have, according to Elster, different modes of explanation. The transfer and adaptation of ideas and concepts between these research traditions has to be done taking differences in underlying modes of explanation into account. This has two implications: first, as already mentioned, we can only expect different research traditions to be able to suggest analogies and questions but not necessarily to provide answers for evolutionary economics; second, this imposes a continuing attention to the fundamental aspects of any concept, idea or theory which is integrated into evolutionary economics.

The presence and the location of intentionality in economics is discussed by a number of authors. To have conscious aims or goals that can be generated or change without fluctuations in the external environment is a peculiar feature of human beings and therefore of the social sciences. Different schools of economic thought in the past have stressed the purposeful character of human actions (Hodgson, 1988, 1991, 1993). The Austrian school is perhaps the one that has laid the greatest emphasis on purposeful behaviour. However, they only recognize purposeful behaviour in individuals and not in organizations or institutions. Furthermore, they tend to disregard any influence of the external environment on individuals and on their purposeful behaviour. A number of choices are therefore open for evolutionary theorists to follow: determinism vs. purposeful behaviour, determinism vs. indeterminacy, individual vs. collective (organizations, institutions), environment dependent vs. environment independent. Choices of this type are unlikely to be testable but they are important components of any theory and it is important for them to be explicitly articulated in the construction of evolutionary theories. In a similar vein, Foster (1985) in attempting to establish an evolutionary basis for macroeconomics maintains that scientific materialism and homo-economicus form part of the core of orthodox economic theories and that they cannot be refuted empirically. An evolutionary approach will need similarly general foundations.

An extremely important aspect of evolutionary theories, which is shared by economics but is not unique to it, is constituted by their predictive power. Both fluctuations and qualitative change, which are amongst their important features, can limit their predictive power. This is an important issue because predictive power is considered to be a fundamental property of a well-developed scientific theory, and it is important to establish whether there are any limits to the predictive power of a science. Such limitations have been found for physics and they have not compromised the scientific character of the discipline. According to Boulding (1981), prediction is possible only in systems that have stable parameters like celestial mechanics. By his definition, evolution leads to a change of parameters and therefore is essentially unpredictable. Similarly, Faber and Proops (1991) maintain that qualitative change, which they define as change in the genotype, is essentially unpredictable. Whether there is some degree of predictability of qualitative change depends on the continuity between the new and the old. At the root of this problem there is the tension between being and becoming, which has been a fundamental one in western philosophy. In recent times this tension, at least in the context of the natural sciences, has been solved in favour of being. One of the most important features of the development of modern science in the last two to three hundred years has been the attempt to reduce the different and changing to the identical and the permanent (Prigogine and Stengers, 1984, p. 293). Thus all changes were reduced in principle to changes in the position and interaction of the various elementary constituents of the universe. In this attempt a central role was played by the concept of time, which became basically 'a geometric parameter that makes it possible to follow the unfolding of the succession of dynamical states' (ibid., p. 293). Naturally, this concept of time implied also the reversibility of processes. The transition to an evolutionary paradigm involves, among other things, a redefinition of the balance between being and becoming. By emphasizing 'becoming' instead of 'being', one would largely abandon any hope to explain and above all to predict events and processes. Some degree of continuity and commonality of constituents between past, present and future is required if the world has to make sense and show some predictability. Thus the concept of time and the nature and invariance of the constituents of the system stated are fundamentally related to the reversibility (or lack) of processes and to the predictive power of science. The acceptance of irreversibility points to a different role of oriented time. Irreversibility is no longer a purely subjective perception but a fundamental characteristic of scientific explanations (ibid., p. 298). It is very unlikely that this debate can be considered concluded now. To abandon the hope of predicting events would be a very serious problem for any scientific discipline. On the other hand, it seems necessary to accept the limitations to our knowledge which are due to the role of fluctuations and possibly to some extent of objective indeterminacy.

The development of neoclassical economics has been dependent on an analogy with classical mechanics (Clark and Juma, 1987, 1988). The same concept of time as a geometric parameter has therefore been used in economics. Furthermore, given the concern of economists with equilibrium states, questions of mutual consistency of given relationships have been highlighted rather than the nature and mechanisms of the corresponding processes which destroy those states. Thus in explaining the sources of economic growth, it is the shifts of the production function and not their timing and origin which are important (Amendola and Gaffard, 1988). It is obviously one of the tasks of evolutionary economics to recover a concept of time which is compatible with becoming, and which gives a substantial role to the nature of processes. This would supply a much needed connection with history.

Evolutionary theories deny the existence of complete determinism and, therefore, of total predictability. The presence of fluctuations near transitions leads to indeterminacy and does not allow us to predict accurately the state(s) after the transition. We can reach an understanding of the states which are possible after the transition, but not know the one that will necessarily be occupied.

This very brief description of some fundamental problems in evolutionary theories does not pretend to be comprehensive. Its aim is simply to point out that problems of this kind are particularly acute at this state and that continuing study and analysis of them is fundamental for the further development of the subject.

Units of Analysis and Taxonomy

Like any science, evolutionary economics must have a conceptual apparatus which is compatible with empirical analysis. This enables economic theories to be applied to particular situations, and that empirical analysis can serve as a basis from which to infer further theories. In this sense an important problem for an evolutionary approach is to establish its units of analysis at different levels of aggregation. Given the central role of technology in these considerations one needs to have units of observation for both organizations and technology. Here it must be observed that units of analysis are not necessarily the same in different studies. Individuals, organizations, innovations, technologies can all be units of observation. While we may not necessarily be able to establish a relationship similar to that between atoms, molecules and macroscopic objects, it is important to establish the relationship and compatibility of the units of analysis of different studies.

Firms are the most common but not the only producer and user of technology. An example of a generalized definition of organizational species, which encompasses both firms and other types of organizations, has been proposed by McKelvey (1982, pp. 171–2) on the basis of *dominant competencies*. An organization has a primary task and a set of managerial activities which are directly related to the implementation of the primary task and which constitute the workplace managerial task. Of all the competencies of the organization, the most important ones are those which are directly related to the primary task and to the workplace management task. The set of all these competencies constitutes the dominant competencies of the organization (ibid., pp. 189, 191). The elements of dominant competence are called comps. An organizational species is then constituted by population of organizations sharing some dominant competences (ibid., chapter 7).

For what concerns the technologies themselves the units of analysis are the products and the processes used to produce them. The previously mentioned contributions by Sahal (1981a and b) and by Saviotti and Metcalfe (1984) are examples of possible definitions of these units of analysis. In the latter, products are represented by two sets of characteristics, one describing the internal structure of the technology (technical characteristics) and one representing the services performed for its users (service characteristics). Processes are represented by different characteristics (capital and labour intensity, structure, types of machines, process layout, batch mass flow process, etc.). By means of these units of analysis, one can represent various types of elementary processes (see next section), measure degrees of technological change and develop a numerical taxonomy.

In addition to a taxonomy of organizations and of technologies one can establish a taxonomy of innovations and innovation strategy. Thus innovations can be classified as product or process, radical or incremental (Freeman and Perez, 1988). Conversely, innovation strategies can be classified as offensive, defensive, imitation, dependent, traditional and opportunist (Freeman, 1982). An innovation taxonomy at a higher level of aggregation has been proposed by Pavitt (1984). In his classification, industrial sectors are classified as supplier dominated sectors, scale intensive sectors, specialized suppliers and science based sectors. These sectors differ with respect to the source of the innovations that they use (they can be imported into the sector, generated internally or sold to other sectors), with respect to size and capital intensity, to the type of process used (mass, flow, etc.) and to the influence of science on the performance of the sector.

A well-developed evolutionary theory will require a better developed taxonomy at all levels of aggregation in such a way that the relationships of the various units of analysis within and between each level of aggregation can be analysed. Naturally, this taxonomy is now far from complete and will need to be extended and refined.

Elementary Processes of Technological Evolution and Other Basic Concepts

Qualitative change linked to the emergence of new products and services and new organizational forms has previously been indicated in this chapter as one of the fundamental components of an evolutionary explanation. How these

qualitative changes are to be measured is a critical problem in evolutionary explanations of economic change.

New products, services, etc., can either substitute previous ones or coexist
alongside them. Depending on the outcome of the substitution process, the
economic system will have a changing variety of surviving 'species'. This is
obviously a very interesting question because the concept of variety can be the
basis for an analytical representation of the qualitative change that is so central
both to economic development and an evolutionary perspective. Therefore, it
is important to understand the nature of variety of the economic system and to
give a rigorous analytical definition of it. This way it will become possible to
map trends in variety in the course of economic development and to analytically relate variety to other important variables characterizing the economic
system.

As already mentioned, new products and services are continuously emerging
in the economic system. If the majority of these do not substitute for previous
products and services but are simply 'added' to the economy, the variety of the
system is likely to increase. Casual observation of the habits of an average
household gives the impression that the number of types of goods and services
used now is much greater than that which was available only two or three hundred
years ago. Product differentiation and diversification have added to this variety.
However, it must be remembered that they are essentially a phenomenon typical
of mature industrialized societies which began on a large scale during the 20th
century. The implications of these considerations are twofold: first, they point
to the number of surviving species (products, services, etc.) as an important aspect
of variety; second, they seem to imply that, at least in recent historical times,
the variety of the economic system might have been increasing. A definition
of this type of variety at the level of aggregation of the economic system as a
whole, is the number of distinguishable products, services, etc., in the system.
This aspect of variety and its implications for technological and economic
evolution is discussed in Saviotti (1988a, 1991a).

Different types of phenomena, closely related to a population perspective,
occur at another level of aggregation in the economic system. During the
evolution of a technology or an industry the number and size of firms is likely
to change. Such changes are incorporated in the models of Nelson and Winter
(1982) and Metcalfe and Gibbons (1989). This amounts to a change in the institutional variety of the supply structure of a given industry during its evolution.
Consequently, the variance of a number of properties of the firms in the industry
changes in response to the forces of competition selection, innovation and institution. Other features of the firms in the industry, such as the number of product
designs at each time, the nature of the process technologies used, etc., which
also contribute to the variety of the system, are likely to change systematically

during the evolution of the industry (Abernathy and Utterback, 1975). Similar changes in the variance of these properties can be expected.

Thus different aspects of the variety of the economic system exist at different levels of aggregation. Furthermore, they are not independent. The main purpose of these notes, however, is not to give a complete description of the concept of variety and of its aspects and methods of measurement but to suggest that variety is a very important concept which promises to have a fundamental role in the development of an analytical treatment of the processes of qualitative change previously described.

Changes in variety can take place by means of a number of mechanisms. For analytical purposes it would be very useful to be able to represent such complex processes, of which there is a great diversity in the economic system, by means of a small number of elementary processes. These would be the common dynamic constituents of complex processes of economic and technological change. To discuss these elementary processes it is useful to adopt the distinction which is often made, although only for didactic purposes, between the act of innovation and its subsequent diffusion. Naturally, this does not imply that these two stages of generation and utilization of innovations are independent. Some elementary processes are more closely related to the generations of innovations, others to their subsequent diffusion; amongst these there are technological substitution, specialization and emergence of completely new products.

Elementary processes can be very useful building blocks in the representation and analysis of complex processes of technological change. Recent research in the economics of technological change has also uncovered a number of general patterns of evolution of technologies. For example, Abernathy and Utterback (1975, 1978) proposed a life cycle in which technologies evolve from a multiplicity of product designs to a dominant design and in which simultaneously the scale and organization of the production process change from small and loosely coordinated to large and rigidly coordinated (systemic). In a somewhat similar way, although starting from quite different premises, Nelson and Winter (1977) introduced the concepts of technological regimes and natural trajectories, Sahal (1981a,b) that of technological guideposts and Dosi (1982) that of technological paradigm. Apart from their specific features, these concepts all point toward some degree of invariance of technological systems with respect to fluctuations in their external environments (Saviotti, 1986) or alternatively a form of self-organization of the system. These developments have therefore redefined the previous need or demand pull/technology push debate (Mowery and Rosenberg, 1979; Coombs, Saviotti and Walsh 1987) by limiting the influence of demand on technology to changes within the existing technological paradigm.

Similar patterns at a higher level of aggregation have been proposed by Perez (1983) and Freeman and Perez (1988). They talk about technoeconomic paradigms as the combination of regularities in the technologies used and in the surrounding institutions. A particularly important role is played for them by the delay with which institutions adapt to the new potential generated by new technologies.

Quite apart from their specific features these concepts imply a considerable discontinuity in economic and technological development and some form of self-organization which gives the technological or economic system a relatively stable and ordered structure which only occasionally undergoes Gestalt switches to different configurations. The nature of such regularities has so far been proposed but very little both empirical or theoretical research has been done on them. Amongst the first analytical treatments are those of Metcalfe (1984) and Heiner (1983, 1988). Furthermore, these concepts imply that some features of technology can change continually while others change only rarely. For example, some elements of the knowledge base are common to the firms operating in a given technology and change only when a transition to a different paradigm occurs. Consequently, one can interpret the knowledge base as the equivalent of the genetic make-up and the paradigmatic transition as the equivalent of a mutation.

In summary, this section has discussed a number of emerging conceptual tools which were not present in orthodox economics. These concepts have originated recently from the generalization of findings of studies of technological change. Such studies were generally not carried out according to an explicitly evolutionary framework but were rather eclectic in their methodology and empirical in their approach (Coombs, Saviotti and Walsh, 1987). This eclecticism reflected the unsuitability of orthodox economics for the purposes of the studies and their policy orientation. Although such studies of technological change were not explicitly evolutionary they helped to formulate a number of important concepts which have become an integral part of a modern evolutionary approach because they analysed one of the main ingredients of qualitative change in the system. As already pointed out, this level of analysis allows the reconstruction of processes of technological change and not only of their outcome. Those studies of technological change were therefore of fundamental importance in providing material which one can consider implicit data and evidence for an evolutionary explanation.

From these empirical studies a natural history of innovation is emerging, from which higher level conceptual structures can be developed. In most cases these are still in a qualitative form and are still non-analytically founded and non-analytically applicable. One can foresee that the next stage of conceptual development will consist of the construction of analytical foundations and structures for basic concepts like those described above. Naturally, this does not exclude that other new conceptual structures can be inferred but it implies that they too will need a sound analytical foundation.

The Role of Technology

Technological change plays a very important part in this book. It is one of the fields of study which has given some of the most important contributions to the development of a modern evolutionary approach. Yet technological change is not accorded a very prominent role by the economics profession. It is hardly mentioned in general economics textbooks and it plays a secondary role even in industrial economics textbooks. Courses on the economics of technological change are very rare and specialized options. Policies for science and technology are conceived outside economics and have very limited relationships with the mainstream of economic policy. All this can make sense only to the extent that technological change is exogenous to the economic system and therefore that the economist has only to register its outcomes and proceed to relate them to other aspects of economic behaviour. To the extent that technological change is itself one of the main aspects of economic change and development then it must necessarily play a more central role in economic theory and policy.

This defence of the role of technological change in economic life and theory does not in any way imply that it is the only cause of qualitative change. Schumpeter is often quoted as one of the main proponents of the importance of technological change in economic development but he included new markets and new forms of organization amongst the main types of change. What is required is not an excessive and one-sided emphasis on technological change but a generalized concept of innovation and experimentation and of their relationship to more routine activities.

SUMMARY

In order to understand the present state of development of evolutionary economics, this chapter analyses the different research traditions that are contributing to it. Biology, evolutionary interpretations in economics, systems theory, non-equilibrium thermodynamics, and firm and organization theories are the research traditions having the greatest influence and converging to a considerable extent in forming modern evolutionary theories. The different research traditions are in a relationship of hierarchical complementarity, in the sense that some of them provide theoretical justification for the fundamental concepts of others. In turn, it is possible to transfer and adapt some of the problematics, concepts and methods between the different research traditions. From this convergence a number of key concepts and processes emerge: variation, selection, reproduction and inheritance, fitness and adaptation, a population perspective, irreversibility and path dependency, elementary interactions and external environments. While this may not be an exhaustive list, the articulation and adaptation of such concepts to economic evolution would constitute a non-negligible achievement. In Parts 2 and 3 of the book an attempt will be made to articulate these concepts in the context of technological evolution and of organizations at different levels of aggregation.

This chapter ends with an analysis of unresolved issues and of directions for further development. The presence and location of intentionality in economics, the predictive power of theories and the concept of time are some important unresolved issues. The definition of units of analysis, of elementary processes in technological evolution and the role of technology are important problems to be faced in approaching the analysis of qualitative change in economic development.

Returning now to the theme started in Chapter 2, the comparison of neoclassical and evolutionary theories, we can see that they have different observation spaces. For example, analysis of the internal structure of technological developments and of organizations are part of the observation space of evolutionary but not of neoclassical economics. Other differences between the two can be found in terms of the use of either a typological or a population perspective, of the importance of random fluctuations and of open systems.

These differences repropose in a more complex way the relationship between evolutionary and neoclassical economics, and clearly have implications for the future development of the former. From the results of the previous analysis one could conclude that evolutionary economics tends to address different problems with respect to neoclassical economics, and therefore to have a different observation space. This would indicate an at least partly complementary role of the two. To the extent that the two research traditions have non-overlapping observation spaces one would expect their relationship not to be one of substitutes and therefore of competitors. In this sense a substitution of neoclassical by evolutionary economics is unlikely. It would be more logical to expect a higher synthesis of the two. By 'adding them up' one would simply expand the scope of economics as a whole. However, it is also true that the two research traditions are competing in overlapping parts of their observation spaces. This implies that although the most important role of evolutionary economics is likely to be to address problems which for choice, 'repression' or inadequate conceptual tools had remained outside the scope of neoclassical economics, a situation of simple complementarity is likely to be problematic. Different conceptual tools, attitudes and values generated and stabilized within each research tradition will hinder the process of comparison of overlapping parts of their observation spaces and of synthesis of the two. In spite of this complexity, at least some features of the path forward for evolutionary economics seem to be clear: the synthesis of the concepts derived from the converging research traditions, the development of formal methods and the integration with static aspects of economics seem to be very important directions for future development.

PART 2

A Model of Technological Evolution

INTRODUCTION

In Chapter 1 the analysis of qualitative change and the need for an explicit analysis of technological change were indicated as the two main themes of this book. Moreover, an evolutionary approach was considered more appropriate to the analysis of technological change and of its role in the economy. After having established a number of methodological points we can now begin with the actual analysis of technological change. As already indicated, the rest of the book will be divided into two parts, the first concerned with artefacts, mostly with product technology, and the second with knowledge. While they do not represent all the characters missing from an implicit approach, they are two very important characters and their analysis constitutes a relevant example of an explicit approach to technological change. In the meantime, their treatment is also a good example of the analysis of qualitative change.

In Chapter 4 a generalized representation of product technology is introduced. By means of such a representation, which separates the internal structure of the technology from the services it provides for its users, it is possible to distinguish analytically radical and incremental innovation. Such a representation allows us to recognize and map an important aspect of qualitative change.

In Chapter 5 a model of technological evolution based on replicator dynamics is introduced. Qualitative change is at the centre of this model, which represents the evolution of technological populations, including the emergence of completely new ones.

Finally, in Chapter 6, the concept of variety is introduced as one of the main variables required to provide an analytical representation of qualitative change. Variety provides also an important link between technological change and economic development. Two important hypotheses are formulated in Chapter 6, implying that (a) variety growth is a necessary condition for the long-term continuation of economic development, and (b) variety growth and efficiency growth in old sectors are complementary tendencies. Finally, by means of the model of technological evolution based on replicator dynamics it is found that intra-technology competition must be greater than inter-technology competition in order for variety to grow.

In summary, insights and methods which are in the meantime relevant for an explicit analysis of technological change and for that of qualitative change are discussed. Naturally, qualitative change is not completely caused by or embodied in artefacts, but knowledge and institutions and organizational structures make a fundamental contribution to its generation. Such other aspects will be discussed in Part 3 of the book. Finally, it must be pointed out that the structure of the models and representations used is in part due to a generalization of the results obtained in a large number of studies of innovation.

4.   A characteristics and population approach to technological evolution

INTRODUCTION

This chapter begins with the double objective of developing an explicit approach to the economic analysis of technological change and of dealing with qualitative change as one of the fundamental aspects of economic development. The characters of technological evolution which will be used here are product models, that is the different variants of each product which are available in markets. Such product models are obviously diversified and will be represented by means of two sets of characteristics. Before proceeding to describe the representation of these characters it is important to note that they do not constitute all the possible characters of technological change. Process technologies, human skills and qualifications are examples of other such characters, but they will not be incorporated in the analysis here. Therefore, the approach developed in this book is not comprehensive, but is intended more as an example of the way to proceed. By means of the characteristics representation it will be seen that the models are represented by points in characteristics space and that, unless they are all identical, the models will be distributed in characteristics space. Such distribution will constitute a technological population. The population approach will be the second half of the representation of product technology used in this chapter. It will be shown that such representation can help us to understand more accurately than is possible at the moment some key concepts, such as when technologies are different, the difference between radical and incremental innovation, the nature of technological regimes, trajectories and paradigms, etc. Also, such representation will allow us to perform technology mapping, that is to trace the evolution of technological populations in characteristics space. Technology mapping is useful both for its strategic implications and because it can allow us to infer generalizations about technological evolution.

A TWIN CHARACTERISTICS REPRESENTATION OF PRODUCT TECHNOLOGY

A theory of technological evolution has to enable us to represent, interpret and predict the changes that we call technological evolution. The minimum requirements for such a theory are a set of units of analysis, some elementary patterns of interaction amongst them, and some criteria to assess the overall evolution of the system. Furthermore, the theory must have connections and links with economic theories and, possibly, with other theories of social behaviour.

In order to define the units of analysis, or characters, of technological evolution, we begin with a biological analogy. We need to define the analogues of organisms, species and populations. For the purposes of this chapter product models will be considered the analogues of organisms, but there is here a fundamental difference with respect to biology. As opposed to biological organisms, technological products cannot reproduce themselves. They are reproduced by organizations (firms etc.) which replicate them using production processes. The real equivalent of a biological organism, or the proper unit of analysis, in this case should be the combination of the producing organization and of its output. An organization has an internal structure and uses knowledge to produce its output. In other words, an organization has a *knowledge base* (Metcalfe and Gibbons, 1987, 1989) and a set of *capabilities* (Teece, Pisano and Shuen, 1990). The nature of the output and the changes that it undergoes in the course of time are related to the organization's knowledge and internal structure. Competition amongst organizations takes place, at least in part, by means of their output. The output constitutes the revealed technological performance (RTP) of organizations. The RTP of firms/organizations at the time of its production is an embodiment of their knowledge and capabilities. Naturally, knowledge and capabilities have to change in the course of time before they can be embodied in new RTP. Firms are always carrying out search activities while replicating existing products/output, which is based on previous search activities. At any time the RTP of a firm is going to be a map of the capabilities the firm had some time before. The attempt to study the evolution of technological artefacts and to find out if there are any patterns or regularities in their evolution does not correspond to the assumption that technologies, interpreted as artefacts, have an existence independent of the organizations which produce them. In other words, there is no implicit assumption of technological determinism. The focus chosen here is determined by the fact that the nature of the output was a variable completely absent in traditional theories (where output was assumed to be homogeneous in each industry). On the other hand, there are two very good reasons for studying changes in RTP: first, it is a fundamental determinant of the variety of the system and, second, it is an extremely important variable for any technology or innovation policy.

Technological models will, therefore, be assumed to be organisms competing for customers/users. Different firms will produce populations of similar but not identical models. There will be variations amongst models. Models with better variations will be selected preferentially and will contribute to increase the economic weight/market share of the producing firm. Better variations will be generated either by improving gradually the properties of pre-existing products (incremental innovation) and/or by introducing radically new ones (radical innovation).

In this way there will be both qualitative and quantitative changes in the existing stock of technologies. Quantitative changes are likely to be more frequent, but qualitative changes have a very important role to play in long-term economic development, as stressed by Schumpeter (1912). It is the innovations, or the new combinations of means of production that allow the economic system to continue in its development (ibid., p. 66). Also, it is the qualitative changes or innovations which increase the variety or diversity of the economic system. Thus, due to innovations like the aircraft, motor car, tape recorder, television, fridge, etc. the landscape of technological artefacts that surrounds us in our everyday life has changed completely and qualitatively in the last two hundred years. New technologies and new industries are created in this process, while some older ones disappear, or become extinct. However, the diversity/variety of the economic system will increase only if pre-existing goods and services survive alongside the new ones. This is not always the case, since one of the most common processes in technological development is the substitution of a pre-existing commodity by a new one. It is, therefore, important to consider the *net* variety of the economic system.

Our units of analysis are then artefacts. The importance of artefacts can be appreciated remembering the distinction, introduced by Lotka and adopted by Georgescu Roegen (1971, pp. 11, 307), between *endosomatic* and *exosomatic* instruments. The former are the biological organs that both animals and human beings are born with. The latter are those instruments which are produced, predominantly by human beings. One can, therefore, talk about endosomatic and exosomatic evolution. Problems of income distribution in human societies are fundamentally related to the onset of the social production of exosomatic instruments, which took place at a very early stage of exosomatic evolution.

What is required is a general representation of artefacts. This chapter will focus on a subset of all artefacts, that of product models. However, before we proceed to describe the representation adopted here, it is important to remember that a very common distinction used in innovation studies is that between product and process technology. In principle, process technology can be reduced to a combination of products (e.g. machine tools) produced by other firms. No attempt is made here to extend the approach illustrated in this chapter to process technology.

The Representation of Technologies

The units of analysis are the products, which constitute the final output of a technology. These products are complex, multicharacteristics and highly differentiable. Each firm using the technology produces a number of different models.

The output is constituted by the sum of the numbers of each model. Each of these models is defined or represented by two sets of characteristics describing the internal structure of the technology and the services performed for its users. The two sets are called *technical* and *service* characteristics respectively (Saviotti and Metcalfe, 1984) (see Figure 4.1). The meaning of this distinction can be understood from a number of points of view. First, technology is the knowledge required to transform materials, energy and labour into final products, which can then satisfy some type of demand. This process of transformation starts with scientific and technological knowledge, and ends with services provided for the users of the products. Scientific and technological knowledge are embodied in the technical characteristics of the technology. These are the only characteristics that can be modified directly by the producers. Thus a motor car manufacturer can only design the engine and the shape of the car body in order to produce a required speed of transport, but not produce directly that speed of transport. Seen from the viewpoint of a producer, technical characteristics are like buttons that, when pushed, produce required services.

$$\textbf{Technical} \qquad \textbf{Service}$$

$$\begin{pmatrix} X_{i1} \\ X_{i2} \\ \cdot \\ \cdot \\ \cdot \\ X_{in} \end{pmatrix} \Leftrightarrow \begin{pmatrix} Y_{i1} \\ Y_{i2} \\ \cdot \\ \cdot \\ \cdot \\ Y_{im} \end{pmatrix}$$

Figure 4.1   The twin characteristics representation of technology i. The double arrow between technical and service characteristics represents the pattern of imaging

Second, technologies can differ for the technical or for the service characteristics or for both. An example can help to understand this aspect of the problem. An aircraft and a bird can be considered two different 'technologies' which supply air transport services. Their services are not entirely equivalent, but there is a certain homogeneity between them. On the other hand, their internal structures are completely different and require qualitatively different concepts and, therefore, different variables to be represented. Two different technologies differ at least for their internal structure. A change in technology implies a change in internal structure. Naturally there are also technologies which differ for both internal structure and services performed, such as a fridge and a personal computer. This gives us a very effective way of conceptualizing the difference between radical and incremental innovation. A radical innovation leads to a completely new technology, that is, according to the previous definition, to a technology that has an internal structure qualitatively different from the previous one. On the contrary, an incremental innovation leads only to a change in the levels (values), but not in the nature, of the characteristics of the existing techology.

Third, technologies/artefacts can be considered as interfaces between an inner environment, 'the substance and organisation of the artifact itself', and an outer environment, the surroundings in which it operates (Simon, 1962, 1981). One can clearly think of the internal structure as the inner environment and of the service characteristics as the interface (Saviotti, 1986).

If we consider scientific and technological knowledge as inputs in a production process and services performed as outputs, we realize that they are both different and related, since the inputs are only used for the purpose of producing demanded ouputs. The pattern of correspondence (or imaging) between technical and service characteristics constitutes the coupling of technological knowledge to market demand. The services performed by a given technology determine how closely it can adapt to the environment in which it operates. If the inner environment is appropriate to the outer environment, or vice versa, the artefact will serve its intended purposes (Simon, 1981). It is in principle possible to define an index of 'closeness of fit' between the services performed by a given technology and the characteristics of the selection environment in which it operates. Such an index of closeness of fit would be nothing else than the fitness of the particular technological model considered. Such a definition of fitness is adopted in Chapter 6. Unfortunately this definition, although correct in principle and useful for heuristic purposes, is difficult to apply. An approximate definition of fitness still based on a characteristics representation but easier to apply will be considered in Chapter 6. In turn, selection by users is based on differential adaptation. Better adapted technologies are chosen more frequently, and, in the course of time, increase their economic weight. In a way, it can be said that the pattern of imaging between technical and service characteristics is the link between scientific and technological knowledge on the one hand and economic activity on the other.

The knowledge that firms possess is, therefore, crucial. This is both the scientific and technological knowledge required to design 'best practice' technical characteristics, and knowledge of the external environment required to determine the types and levels of services required. These different types of knowledge will usually be embodied in different parts of the firm. For example, scientific knowledge will be predominantly 'contained' in the R&D department, technical knowledge in the production department, and knowledge about the external environment in the marketing department. The intellectual division of labour within a firm will be related to the two sets of characteristics used for the representation: marketing knowledge will be predominantly about the correspondence between service characteristics and the environment; R&D knowledge will be predominantly about the correspondence between scientific theories and technical characteristics; engineering knowledge about the correspondence between process technology and technical characteristics on the one hand and about that between technical and service characteristics on the other (see Figure 4.2).

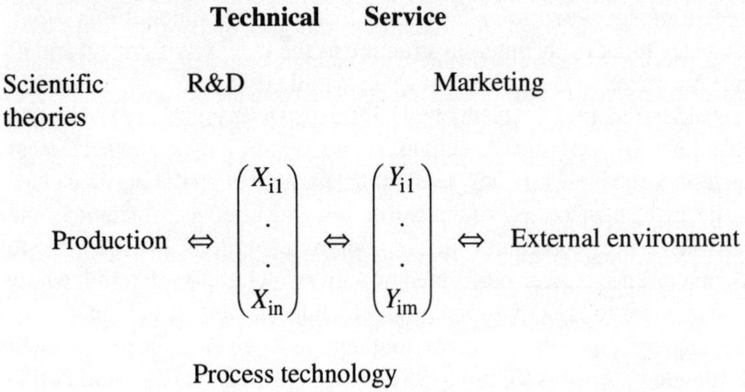

$$\text{Production} \Leftrightarrow \begin{pmatrix} X_{i1} \\ \cdot \\ \cdot \\ \cdot \\ X_{in} \end{pmatrix} \Leftrightarrow \begin{pmatrix} Y_{i1} \\ \cdot \\ \cdot \\ \cdot \\ Y_{im} \end{pmatrix} \Leftrightarrow \text{External environment}$$

Technical **Service**

Scientific   R&D   Marketing
theories

Process technology

Figure 4.2   *Relationships between technical and service characteristics, and different types of knowledge used in production and innovation*

From a related point of view we can point out that demand theories need to be concerned only with service characteristics, since they are the only ones that a user is concerned about. Theories of supply have to be concerned with the production of technical characteristics either from scientific theories or from process technology, but also with the correspondence between technical and service characteristics. In this sense it is worth pointing out that Lancaster's (1966) approach to the demand for multicharacteristics products would apply only to service characteristics. The representation proposed in this chapter allows us to couple demand and supply by means of the factors influencing the production of technical characteristics and their correspondence with service characteristics. The representation provided in this book constitutes an extension of Lancaster's approach to a completely new territory, that is to the generation and diffusion of technological innovation. The inclusion of the internal structure of the technology is necessary to provide an explicit representation of the characters of technological change emphasized in this chapter, that is product technologies.

Finally, we can note that the sources of discontinuities in technological evolution come more from the internal structure of technologies than from the services they perform. For example, cars, trains and aircraft all provide transport services, qualitatively not entirely dissimilar from those provided by previous technologies, such as horse-drawn carriages or canoes. It is possible for services to undergo a certain degree of specialization. For example, transport services can be split into air, land and water based, but at least some of the variables required to describe them remain constant (e.g. speed of transport, payload, energy input). On the other hand, qualitatively new technologies require completely different technical characteristics to be described. In other words, the extent of qualitative change caused by the internal structure of technologies is greater than that due to their services. In the meantime, the greater continuity existing between the services of radically different technologies can help us to understand the pattern of emergence of new ones. Thus bottlenecks in the provision of services could provide inducements to the creation of new technologies/internal structures.

An example of this type of representation applied to helicopter technology is given in Table 4.1, where geometry and engine type can be the following: geometry – 1 rotor, 1 shaft (1R,1S), (1R,2S), (2R,2S); engine type – piston (P), turboshaft (TS). Characteristics such as length, rotor diameter and engine power are continuous and constitute characters of the technology. Characteristics such as engine type, number of engines and geometry describe qualitatively different species (or subspecies).

Table 4.1   Characteristics representation of helicopter technology

Technical characteristics	Service characteristics
Length Rotor diameter	} Maximum take off power
Engine power Engine type	} Maximum speed
No. of engines Geometry	} Range

Population Perspective

Quite often in the social sciences and sometimes even in the biological sciences a typological perspective is adopted. According to this perspective a given species/class of products/class of organizations, etc. can be adequately represented by the properties of the average or representative individual within the species/class. The opposite approach, a population perspective (Saviotti and Metcalfe, 1991), stresses that the variance in properties amongst the members of a population is as important as the values of the properties of the average/ representative individual.

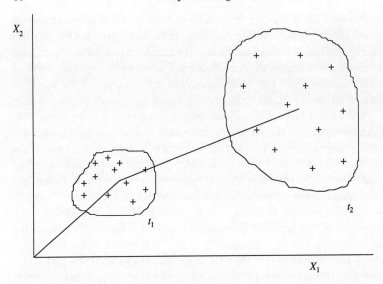

Figure 4.3   The position and density of the technological population change between times t_1 *and* t_2*. The centre of the technological population describes a trajectory*

A population perspective is a fundamental component of evolutionary theories and complements naturally the twin characteristics representation of a technology. A technological model is represented in characteristics space (X space) by a set of values/levels of the N defining characteristics. Such a model is, therefore, represented by a point in an N dimensional space. Different models/members of a technological population are represented by points contained in a region of X space. The whole technological population is represented by a cloud of points (see Figure 4.3).

Based on the previous considerations we can expect a number of types of change to take place during technological evolution.

Changing position
If we assume that all characteristics are measured in such a way that their value increases in the course of time, we can expect that, due to technological progress, a technological population will move away from the origin in the course of time. The previous assumption is not as limiting as it would seem. Some important variables required to characterize a technology are externalities or costs (e.g. pollution, fuel consumption, etc.). Even in these cases, however, it is possible to define the variables in such a way, for example as fuel efficiency or degree of cleanliness, that their value will tend to increase in the course of time. At any given time a trade-off exists for which a given characteristic's value can

be increased only at the expense of other characteristics. However, in the course of time all characteristics can increase, even if we cannot expect them to increase by the same extent. In summary, we expect technological populations to move away from the origin of their characteristics space. The centres of a technological population, as they move in the course of time, will describe a trajectory of change (see Figure 4.3).

Changing density
As a technological population moves away from the origin of X space its density may change (see Figure 4.3). According to the discussion on p. 86 this implies a change in the intensity and/or in the type of competition. For example, a growing density of the population would indicate an increasing intensity of competition and a falling internal differentiation of the population, that is a competition which moves away from the Schumpeterian type and towards the perfect one.

Fragmentation/specialization of the technological population
The growing intensity of competition within a given technological population could provide a motivation for some of the existing producers to exit the core of the technology and to acquire a degree of monopoly by establishing themselves

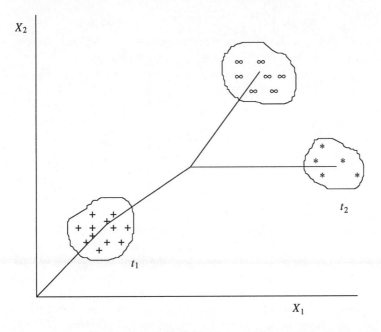

Figure 4.4   During the evolution of the technological population specialization/fragmentation takes place, giving rise to a bifurcation in the trajectory

A model of technological evolution

in niches (see pp. 105–7). This corresponds to a process of specialization and increases the net variety of the economic system within which it occurs. Such an evolution can give rise to the fragmentation of a technological population into several, or to the development of an increasingly asymmetric structure in an existing population (see Figure 4.4).

Elementary Mechanisms and X Representation

It would be useful to be able to represent large numbers of processes of technological evolution in terms of a much smaller number of elementary mechanisms. These elementary mechanisms would then be like the bricks or the modular elements with which a building is constructed. In what follows, some examples of elementary mechanisms are discussed in terms of the twin characteristics framework previously presented.

Pure substitution

A new technology T_2 replaces a pre-existing technology T_1. T_1 and T_2 provide the same quality of services but have different internal structures/technical

$$
T_1 \begin{pmatrix} X_{11} \\ X_{12} \\ \cdots \\ \cdots \\ \cdots \\ X_{1n} \end{pmatrix} \Leftarrow \Rightarrow \begin{pmatrix} Y_{11} = \\ Y_{21} \\ Y_{12} = \\ Y_{22} \\ \cdots \\ \cdots \\ \cdots \\ Y_{1m} = \\ Y_{2m} \end{pmatrix}
$$

$$
T_2 \begin{pmatrix} X_{21} \\ X_{22} \\ \cdots \\ \cdots \\ \cdots \\ X_{2n} \end{pmatrix} \Leftarrow \Rightarrow
$$

Figure 4.5 Characteristics representation of pure substitution.
T_1 = *pre-existing technology;* T_2 = *new technology*

characteristics. The advantage of T_2 consists of providing the common services at a lower unit cost (see Figure 4.5).

Specialization

T_1 and T_2 provide qualitatively the same services with a different distribution of service levels or each one of them may provide a common core of services and some other services which are specific to each technology. T_1 and T_2 may have the same or different internal structures (intra- and inter-technology specialization) (see Figures 4.6 and 4.7).

$$T_1 \begin{pmatrix} X_{11} \\ \vdots \\ X_{1n} \end{pmatrix} \Leftarrow \Rightarrow \begin{pmatrix} Y_{11} \\ \vdots \\ Y_{1k} \\ \vdots \\ Y_{1p} \\ \vdots \\ Y_{1m} \end{pmatrix} \begin{matrix} \text{Only } T_1 \\ \\ \\ \text{Common} \\ \\ \text{Only } T_2 \end{matrix}$$

$$T_2 \begin{pmatrix} X_{21} \\ \vdots \\ X_{2n} \end{pmatrix} \Leftarrow \Rightarrow$$

Figure 4.6   Twin characteristics representation of inter-technology specialization. T_1 = *old technology;* T_2 = *new technology*

$$T_1 \begin{pmatrix} X_{11} \\ \vdots \\ X_{1n} \end{pmatrix} \Leftarrow \Rightarrow \begin{pmatrix} Y_{11} \\ \vdots \\ Y_{1m} \\ \vdots \\ Y_{21} \\ \vdots \\ Y_{21} \end{pmatrix} \begin{matrix} T_2 \\ \\ \\ T_3 \end{matrix}$$

Figure 4.7   Twin characteristics representation of intra-technology specialization. T_1 = *precursor technology;* T_2, T_3 = *new technologies arising from specialization*

Partial substitution

T_2 provides all the same services provided by T_1 and some additional new services. This case is intermediate between pure substitution and specialization both logically and chronologically (see Figure 4.8).

$$
T_1 \begin{pmatrix} X_{11} \\ \vdots \\ X_{11} \end{pmatrix} \Leftarrow \Rightarrow \left. \begin{pmatrix} Y_{11} = Y_{21} \\ \vdots \\ Y_{1k} = Y_{2k} \\ \vdots \\ Y_{2m} \end{pmatrix} \right\} \begin{array}{l} \text{Both } T_1 \\ \text{and } T_2 \\ \\ \text{Only } T_2 \end{array}
$$

$$
T_2 \begin{pmatrix} X_{21} \\ \vdots \\ X_{2n} \end{pmatrix} \Leftarrow \Rightarrow
$$

Figure 4.8   Twin characteristics representation of partial substitution. T_1 = *old technology;* T_2 = *new technology*

Completely new product

T_2 has a qualitatively different set of both technical and service characteristics with respect to T_1 (see Figure 4.9).

$$
T_1 \begin{pmatrix} X_{11} \\ \vdots \\ X_{1n} \end{pmatrix} \Leftarrow \Rightarrow \begin{pmatrix} Y_{11} \\ \vdots \\ Y_{1m} \end{pmatrix}
$$

$$
T_2 \begin{pmatrix} X_{21} \\ \vdots \\ X_{2n} \end{pmatrix} \Leftarrow \Rightarrow \begin{pmatrix} Y_{21} \\ \vdots \\ Y_{2k} \end{pmatrix}
$$

Figure 4.9   Twin characteristics representation of the emergence of a completely new product. T_1 = *old product;* T_2 = *new product/technology*

Recombination of subsets of existing products

This process can lead to a new product by means of the combination of parts of existing products. For example, the Wright brothers built an airplane by combining bicycle wheels, airfoils and a petrol engine (Kauffman, 1988).

IMPLICATIONS OF THE FRAMEWORK FOR TAXONOMY AND INNOVATION THEORIES

The previous framework can be easily related to some basic taxonomic problems of innovation and to a number of theories and innovation studies.

Radical vs. Incremental; Species vs. Characters Characteristics

A very fundamental distinction in studies of technological change is that between radical and incremental innovation. The representation of product technology illustrated in this chapter helps to put this distinction on a more logical basis. Thus radical will be an innovation which leads to a new internal structure and incremental will be an innovation which improves services without any qualitative change in internal structure/technical characteristics. A radical innovation is one that gives rise to entirely new technical characteristics, which need to be represented by different variables. For example, power to an aircraft can be supplied either by a piston engine or by a jet engine. The two technologies have qualitatively different internal structures and require different variables to be represented. The transition between the two has evidently been a radical innovation. At a different degree of detail the two technologies could either be represented by two different sets of variables or by two values of the dummy variable engine type. The latter approach is used in this chapter. All the characteristics representing a technology can then be classified as characters (which undergo only quantitative change) or species (which undergo qualitative change). Alternatively, changes in characters are incremental innovations and changes in species characteristics are radical innovations.

It is important to remember that the degree of change in characteristics is likely to be related to the degree of change in the knowledge base and in the capabilities of the producing firm. In other words, completely new capabilities and knowledge are likely to be required to produce a model with a completely new internal structure. The distinction between competence enhancing and competence destroying innovations introduced by Tushman and Anderson (1986) is relevant here. Innovations which have a completely new internal structure are likely to be competence destroying, leading to the obsolescence of the skills and knowledge of existing firms, while innovations which improve the levels of existing technological characteristics enhance the knowledge of existing organizations.

The Twin Characteristics Framework and Demand Theory

The characteristics framework presented in this chapter is almost exclusively concerned with the supply side. However, such a framework can be related to demand theories for complex, multicharacteristics products. For example, the existence of multiple wants for multicharacteristics products has been theorized by Lancaster (1966, 1971, 1979). However, that theory was exclusively concerned with demand. In terms of the present framework one could say that it is the services supplied by a good from which utility is derived. Clearly a user may be completely uninterested in the internal structure of the technology and, logically, no attention was paid to it in Lancaster's treatment. The internal structure and technical characteristics have to be added when technology becomes an important variable to be studied. As noted above, technical characteristics are the only ones to be directly produced. Thus costs are incurred in the production of a given level of technical characteristics, from which the desired level of services will flow. A theory of costs will have to deal primarily with technical characteristics while a theory of demand will have to deal primarily with service characteristics.

Furthermore, the present approach is much more suitable for capital goods or for consumer durables which are not heavily influenced by fashion or by completely subjective judgements. A demand theory for these goods could be potentially quite different from one appropriate for most 'subjective ' consumer goods. The construction of a demand theory appropriate for the type of goods treated here and compatible with the present framework is certainly an important goal, but one which is beyond the scope of this chapter. Only a few specific remarks about this theme will be made here.

Commodities/products treated in this way are multicharacteristics. In this case consumers/users face a two tiered decision problem (Lancaster, 1979): first, what product model to choose within a group/technological population of varying specification (the mixture of characteristics of a given commodity); and, second, how much to purchase of the model they have decided to buy. These two dimensions of choice correspond to what Lancaster has called *market width* and *market depth*, respectively. The nature of the specification is an extremely important variable influencing consumers'/users' demand. Within the present framework the characteristics which should influence demand most are service characteristics.

In this context it is interesting to notice that substitutes and complements can be represented in terms of the previous framework. Thus substitutes will be two products which have the same service characteristics, although they may have different internal structures/technical characteristics. On the other hand, complements will be two products which have generally different service characteristics, but in which one of the two products can influence some characteristics of the other. Thus petrol can influence the service characteristic 'fuel consumption' of a motor car. It would thus be possible to calculate the elasticity of substitution for two products on the basis of the similarity of their service characteristics.

The Role of Demand and Supply in Directing Innovative Activity.

There has been a long-standing debate among students of innovation about the relative roles of demand and supply in stimulating successful innovation. The debate has never been properly concluded (Coombs, Saviotti and Walsh, 1987;

Mowery and Rosenberg, 1979). The twin characteristics framework allows one to approach the problem from a more rational point of view.

One of the few possible generalizations of innovation studies seems to be that attention to users' needs is an important determinant of success in innovation (Freeman, 1982; Coombs, Saviotti and Walsh, 1987). In terms of the present framework this means that firms competent only in the internal structure of the technology are unlikely to be successful. Knowledge of the selection environment is required as well to decide what services the users want and how much they are prepared to pay for them.

The relative roles of demand and supply are unlikely to remain the same during the whole process of generation and diffusion of an innovation. This had already been foreseen by Schumpeter (1912, p. 65), according to whom producers might even have to 'educate' the consumer to want the new commodities. Two types of considerations are important here. First, demand is based on learning. The greater the novelty of a product, the less the potential consumer will be able to estimate how useful this new product will be. However, as consumers/users start using it, they will begin to learn the properties of the new product and how it can serve their purposes. The importance of learning by doing has long been known in economics (Arrow, 1962; David, 1975). More recently Rosenberg (1982) pointed out that *learning by using* is important as well. Many improvements in the performance of some technologies take place as they start to be used. Customer feedback is essential in this respect (see also von Hippel, 1976). Aspects of technological performance and reliability, such as service intervals and the progressive improvement of different parts of the technology (e.g. the engine and wings of an aircraft) are gradually improved due to information gathered by using the technology. This same information gathered through learning by using, allows users to improve their understanding of the performance of the technology for their purposes. The demand for a given technology is going to be influenced by learning by using. More specifically, the present demand for a product /technology is based on learning how to use the services supplied by previous vintages of the same product. Alternatively, one could say that consumers learn how to form expectations about the performance of given products/technologies.

This has two types of consequences: it reduces the uncertainty (expressed as a standard deviation) in the customers' estimate of the performance of the technology; and it determines an irreversible and path dependent demand behaviour (Georgescu Roegen, 1982). Adapting those considerations to the present case one could say that once a new commodity has become part of the consumption pattern it will not necessarily disappear even if some of the circumstances that brought it about were to recede.

From the first consequence, the progressive reduction in the uncertainty surrounding consumers' estimate of the properties of the new commodity, it follows that there will be a corresponding uncertainty in the estimate of the demand by producers. This estimate will then become progressively more accurate during the maturation of a product. Estimates of expected revenues and, therefore, of expected profit are likely to be highly inaccurate (greater uncertainty) at the beginning of the life cycle of the new product. Consequently, the risk associated with the production of a product is at a maximum at the stage of introduction of the new product. It is precisely at this stage, rather than in the later and more mature phases of the product life cycle, that entrepreneurial initiative/supply can be expected to play a relatively greater role. Of course, if a product is radically new only for what concerns its internal structure (i.e. different Xs), but provides services qualitatively equal (same Ys) to those of existing products, no such discontinuity will be experienced by users, to the extent that they can use the services without having to know very much about the internal structure.

The second type of consideration which is relevant here is that what a user needs is not a product, but the services it can provide. Sometimes these services are provided by the product itself, but at other times the product has to be combined with 'complementary inputs' to provide the required services. Examples are a watch in the first case, and a motor car or computer in the second. A watch can provide services on its own (except for the occasional need for a new battery or for some repairs) while a motor car needs petrol stations, special roads, traffic equipment, etc. Similarly a computer needs electricity, software, communications facilities, etc. The complementary inputs needed to provide the final services sometimes require such a large investment that they have to be supplied by different institutions from those producing the product considered. Often the complementary inputs are infrastructures. These infrastructures expand the scope of the product/technology by allowing it to be used more productively and in more circumstances than would otherwise have been possible. In other words, the complementary inputs expand the range of the selection environment in which the product/technology can operate. Conversely, the absence of complementary inputs can make the product virtually worthless and, therefore, severely limit its diffusion. Thus expansion of the relevant portion of the selection environment would have an effect similar to post-innovation improvements on the diffusion (Metcalfe, 1981, 1988). This situation is very similar to the one described by Kauffman (1988) as an *economic web*, or a web of transformations of products and services among economic agents. The web has nodes constituted by commodities (products or services) which are linked either by technical relations (e.g. parts to the whole commodity) or by needs (e.g. the previous examples of cars, roads, etc.). A web can be coherent when all commodities are linked to other commodities in a need network. The introduction of new commodities requires a restructuring of the web, which is likely to require a considerably longer time than the innovation of the commodity itself. Both supply structure and demand will develop relatively slowly after the innovation of the new commodity. The learning effects required to create a demand for the product in the strict sense of the word would then depend on the 'joint' production of the product and of the complementary inputs required to provide services. The requirement for the joint production of a product and of its complementary inputs/infrastructures increases the discontinuity of the introduction stage of the new product.

In summary, the greater the degree of novelty of the new product's services and the less totally embodied in it (or, alternatively, the greater the weight of complementary inputs) the lower will be the relative role of demand in directing innovation in the early phases of introduction of a new product.

Pattern of Imaging and Technological Paradigms etc.

The pattern of imaging has been defined before as the pattern of correspondence between technical and service characteristics. Engineers/designers have a knowledge, at least qualitative, of the pattern of imaging and know what technical characteristics (Xs) to change to improve services (Ys). Once a technology becomes established, its pattern of imaging becomes part of the existing heuristics and knowledge base used by engineers/designers. It is then possible to relate the pattern of imaging to concepts like dominant designs, technological regimes, technological paradigms, etc. These concepts are somewhat different, but they have a common core: they imply a discontinuity at the transition between two paradigms and the convergence of all the participants in a given technology on a set of technical solutions (internal characteristics) narrower than the one that could in principle be available. During such convergence a degree of self-regulation of the technological systems thus created is achieved (Saviotti, 1986). In terms of the twin characteristics representation a dominant design (Abernathy and Utterback, 1975, 1978) or a technological regime (Nelson and Winter, 1977) can be conceptualized as the presence of a constant set of technical characteristics. During the evolution of the design/regime, only changes in characteristics levels/incremental innovations take place.

A trajectory can be defined for a technological population as the locus of all the positions occupied in characteristics space by the centres of the technological population at different times. Such trajectory can imply either a general displacement away from the origin of X space or, in the case of specialization/fragmentation, a bifurcation of the trajectory (see Figure 4.4). A technological paradigm (Dosi, 1982) includes the dominant design/regime, the trajectories implied, and the knowledge and social relations of the institutions involved in producing the technology. The presence of a dominant design/regime implies a constant set of technical, and, through the pattern of imaging, of service characteristics. The knowledge of engineers, scientists, managers, technicians, etc. involved in the implementation of the technology becomes specialized around the process, technical, and service characteristics used (see Figure 4.2). This specialization creates networks of communication and power which reinforce the stability of the artefact dimension of the technology.

Fundamental and Adaptive Variables

Fundamental variables/characteristics of a technology are those which led to the introduction of the technology in the first place. Adaptive are those variables which improve the fit of the technology into its environment (Ashby, 1956; Saviotti, 1986). Examples of these different types of variables can be found in the motor car and tractor technologies. In both cases an initial period, during which convergence on a dominant design took place, was followed by another, in which further variables were added, which improved the fit of the technology into its environment. Examples of these changes are the addition of hydraulics and later of a cab to agricultural tractors, of improved suspensions and of lower cars to take advantage of the smoother road surfaces which are now commonly encountered in industrialized countries. It is possible to expect that similar patterns could be followed by other technologies. In other words, as a technology ages, fundamental variables could become very similar in all models/members of the technological population while adaptive variables could constitute the locus of differentiation and competition in the technology. The concepts of fundamental and adaptive variables on the supply side have some analogue concepts on the demand side. Thus different authors have postulated a hierarchy of consumption, according to which the products in a class will perform some basic function to much the same degree but will vary greatly in attributes ranking lower in the hierarchy (Lancaster, 1979, p. 10).

A possible pattern of evolution would be constituted by a decreasing intra-technology variance of the fundamental variables and by an increasing intra-technology variance of the adaptive variables. It is worth emphasizing that this pattern represents a variant of a life-cycle model, such as that of Abernathy and Utterback (1975). According to their model, when the mature phase of the life cycle has been reached after the convergence on a dominant design, the locus of innovation shifts from product to process technology. According to the pattern analysed here the locus of innovation would move from fundamental to adaptive variables, which means between two different types of product characteristics. These changes of the locus of innovation, from product to process and from fundamental to adaptive, could take place simultaneously, so that a mature technology would be characterized by process and adaptive variables innovations.

The Technological Frontier

In a general sense the concept of technological frontier represents the limitations in what can be achieved by existing technologies. Thus at any time it is not possible to obtain more than a given level of output from the available inputs (e.g. labour and capital). Traditionally, within a production function approach, the frontier represented the locus of the output that could be obtained from the possible combinations of labour and capital using the most advanvced techniques available at the time.

In spite of its apparent ease, the concept of technological frontier needs a little more clarification. Thus, at each time there is a scientific frontier, which could be developed using the most advanced set of techniques compatible with existing scientific knowledge, even if at an infinite cost. The scientific frontier is never achieved. Somewhat below it there is the technology frontier or metaproduction function, which represents the set of techniques used by the most advanced firms in the most advanced countries (Ahmad, 1966; Binswanger and Ruttan, 1978). These techniques constitute the technological best practice at the time. Below the technology frontier there is the distribution of achievements of all the non-best practice firms, wherever they are located.

In this chapter, which is mainly concerned with technological characteristics, the concept of the technological frontier can be represented as the locus of the characteristics of the most advanced technologies. By representing technologies in characteristics space we obtain for a technological population a cloud of points/models. These points/models are at different distances from the origin of the axes. The models which are furthest away from the origin are the most advanced within the technological population. By joining all the most advanced points/models we can obtain a surface in an N dimensional space (manifold). This surface represents the technological frontier, the limit that at the time of the experiment no producer can overcome. It is worth stressing that this is not the maximum achievable performance (i.e. the scientific frontier or Ahmad's (1966) innovation possibility curve (IPC)), but the maximum performance 'achieved'. The knowledge existing at the time of the 'measurement' might allow the production of more advanced models. However, the cost of producing them might be so high that in fact they will not be produced even as prototypes. In other words, by using models characteristics one would construct a technology frontier for specific products, with the distribution of achievements of existing producers.

It is difficult to predict what distribution of models with respect to the frontier to expect. Two examples of technological frontier in characteristics space are given for helicopter technology (Figure 4.10) and for aircraft technology (Figure 4.11). Both technologies are represented by means of six characteristics (see Table 4.1 for helicopters), but the figures are obtained by means of principal

A model of technological evolution

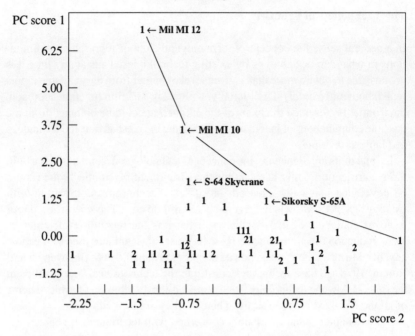

Figure 4.10 Results of principal components analysis (PCA) applied to helicopter technology for the period 1960–72. The figures 1 and 2 indicate the number of models superimposed on each point. Some of the models outside the core of the technology have been identified in the diagram (e.g. Mil MI 12, Sikorsky S-65A). The technological frontier is indicated by the line joining the points/models furthest away from the origin

component analysis (PCA). PCA is a technique by means of which an *N* dimensional problem can in some cases be reduced to a bidimensional one (Chatfield and Collins, 1981; Cooper and Weekes, 1983; Pielou, 1984). Each point in PCA space corresponds to a model in characteristics space. In both cases we can note that the populations of models of the two technologies are not homogeneously distributed with respect to the technological frontier (TF). The majority of the models are concentrated in a region at some distance from the frontier. Starting from that region and moving away from it, either towards the TF or in the opposite direction, the concentration of models falls. The region of *X* space occupied by a technology can be divided into a *core*, where most producers concentrate their models, and outlying regions, where very few producers are present. These outlying regions are heterogeneous. For example, the region which is furthest away from the frontier could be one where the less advanced producers concentrate or one where only very specialized products (very small, slow, etc.)

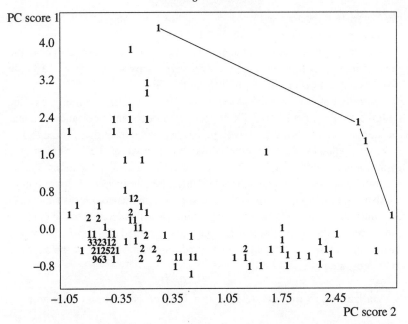

Figure 4.11 Results of principal components analysis (PCA) applied to aircraft technology for the period 1966–84. The figures 1, 2, etc. indicate the number of models superimposed on each point. The technological frontier is indicated by the line joining the points/models furthest away from the origin

are present. On the other hand, the region immediately adjacent to the techno-logical frontier contained the most advanced models, which require the highest technological capability (that few producers have) and which are very expensive, and therefore used only for very specialized applications. One could consider the outlying regions as specialised niches, in which not all producers will be present. To the extent that these results are generalizable we can then say that technologies will have models distributed in X space in such a way that the majority are concentrated in a region, the core, at some distance from the frontier in which most producers are present, and in some niches, either very close or very far from the frontier, in which few producers will be present. The core is likely to be where most producers are present both because it does not require the highest technological capabilities and because most of the demand, and therefore sales, is going to be concentrated there. It can also be noted that this TF is equivalent to a production possibility frontier (PPF) in X space. As in the case of a common PPF this one implies a trade off between different char-acteristics. We can see, however, that all the possible combinations of characteristics are not used in every case. For example, in the case of aircraft technology the closer one gets to the TF, the more concentrated in two regions of X space are the models. For the moment it is important to notice that not only the distribution of models is not uniform as one moves away from the TF, but that it is not uniform as one moves along the TF.

Naturally both of these distributions are not static. They are likely to change with the displacement of the TF. If specialization is an important elementary mechanism in technological development, we can expect that even a technological population which is approximately spherical at the beginning of its evolution will tend to fragment into separate technological populations. The distribution of models along the frontier will then necessarily become discontinuous.

Also, the cloud/population is not necessarily homogeneously distributed. On the contrary, its distribution and the changes that it undergoes in the course of time is one of the most interesting aspects to be studied. This issue will receive further discussion in the context of competition and of some of the examples to be presented later.

Specialization, Dominant Designs and Trajectories for Development

It was mentioned at the beginning of this chapter that technological evolution seems to follow a 'punctuated equilibria' mechanism rather than a gradual one. A number of concepts which have been developed recently in innovation studies imply a similar type of development. Abernathy and Utterback (1975, 1978) first pointed to the existence of a life cycle in the development of technologies. They proposed that technologies are characterized at the beginning of their evolution by a multiplicity of product designs, by a predominance of product innovation and by a flexible process technology. As technologies mature they converge on a dominant design, their innovations become more process oriented, and their process technology more specialized and rigid. Nelson and Winter (1977) introduced the concepts of *natural trajectories* and of *technological regimes*. Both concepts imply that particular technological variables/parameters and trends are acquired within the development of a technology and that they have a short- to medium-term stability. Similarly, Sahal (1981a and b) argued that *technological guideposts*, established at particular times, determine the subsequent develpment of technologies. Dosi (1982) called *technological paradigms* the combination of a series of technological features, which remain stable for a period of time, and of the related knowledge, organizational structure and social relations.

All these concepts imply a pattern of technological discontinuities followed by relatively long periods of incremental innovation within an established framework.

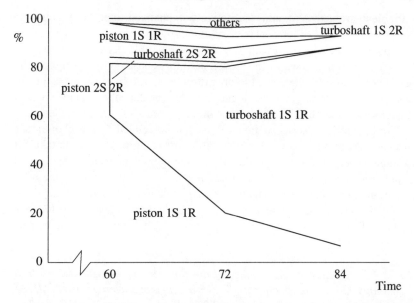

Figure 4.12 Proportion of helicopter types (species) over time. Each helicopter type is identified by engine type and geometry

Such concepts can be adequately represented by means of the characteristics approach described in this chapter. Thus dominant designs or technological regimes can be defined by means of a constant set of technical characteristics lasting for a relatively long period of time. An example of the emergence of a dominant design/technological regime as detected by means of a characteristics approach is given in Figure 4.12, which shows the share of new models accounted for by different types of helicopter design, where a design is defined by engine type, number of shafts and number of rotors. Initially the majority of models was accounted for by the (piston: 1 Shaft, 1 Rotor) design. In the period 1940 to 1986 the (turboshaft: 1 Shaft, 1 Rotor) design emerged as dominant. Some alternative designs, such as (turboshaft: 2 Shafts, 2 Rotors) survive with very small percentages of new models. These are 'niche' models, which can be found very close to the technological frontier or very far from it. In consequence, for a heterogeneous technology, a dominant design can be expected to account for the majority of (or all) the models in the core of the technology, but not necessarily for the models to be found in the specialized niches of the same technology.

Technological regimes and dominant designs refer, in terms of this approach, to a set of characteristics which remain common to most (or all) producers within an industry for a relatively long period of time. Although these variables/parameters remain qualitatively unchanged, their levels change. Natural trajectories are coherent patterns of improvement in established variables and parameters which predominate for considerable periods of time. For example, the trends towards the reduction in fuel consumption for motor cars and that towards raising the lift to drag ratio in aircraft have shown a considerable stability in these two technologies. Naturally, an important feature of natural trajectories is that they are stable even in the presence of changes in demand.

The previous patterns of innovation can be related to the elementary mechanisms in technological evolution described on p. 70. Let us take for example specialization. This occurs if an initially homogeneous technological population fragments into two or more populations. This is one of the most important elementary mechanisms and gives rise to a growing variety of the economic system. If specialization is common to many technologies for long periods of time, it can constitute a trajectory, which can be observed in characteristics space.

Table 4.2   Change in the number of members in each cluster for aircraft technology. Cluster designations: AS/AS = average size, average speed; ML/AS = medium/large size, average speed; LSS = light, small, slow; SMF = small, medium, fast; MS = medium, slow; B = big; MLS = medium/large, slow; LF = large, fast.

Cluster designation	AS/AS	ML/AS	B		
1905–1925	67	8	2		
Cluster designation	LSS	SMF	MS	B	
1926–1935	121	3	4	11	
Cluster designation	LSS	SMF	MS	B	
1936–1940	82	1	23	2	
Cluster designation	LSS	SMF	MS	B	
1941–1945	65	1	10	2	
Cluster designation	LSS	SMF	MS	B	
1946–1955	106	6	14	2	
Cluster designation	LSS	SMF	MS	B	
1956–1965	67	10	24	1	
Cluster designation	LSS	SMF	MLS	LF	B
1966–1984	106	6	12	2	2

Let us consider as an example the evolution of aircraft technology. Population changes between 1905 and 1984 have been followed by means of PCA. In this period the population of aircraft technology changed from a relatively uniform, almost spherical, cloud to an L-shaped cloud (see Figure 4.11). In the latter state the two branches of the population/cloud correspond to different trajectories for development, one containing large and relatively slow aircraft models, and the other containing small and fast models. This change in shape of the population implies that the models at the frontier of the two trajectories have become progressively less similar during the evolution of the technology. In other words, aircraft technology has been characterized by a growing tendency to specialization during its development.

This same tendency to specialization can also be detected by means of cluster analysis. The number of aircraft clusters increased from 3 to 5 during the period 1905 to 1984 (see Table 4.2).

COMPETITION

Competition is a concept which is used with different meanings in economics and in biology. In economics the most used concept is that of perfect competition. Perfect competition defines a situation in which firms are price takers, there is free entry which establishes a position of normal profitability, and, what is particularly important for a characteristics approach, all firms produce a homogeneous and equal product. Essentially different was the competition described by Schumpeter, for whom the introduction of 'new combinations' by entrepreneurs (Schumpeter, 1912, pp. 65–6) was the driving force of capitalist economic development. This type of competition, in which firms compete not by varying the quantity of their output or price but by trying to be first in the introduction of new products, has been called *innovation competition* by Metcalfe and Gibbons (Metcalfe, 1984; Metcalfe and Gibbons, 1987). Another case, which could be considered intermediate between these two, is that of product diversification (Chamberlin, 1933). Here, producers gain a limited degree of monopoly by diversifying their products.

Competition cannot in principle be perfect for multicharacteristics products because they are not homogeneous. However, even for these products we can obtain important indications about the nature of competition by means of a characteristics representation. As explained previously, a technological population will consist of a cloud of points/models in X space. The distance between any pair of models gives us an indication of their similarity. In the extreme case in which all the models had the same characteristics the population would collapse into a point. The greater the average distance between any pair of models, or, equivalently, the lower the density of the cloud, the lower the similarity of the models constituting the technological population. Changes during the development of the technology can lead either to a higher or to a lower density of the population, indicating a growing or decreasing internal similarity respectively.

Returning now to the two types of competition (perfect, innovation) described initially we notice that innovation competition, by leading either to the introduction of completely new products or to considerable differentiation in existing products, would generate new dimensions in X space or it would lead to changes in the location and shape of the cloud of points representing the technology. In particular, product differentiation would lead to a fall in the density of the population. On the contrary, if the type of competition were to approach perfect competition it would tend to reduce the size, and hence increase the density, of the cloud of points representing the technology.

Considerably different is the model of competition used in biology. In biology species compete for resources present in the habitat where they live (e.g. birds compete for seeds). In a habitat there is a distribution of resources, for example different seed sizes, which determine the number of species which can survive in that habitat. The habitat itself can be divided into a number of niches, each corresponding to the resource utilization function of a species. The intensity of competition is greater the greater the number of species using similar resources. Also, niche theory tells us that in the presence of very small to medium environmental fluctuations, only one species per niche can survive in a given habitat (May, 1973; Maynard Smith, 1974; Roughgarden, 1979). The last result is equivalent to Gause's exclusion principle, that two species with identical requirements cannot coexist in a given habitat (Maynard Smith, 1974).

The previous ideas can be adapted to technological evolution. Technologies compete for users, or more accurately, for users' requirements, by supplying services. The range of services supplied corresponds to the biological habitat. In these conditions the intensity of competition increases the greater the number of species producing similar services. Furthermore, a niche can be defined as the distribution function of the services produced by a given product technology.

Such a concept of competition has an interesting interpretation in terms of orthodox and less orthodox concepts of competition present in economics (Saviotti, 1991b). The more similar the services produced by the models constituting a given technological population, the higher the population density, and the more intense competition. The limiting case in which all the models produce exactly the same services, and in which the population collapses into a point, provides the multicharacteristics analogue of perfect competition. Alternatively, if a technology becomes progressively more diversified, the corresponding population expands in characteristics space. Population density and intensity of competition fall, corresponding to the limited degree of monopoly that can be achieved by means of product diversification. This concept of competition can, therefore, encompass a range of situations included between the two extremes of perfect competition and Schumpeterian competition. In the latter, producers compete by establishing themselves in a new and unoccupied region of characteristics space, and by acquiring a temporary degree of monopoly. Such a representation of competition is also very similar to monopolistic competition (Chamberlin, 1933), especially in the version which uses a characteristics representation of products (Lancaster, 1975, 1990).

Another application of this model is the distinction between intra- and inter-technology competition. Different models within the same technological population compete amongst themselves giving rise to intra-technology competition. Also, different technologies supplying qualitatively similar services (e.g. transport services for cars, trains and aircraft, or communications for fax machines and E-mail), but with a different internal structure, compete amongst themselves giving rise to inter-technology competition. The balance between inter- and intra-technology competition will turn out to be particularly important in determining the emergence of new technological populations.

During the course of technological evolution, as different technologies compete (inter-technology competition), there is internal competition amongst the existing producers (intra-technology competition). However, in a large population/cloud models which are very far apart correspond to very different characteristics levels and are not direct competitors. Consequently, intra-technology competition occurs amongst models located in close proximity in X space, which we can call *nearest neighbours* (Lancaster's (1979) *adjacent models*).

We can also relate changes in the nature of competition to the distance of models/manufacturers from the technological frontier. When a technology is sufficiently diversified there will be more 'downmarket' and more sophisticated products. Only few manufacturers are likely to have the capabilities to produce the most sophisticated products and, therefore, to occupy positions near the technological frontier. Competition is likely to be more intense near the average practice/core of the technology, located in areas of characteristics space relatively far from the frontier. We can also expect that the relative distribution of models/manufacturers with respect to the frontier will change in the course of time.

SOME EXAMPLES

Examples of such trends have been observed in the aircraft (Saviotti and Bowman, 1984; Saviotti, 1988a) and motor car technologies (Saviotti, 1985). In aircraft technology such a phenomenon was followed by means of cluster analysis. Changes in model density were calculated for different clusters (see Table 4.2). Only in one cluster, constituted predominantly by light business aircraft, did the density rise constantly between 1905 and 1984 (see Figure 4.13). In the other clusters, constituted for example by military or by large passenger aircraft, model density did not show any systematic trend. Studies of the industry indicate that competition in the light business aircraft sector is very similar to that of many consumer durables, while it is quite different in other clusters. For example, military aircraft is a technology with very few producers, quite often only one per country, and with a selection environment which is less constrained by cost considerations than civilian technology.

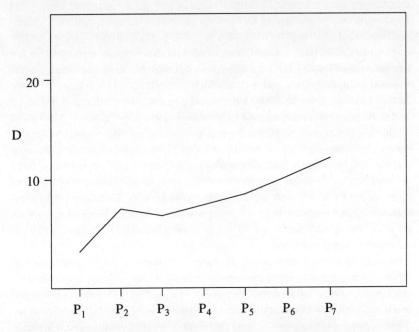

Figure 4.13   Change in density D (number of models per unit of cluster volume) of the LSS cluster (see also Table 4.2) containing light, small, slow aircraft models. P_1 = 1905–25; P_2 = 1926–35; P_3 = 1936–40; P_4 = 1941–45; P_5 = 1946–55; P_6 = 1956–65; P_7 = 1966–84.

A trend towards a growing density of the population can be found for motor car technology between 1955 and 1983 (Saviotti, 1985). In this case population density grew constantly, while the number of distinguishable models offered by producers rose. A growing density of the technological population indicates that the outputs of different producers became more and more similar when each one of them was offering a wider and wider range of products.

Such trends can be explained in the following way. Producers have some degree of feedback about the appropriateness of their product(s) to the intended user environment. At the beginning of the life cycle of the technology there is likely to be a considerable difference in the knowledge base of different producers. Such differences in knowledge base lead to different product characteristics. The subsequent process of selection sends a feedback to those producers and leads to convergence of output characteristics towards the preferences revealed by users. An extreme case of this feedback would be represented by firms which cannot adapt their product characteristics and disappear from the competition. Either through elimination or through characteristics convergence the variance of the characteristics of a given model type (e.g. Ford Escort) falls. This convergence is not the same as that predicted by Abernathy and Utterback (1975, 1978), but is more reminiscent of the expected fall in the variance of the fitness of a species during its evolution predicted by Fisher's fundamental theorem (R). This convergence can occur both when the output variety of the technology rises or falls. In other words, producers' outputs, or equivalently their RTP, are changing, but they are increasingly changing in the same way.

A peculiar combination of perfect and innovation competition is found here. While the growing similarity of the products of light business aircraft and of motor car technology can be interpreted as a move in the direction of perfect competition, in the meantime the output variety of motor car technology rises, showing a move towards innovation competition. It seems that a characteristics representation of technological evolution can give us very important insights about the nature of competition, in particular technologies and about its change in the course of time.

Similar concepts have been introduced by Foray and Grubler (1989, 1990a). They apply morphological analysis to the evolution of technologies. Each technology is represented by a point in morphological space. They define a neighbourhood as the region of morphological space contained within a critical distance (the radius of the graph), from a given point/technology. Technical change can take place within the same neighbourhood (incremental change) or outside it. In the latter case, the technology generated would be a new and qualitatively different rival to the existing one(s) contained in the neighbourhood. Competition can only occur between technologies which (a) assume a similar basic function (e.g. mass production, degree of complexity of products), and (b) are within a given morphological distance. Competition between technologies within the same neighbourhood can be related to intra-technology competition while competition between technologies contained in different neighbourhoods to inter-technology competition.

CONCLUSIONS

At the beginning of this book it was pointed out that conventional economic treatments of technological change have two shortcomings: first, they are implicit analyses of the phenomenon, and, second, they deal only with the growing output and increasing efficiency of economic development, but neglect the growing output variety aspect. Conventional economic treatments are implicit because they only describe the effects of technological change on economic variables, but they do not deal with the 'characters' of technological change, such as machines, knowledge, human capital, etc. This treatment is quite adequate for a number of purposes, but prevents one from dealing theoretically with questions such as: What new products can we expect to appear? What features will these new products have? Are there any basic processes which are repeated systematically in many cases of technological development? It is therefore argued that a complete treatment of technological change needs to incorporate explicitly a representation of the characters of technological development.

The same entities which are the characters of technological development are those that contribute to the variety of the system, intended as the number of its distinguishable products, processes, activities, etc. The twin characteristics approach presented in this chapter is intended to solve both of these problems, at least for what concerns product technology.

The approach was used to define a number of elementary interactions and processes, to discuss several concepts used in the innovation and technical change literature, and to create maps of the evolution of some technologies. This approach is still at a development stage and it is by no means complete. It needs to be developed both for what concerns its internal structure and for its compatibility with economic theories, existing and under development. In this chapter a choice is made in favour of an evolutionary framework, although some extensions of more conventional theories are discussed.

The definition of evolution used here is relatively limited, being based on (a) the presence of qualitative change, and (b) the processes of variation and selection, which bring about that change. Even this relatively limited definition allows one to interpret a number of phenomena and patterns of interaction according to an evolutionary framework.

In summary, the concepts developed in this chapter can be useful (a) to construct a taxonomy of technology which can extend the range of technological entities and phenomena analysed by economic theories, and (b) to develop a model of technological evolution which can extend the types of technological processes studied by economics.

In addition to extending the range of entities and processes considered by economics the aim of this chapter can be seen in the light of the dichotomy: replicating existing routines vs. innovating, that is introducing qualitative change into the system. The phenomena traditionally analysed by economics resemble more replication of routines, but innovation/qualitative change is one of the fundamental determinants of long-term economic development and has to be addressed.

The twin characteristics framework is essentially supply oriented. It is particularly important to integrate it with demand theories. A very limited attempt in this direction has been made here for what concerns demand for multicharacteristics products. However, this integration needs to be adequately developed.

It is very important to couple elements of this framework with other necessary developments of evolutionary theories. For example, the RTP of a firm/organization is closely related to its knowledge base. This chapter was almost exclusively concerned with the RTP, but connections with theories dealing with the knowledge base must be developed. Furthermore, since RTP is produced by firms/organizations, the twin characteristics framework needs to be integrated with organization theories. Finally, articulation of the concept of the selection environment is a necessary development of evolutionary theories. Technology is an important component of the selection environment and this framework should help to improve the articulation of its concept.

5. Variety, economic and technological development

INTRODUCTION

Two of the most important aims of this book, which have already been discussed at different stages, are to construct an approach to the economic analysis of technological change which is at the meantime explicit and general, and to develop an approach to the treatment of qualitative change in economic development.

The representation of product technologies developed in Chapter 4 constitutes an example of an explicit approach. It is of considerable generality and it is potentially compatible with a number of economic theories (e.g. theories of demand). Within that representation there are several elements which cause qualitative change in the economic system. For example, some of the elementary processes (see p. 70) in technological evolution, such as specialization and the emergence of completely new products, lead to products which are clearly distinguishable from the previous ones since they occupy separable positions in characteristics space. Such processes give rise to an increase in the number of technological populations. This is a qualitative change in the economic system, which in turn gives rise to changes in activities (qualifications, processes, etc.) and in actors (new firms, institutions, etc.). The explicit representation of Chapter 4 captures several features of qualitative change.

The problem is then to be able to relate qualitative change to economic development. A variable that can capture the effects of qualitative change in a way which is compatible with the analysis of economic development is variety, defined as 'the number of *distinguishable* types of actors, activities and outputs required to characterize an economic system'. This concept of variety is similar but not identical to that already used in the economics literature (see p. 00 for a very brief survey of this literature) where variety was considered in the context of a product group. The definition of variety used here is conceived at the level of aggregation of the whole economic system and it resembles more the concept of diversity as used by biologists (Pielou, 1977). As the concept of diversity is related to the number of species surviving in a given environment, variety is used here as the number of distinguishable actors, activities and outputs in the economic system.

The general point to be made now, before embarking on more detailed considerations of variety, is (a) that the generation of variety requires innovation, and (b) that the generation of variety is one of the fundamental trends in the development of economic systems, but one which has systematically been neglected in economics (at least for the purposes of this chapter). Traditionally, economics has taken into account only the productivity raising effect of technological change, that is, its quantitative aspect. However, innovation has at least the potential to change the variety of the economic system and casual observation suggests that the variety of the economic system has indeed changed quite dramatically, if we consider only the last two hundred years (i.e. the period following the Industrial Revolution). Specifically, the hypothesis that will be followed in this chapter is that the variety of the economic system has continuously grown, and that this is one of the main trends in economic development. A trend towards growing variety is, therefore, considered one of the fundamental trends in economic development. Such a trend has to be incorporated into models of economic development together with the trend towards increasing productivity. Furthermore, in this chapter it is argued that these two trends are not independent but complementary.

According to Schumpeter, long-term economic development requires innovations to continue (Schumpeter, 1912, 1942). Innovations certainly have an impact on the variety of the economic system. Consequently, if there is a relationship between variety and innovative activity, variety itself must be an important variable in the construction of an analytical framework for a Schumpeterian theory of economic development.

DEFINITION AND ANALYSIS OF THE CONCEPT OF VARIETY

The definition of variety given above is quite general, and needs to be specified better to acquire any operational value. First, a criterion of distinguishability is required. While it seems quite clear that a computer is qualitatively different from an abacus, or a train from a stage coach, more subtle and quantitative criteria would be required to distinguish different types of watches, machine tools, lorries or stereo equipment. Provided these products can be represented by means of a set of characteristics then their distances, or their degrees of similarity (the inverse of distances) (Pielou, 1984) enable us to develop a quantitative criterion of distinguishability (Saviotti, 1991a). There may be a number of cases in which distinguishability has to be based upon subjective criteria, but this does not detract from the value of this approach. The number of types of output, activities and actors which can be distinguished within the economic system is large and an analysis based on this approach can be very useful.

Assuming, then, that we have a criterion of distinguishability and that consequently we can count the number of actors, activities and types of output, we can ask the question: How is variety related to the number of these 'species'? A number of definitions have been used in information sciences (Ashby, 1956), or by biologists and ecologists (Pielou, 1977). In particular, in biology and ecology where variety is often called diversity, the nature of the problem is very similar, given that biological species can be represented by means of characters. Also, recently Weitzmann (1992) has proposed a measure of diversity based on distances/indices of similarity, which is more general than the previous ones and that contains them as a special case.

The problems in the measurement of variety can be either methodological or of data availability. For what concerns the former problem the previous considerations show that there is a reasonably established methodology to attack the problem, even though more developments are needed. Alternatively, it would be virtually impossible to calculate variety on the basis of the most aggregate type of published statistics/data. This does not prove the irrelevance or the lack of validity of this hypothesis, but only that the data had been collected without bearing in mind the concept of variety. Data for the calculation of variety are much more easily available at a lower level of aggregation, that is of particular technologies or product groups. In summary, the measurement of variety presents considerable difficulties, which will require both empirical and methdological developments, but which do not seem insuperable.

Several of the examples given in this chapter refer to the variety of some technologies. It is possible in principle for the technological variety to differ from the economic variety of a social system, and for the trends followed by the two in the course of time to differ. Following the previous definition of variety we can consider that some, but not all, the activities and the types of output of an economy are technologically based. Consequently, at any given time the economic variety of the system will be greater than, or at least equal to, its technological variety. If the technological variety grows in the course of economic development, so will economic variety.

An objection which is often made to the hypothesis that variety grows in the course of economic development is that craft products have a far more variegated nature than industrially made products, and that variety has actually been falling with the onset of industrial methods of production. This apparent contradiction is due to a confusion between variance and variety. Craft products have a much greater variance of characteristics, but cannot be produced in more than a few basic types due to the inefficiency of their production methods.

Other relevant distinctions are that between potential and net (or actual) variety, and that between process (V_p) and output (V_q) variety. Search activities give rise to a very large number of potential production activities and types of output, but not all these acquire economic weight. Only the potential activities and types of output which survive the process of economic selection contribute to net variety. At any time, potential variety is greater, and generally much greater, than net variety. An example of this situation can be found in the relatively low percentage of patents taken out which are actually used in production processes. Finally, for a number of purposes it is useful to distinguish between output variety, V_q (the number of distinguishable types of output) and process variety (the number of distinguishable types of processes) V_p, since the two are not necessarily going to vary in the same way in the process of economic development.

Given these definitions, is it possible to model the concept of variety, that is to establish its relationship to other economic variables, and to measure it? An answer to these questions is difficult to give ex-ante. Attempts to model and measure variety are required to test the validity of these definitions and of the hypotheses based on them. In this chapter the relationship of variety to a number of economic variables will be explored in order to provide the basis for the modelling of variety.

IMPLICATIONS OF THE CONCEPT OF VARIETY

Let us then assume that we have a reasonable definition of the concept of variety that allows us to translate the definition, 'The number of distinguishable actors, activities and types of output' present in an economic system at a given time, into an analytical formulation for variety, V, and to apply this definition by measuring variety. On this basis it is then possible to proceed to examine the relationship of variety to a number of economic phenomena and variables.

Variety and Economic Development

A very large number of artefacts and activities that most people in industrialized countries use, practise and/or observe have come into being quite recently, in historical terms. Aircraft, computers, video-recorders, stereo equipment, watches, aeroplane pilots, mechanics, computer programmers, provide only a few examples of what could be an enormously long list. This does not necessarily prove that *net* variety has increased, but a number of examples create a very strong suspicion that this has been the case. Let us look at some such examples.

The family trees of some technologies, at a fairly high level of aggregation that I will call here 'macrotechnologies', display a growing variety in the course of their development. Examples of such technologies are transport (see Figure 5.1) and telecommunications (see Figure 5.2).

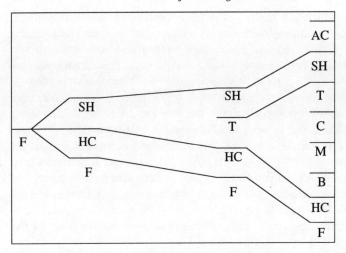

Figure 5.1   Change in variety of transport technologies. AC = aircraft, SH =
ship, T = train, C = car, M= motorcycle, B = bicycle, HC = horse drawn carriage,
F = foot

At a slightly lower level of aggregation, a technology such as agricultural
tractors (see Figure 5.3) has a family tree which, at least during some periods
of its development, shows a growth in variety. Other technologies, such as cars,
behave in a similar way. More examples can be found, but the ones given here
will be considered sufficient to demonstrate the actual growth in variety.

It is important to stress that different results can be obtained depending on
the level of aggregation at which observations are made. In particular, the
hypothesis that variety increases with economic development is likely to be valid
only at relatively high levels of aggregation, such as a national economy, or a
macrotechnology, that is, a technology supplying some broadly defined types
of services (e.g. transport, telecommunications), including several subsets of
this technology (e.g. trains, cars, aeroplanes, etc. for transport) and aggregat-
ing them over several countries (potentially the whole world system) for long
periods of time. The reasons for which variety might not increase in the course
of time at all levels of aggregation will be discussed in a later section.

For the moment let us formulate more explicitly the hypothesis about growing
variety (Saviotti, 1994a):

(a) The overall variety of the economic system increases in the course of
     economic development.
(b) The growth in variety is a necessary requirement for long-term develop-
     ment.

Figure 5.2 — The growing variety of telecommunications technology

1847	1877	1920	1960	1975	1984	2000
Telegraphy	Telegraphy	Telegraphy	Telegraphy	Telegraphy	Telegraphy	Telegraphy
	Telephony	Telex	Telex	Telex	Telex	Telex
		Photo	Data	Medium speed data	packet switched data	Broadband data
		Facsimile	Photo	Low speed data	High speed data	packet switched data
		Telephony	Facsimile	Photo	Circuit switched data	Circuit switch data
		Sound	Facsimile	Facsimile	Telemetry	Telemetry
		Television	Telephony	Facsimile	Facsimile	Teletex
			Stereo hifi sound	Telephony	Teletex	Textfacsimile
			Colour tv	Stereo hifi sound	Facsimile	Facsimile
			Mobile telephony	Stereo hifi sound	Videotex	Colourfacsimile
			Mobile telephony	Colur television	Telephony	Electronic mail
				Colur television	Videoconference	Telenewspaper
				Paging	Stereo television	Videotex
					Mobile telephony	Speechfacsimile
					Paging	Telephony
						Hifitelephony
						Telephone conference
						Videoconference
						Videotelephony
						Stereo hifi sound
						Quadraphon
						Colour television
						Stereo television
						High def. colour television
						Mobile video
						Mobile telephony
						Mobile text
						Mobile facsimile
						Mobile data
						Mobile video
						Paging
						2000

Figure 5.2 The growing variety of telecommunications technology

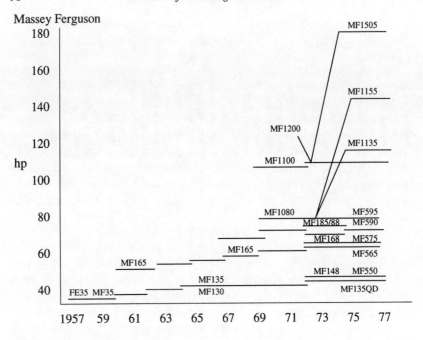

MF = Massey Ferguson, FE = Ferguson

*Figure 5.3 Changes in output variety for a tractor manufacturer in the period
1957–77. Tractor engine powers are represented on the vertical axis and they
are measured in hp*

(c) Growing variety and growing productivity are complementary, and not independent aspects of economic development.

Part (a) of the proposition has already received a limited degree of support
by means of the examples previously quoted.

Part (b) of the proposition implies that not only overall variety grows in the
course of economic development, but that this growth is a necessary requirement for economic development to continue in the long term. The most
convincing support for this part of the hypothesis comes from Pasinetti's (1981,
1990) model of structural change and economic growth. According to Pasinetti
the economy can be modelled as an input–output system, where the flows take
place between the various vertically integrated sectors (VISs) constituting the
economy. In the most complex scenario that he examines, Pasinetti considers
an economy with a growing population, with technical change leading to a rate
of productivity growth which differs amongst VISs, and to a rate of demand

growth which also differs amongst VISs. Demand growth is also likely to follow a life-cycle pattern, that is to achieve saturation in the course of time.

There is in Pasinetti's model an effective demand condition for maintaining full employment (1981, p. 86). Such a condition would only be satisfied if productivity and demand grew at the same rate in each VIS. This is very unlikely to happen in general. If the rate of demand growth for existing commodities tends to follow a life-cycle pattern, rising rapidly at first and then reaching saturation, and if the rate of productivity growth is constant, as Pasinetti assumes, then a situation of demand deficiency may arise within particular VISs. This need not yet produce aggregate unemployment since the opposite condition might arise in another VIS. However, if a situation of demand deficiency were to occur in many VISs simultaneously this could lead to unemployment and under-utilization of productive capacity. Such a situation would be obtained by means of an imbalance between technical change and rate of demand growth.

Fortunately, productivity growth is only one of the effects of technical change. Another effect of technical change (ibid., p. 89) is to introduce new goods. For Pasinetti's scheme this means that as time goes on, new equations have to be added to the system in order to represent the new goods. Thus while existing coefficients (ibid. Eq. V.4.4, p. 86) fall, new goods keep adding new coefficients, which counterbalance the tendency to underemployment generated by the time path of the old coefficients. In other words, in the long run, under-employment of labour and of other resources is likely to occur unless new goods keep being added to the economic system. Translated into the language of this chapter this means that growing variety is a necessary requirement for the long-term continuation of economic development.

The examples previously given and Pasinetti's model of economic growth provide some evidence for the existence of growing variety and for it being a necessary requirement for long-term economic development. Let us now turn to the third part of the hypothesis (c), concerned with the complementarity between productivity growth in existing sectors and growth in variety. What has been established previously is that output variety is a requirement, or a cause, of long-term economic development. However, variety itself can only be generated if a growing efficiency/productivity in existing sectors can 'liberate' the resources required to generate completely new commodities and, therefore, to increase variety.

The situation is very similar to the one described, for example by Kuznets (1965, p. 197), about industrialization. The transition from pre-industrial societies, where the majority of the population is employed in agriculture, to industrial societies can only be achieved if a smaller proportion of the labour force and of capital can produce the same amount of food and raw materials, and thus release a larger share for other uses, industry among them. Thus, in the same way as growing efficiency in agriculture can free resources for industrialization, growing efficiency in existing sectors can free resources for the generation of new commodities, and, therefore, of new sectors.

Variety, Economies of Scale, Consumer Welfare

There is in this field a vast literature to which only some limited reference will be made here. While this statement seems to contradict the previous one, according to which variety has not been given the right place in economic analysis, in fact all the analyses described in this section were addressed to a specific type of problems which, while very important in themselves, constitute only a subset of those which this chapter intends to address. Variety in this context has almost exclusively been referred to as the number of variants within a specific *product group* (Lancaster 1979, 1990). The debate in this area has addressed the relationship between product differentiation, market structure, economies of scale and consumer welfare. The generation of completely new products outside the original product group is usually not taken into account. Thus the contribution of variety to long-term economic development which was analysed before is ruled out ex-ante. In other words, this part of the literature has analysed the concept of variety in such a way that several of its implications, in particular those with which this chapter is concerned, have not been taken into account. Nevertheless, there are still a number of important potential connections between this literature and the present chapter. Only a brief reference to some aspects of it will be made.

Two traditions of thought, linked to the work of Chamberlin (1933) and of Hotelling (1929), have given rise to this literature. The former stressed the differentiation and limited substitutability of products within an industry/product group, and the effects it would have on competition, by giving each firm a degree of monopoly. The latter examined the problem of where different sellers of a given commodity would locate in a one-dimensional space (e.g. a street). In this case the growing dispersion of sellers would imply a greater product differentiation or variety. According to Chamberlin, monopolistic competition would lead to an excessive variety, while for Hotelling the minimum possible differentiation would take place. Neither of these conclusions is particularly robust. Several neo-Chamberlin (Dixit and Stiglitz, 1977) and neo-Hotelling (Salop, 1979; Eaton and Lipsey, 1975; Lancaster, 1979) models arrive at different results.

An important development in this area was constituted by Lancaster's demand theory (1966). Using this theory it was possible to replace geographic space by a virtual space of goods, or of their characteristics, in locational analogue models (Lancaster 1979, 1990).

The basic models and their variants lead to many different types of outcome, depending on the assumptions made. The conclusions which are relevant for the purposes of this chapter are as follows. The equilibrium product variety will be greater:

(a) the smaller the economies of scale;
(b) the lower the substitutability of goods within the group and/or between group goods and outside goods;
(c) the larger the market size;
(d) the more important the share of the group in the economy.

The equilibrium product variety will also depend on the width of the market (the degree of dispersion of preferences) and the depth of the market (density of consumer purchasing power at each location).

What is relevant here is that all the models considered predict an equilibrium product variety which is a trade-off amongst the factors previously described. The models differ about the trade-off achieved, depending on their assumptions, but none of them predict a zero degree of variety. In this respect they provide a microeconomic foundation for a concept of variety which is not too dissimilar from the one used in this chapter. Alternatively, the problematic of this sector of the literature – the optimum variety as determined by given consumers' preferences and welfare, industrial structures and scale economies – is a perfectly static one, not easily compatible with the analysis of the relationship between variety and long-term economic development. The general exclusion of the effect of completely new products, which as it will be argued later, give a dominant contribution to variety growth, compound the problem. In summary, the literature briefly referred to in this section has been 'designed' for purposes different from those of this chapter and is, therefore, only partly relevant here.

Mechanisms of Variety Generation

In this chapter so far it has been argued that a growing variety is a necessary requirement for long-term economic development. Now it is necessary to analyse the processes whereby this growing variety can be created. According to Schumpeter (1912) the economy contains two parts, called the circular flow, which for the present purposes could be considered the set of all routine activities in the economy, and the innovations, introduced by entrepreneurs. Entrepreneurs are the main variety-enhancing actors in the economic system. The Schumpeterian framework only implies that entrepreneurs increase temporarily net variety. If an innovation led to the disappearance of a previous good/artefact/technology the net variety might remain unchanged. Conditions and mechanisms leading to a growth in net variety are required.

Biological analogies offer some help. As in biology, we can assume that two basic evolutionary processes are variation and selection. There may be differences between the nature of these two mechanisms in the biological and in the social spheres. Thus variation in economics is more likely to be Lamarckian than Darwinian (Saviotti and Metcalfe, 1991). Also, following some recent developments in biology and their adaptation to economic and technological history (Mokyr, 1990a and b), we can also say that *punctuated equilibria*, an evolutionary pattern in which radical innovations are followed by long periods of incremental innovation, seems to be a better analogue for economic evolution than a more traditional Darwinian pattern, in which long-term qualitative changes are produced by the accumulation of very many small, quantitative changes.

Such mechanisms are, however, very general, and they have to be given a specific economic and technological meaning. For example, an approach to the problem of variety generation consists of identifying elementary mechanisms in technological evolution (Saviotti 1988a, 1991b). Processes like substitution, specialization and the emergence of completely new products can be considered the basic components of all the more complex processes found in real economies. Such processes, which can be accurately defined by means of a twin characteristics approach (Saviotti and Metcalfe, 1984), constitute three ideal types. There can be several intermediate possibilities. In pure substitution a new product, (T_2) defined by a new internal structure, supplies the same services as an old one (T_1), but it does so either at a lower price or providing higher levels of the same services. If T_2, in addition to the services of the old technology, supplies some extra services, then the process becomes intermediate between substitution and specialization.

The elementary processes listed above have very different implications for what concerns variety generation. Thus pure substitution, in which an old product is replaced by a new product supplying the same services, does not change the number of distinguishable types of output and makes a zero contribution to variety change. On the other hand, specialization, in which a relatively homogeneous technology in the course of time specializes and fragments into two or more distinguishable technologies, leads to a growth in variety. The highest contribution to the growth in variety of the system is made by the emergence of completely new products, with new internal structures and providing completely new services. Clearly, the growth of the overall variety of the economic system implies that the variety-enhancing processes (specialization and the emergence of completely new products) (see Table 5.1) predominate over the variety conserving process pure substitution.

The examples of the evolution of transport and telecommunication technologies shown before indicate that this is the normal pattern in at least a number of cases. We can then conclude that specialization and the emergence of completely new products are the dominant elementary processes in technological evolution and that substitution has to play a much more limited part.

Table 5.1   Examples of the contribution to variety of elementary processes in technological evolution

Process	Example	ΔV_0
P_2 substitutes completely P_1	P_2 = digital watch, supplying time and date P_1 = mechanical watch, supplying time and date P_2 cheaper	0
P_2 almost identical to P_1 except for few new technical and service characteristics	P_2 = digital watch, supplying time, date, stopwatch, appointments P_2 = digital watch, supplying time, date, stopwatch	> 0 small
P_2 new internal structure, some services similar to P_1, some new services	P_2 = digital watch, supplying time, date, stopwatch P_1 = mechanical watch, supplying time and date	> 0 larger
P_2 new internal structure, new services	Personal computers, 1976–79	> 0 maximum

This conclusion has interesting implications for the Schumpeterian concept of creative destruction. One could interpret such a concept as the replacement of old commodities/services by new commodities/services. As seen before, if the net variety of the system is to grow, some of the old commodities/services will survive, although in a modified form, together with the new ones. Creative destruction will in some cases displace the old commodities/services, but in other cases it will lead to specialization, in such a way that the old commodities/services will concentrate on a particular niche and the new ones on a different niche.

Technology in general is a means by which human beings adapt to their environment. In fact one can define technologies as *exosomatic instruments* used by human beings in this process of adaptation (Georgescu Roegen, 1971). A growing variety could be generated by an increasingly better adaptation to the external environment, whether in its 'given' form or after it has been modified by firms to adapt it to their own requirements. By specializing and occupying various niches in the environment firms give rise to a growing variety.

However, according to Basalla (1988), the existing variety of technological artefacts cannot be explained by adaptation alone. Much of the existing variety is due to cultural reasons. In this chapter there is no intention of denying the importance of cultural factors in determining resultant variety, but the analysis used is more relevant for the adaptation based mechanisms of variety generation. In other words, it is argued that variety would increase even if the only mechanisms contributing to it were adaptation based. Further contributions to growth in variety can then be made by cultural factors.

In addition to the mechanisms that contribute to generation of variety there are others that either destroy variety or affect its distribution within the economic system. Some variety generating mechanisms create costs or negative externalities and limit the further growth of variety. Also, variety is generated asymmetrically in the world economic system (see, for example, Dosi, Pavitt and Soete, 1990), but diffusion processes tend subsequently to homogenize its distribution. In a way similar to that proposed by Prigogine (Prigogine and Stengers, 1984) for the case of physico-chemical phenomena, we can consider that all economic phenomena are the results of forces and fluxes, where forces (e.g. innovations) create heterogeneity in the system and consequently a potential for change, while fluxes (e.g. diffusion) tend to reduce this heterogeneity.

OTHER IMPLICATIONS OF THE CONCEPT OF VARIETY

Variety, Organizational Structures and Information Costs

The rise in variety of the economic system in the course of time, in addition to a number of advantages, such as greater consumer satisfaction, creates growing information requirements for producers. The information required for the production of one unit of ouput variety, V_Q, has to be transferred, stored, processed. We can expect producers to try and reduce costs, as with all other costs, while maintaining product variety unchanged or growing. This can be achieved in two ways: (a) by reducing the quantity of information required to generate one unit of V_Q, or (b) by increasing the efficiency of the transfer, storage and processing of the information required to produce one unit of V_Q. The former can be obtained by organizational changes, the latter by means of technologies which allow the same quantity of information to be processed more efficiently (Saviotti, 1988b). Examples of organizational changes which can reduce the information costs required to produce one unit of output variety are changes in the division of labour or in the hierarchical structures of organizations. Such examples will be discussed in detail in Chapter 7. Alternatively, information technologies can be used to process information more efficiently.

Variety and Competition

There are different types of competition, ranging from perfect competition to Schumpeterian or innovative competition (see pp. 85–7). The difference between these two types of competition, for the purposes of this chapter, is that perfect competitors compete by producing an identical and homogeneous output more (or less) efficiently, while Schumpeterian competitors produce something completely new, making themselves qualitatively different from other competing firms. These two types can be considered the extremes of a range, with several types of competition falling in between them. In characteristics space a technological population is a cloud of points, each point representing a model (Saviotti, 1991a and b). The density of the population increases the more similar the product models are, that is, the lower the distance between their representative points. A growing population density indicates a trend towards perfect like competition, while a falling population density indicates a growing differentiation.

The question, then, is whether there is a relationship between these changes in competition and changes in variety. The relationship can be twofold: first, it is possible, and indeed likely, that a growing population density, implying a rising intensity of competition, acts as a motivation for at least some producers to 'move out' of the existing population, in order to lower competitive pressures. In this sense a growing intensity of competition within an existing population can act as a motivation for the system to increase its output variety. Second, after the transition to a greater specialization or to completely new products has been achieved, density in the new technological populations is likely to be lower than in the original one. This seems plausible considering that the 'new' technological populations are either specialist niches or completely new products. In both cases only a few producers are likely to possess the capabilities required to operate in the corresponding portion of the characteristics space. In the case of a completely new product this would correspond to the temporary monopoly enjoyed initially by a Schumpeterian innovator. In other words, types of behaviour leading to growing variety may be perceived by firms within existing technologies as one of the possible ways of lowering competitive pressures.

However, the fragmentation of the technological population leading to specialization does not take place automatically. Some conditions have to be satisfied in order for the process to occur. Such conditions can be understood by means of *niche theory* (May, 1973; Maynard Smith, 1974; Roughgarden, 1979). According to this theory, a series of species compete for a resource, which for simplicity is assumed to vary along a single dimension. An example could be seed-eating species taking seeds of different sizes. Each species has a resource utilization function, which, in the previous example, would be the portion of seeds of each size entering the diet of the species. Assuming that the resource utilization function is the same for all species, competition will be more intense the more the resource utilization functions of different species overlap. The degree of overlap is measured by w/d, where w is the standard deviation of the resource utilization function, and d is the spacing between the species (see Figure 5.4).

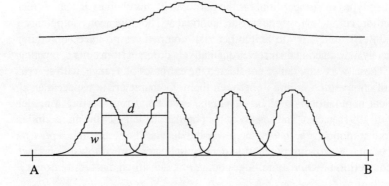

Figure 5.4   The upper curve represents the total resource available. The lower curves represent resource utilization functions for different species. The horizontal axis represents the single dimension of the resource which differs amongst the different competing species. The distance AB is the range of D (or Ry) which represents the total resources available (or the complete range of services performed by the macrotechnology); w is the width of the resource utilization function, or the width of a niche; and d is the distance between niches.

The number of species which can survive in equilibrium in the niche is determined by the extent of environmental fluctuations. If all the environmental parameters are strictly constant, that is for a deterministic environment, in general the system can remain stable, even if an arbitrarily large number of species are packed in arbitrarily close. For severe fluctuations in the resource spectrum, the number of species that can survive is given by D/σ where σ is the level of environmental noise. For fluctuations ranging from moderate to exceedingly small, the number of species able to survive in the niche is D/d. In these circumstances this model leads to the cause principle of competitive exclusion, namely that two species with identical requirements cannot coexist in a given habitat.

It is possible to set up an analogue of this model of competition for technological populations in characteristics space. Let us begin by assuming that a number of technologies can be represented by means of the same service characteristic Y, and that the range of possible values of Y represents the habitat of the combined technologies, which could constitute a macrotechnology (MT). Each particular technology T_i within the set will have a distribution function of the characteristic Y. The distribution function can be considered, for example the fraction of users of the MT using T_i for the provision of a given level of service Y (for example, the users of transport MT using a bicycle, supplying a given range of speeds of transport).

If we transfer to this case the conclusions of the biological model previously described, we can say that for moderate to small environmental fluctuations, the number of distinguishable technologies that can have long-term stability (variety of MT), is equal to the ratio R_y/d_y, where R_y is the width of the complete range of services supplied by the macrotechnology MT, and d_y is the inter-technology distance in characteristics space. Of course, in these conditions d_y is approximately equal to w_y, the standard deviation of the distribution function of Y.

It follows from these considerations that a necessary condition for the growth in output variety in the course of time is the expansion of the range R_y of services performed by the macrotechnology MT. Similarly, we can say that if the width w_y of the resource utilization function of a technology T_i in MT were to grow, we could expect a tendency for the T_i to fragment and specialize into several, each having a smaller value of w_y. In other words, we can expect the rate of growth of variety, both for the whole MT and for each of its constituent members, to be proportional to the rate of growth of R_y or of w_y.

Such a hypothesis would explain, for example, why a technology which provides a very wide and growing range of services, such as aircraft, has undergone a much greater degree of specialization than one which provides a narrow and almost constant range of services, such as helicopters.

Variety and International Trade

The variety of the economic system can be expected to grow in the course of time. Two important processes which contribute to this change are innovation and diffusion. The emergence of an innovation increases the heterogeneity of the system. This is particularly true at an international level. The variety of the world economic system is not likely to be uniformly distributed. Innovations are often introduced first in one country. After having been introduced into use, innovations tend to diffuse nationally and internationally by means of exports and manufacture in other countries. This asymmetric distribution of innovations and the consequent trade flows constitute the basis for the so-called new technology theories of international trade (Posner, 1961; Vernon, 1966; Dosi, Pavitt and Soete, 1990). Thus one could say that the local variety changes in the place(s) where the innovation is introduced first, and that this heterogeneity creates an imbalance between local and global variety in the system. This imbalance induces trade and diffusion of the innovation, which tend to eliminate the imbalance itself. Innovation and diffusion are, therefore, two complementary aspects of technological change.

A model of international trade explicitly based on product variety has been proposed by Barker (1977). The demand for variety available nationally is, in general, lower than that available internationally, and this is going to give rise to a demand for imports. Other models of international trade in which variety plays a role have been proposed by Krugman (1979) and by Helpman (1981). In both cases trade takes place in presence of economies of scale, product differentiation and monopolistic competition. In Krugman the range of products produced by each country is large, but much smaller than the range of products that the country can produce. More specifically, the number of goods that each country can produce is given by $n = L/(\alpha + \beta x)$, where L is the total labour force, α is constant cost, β is constant marginal cost and x is output. The number of goods produced in each country increases with the size of the labour force and with falling costs. From this model, growing productivity or efficiency are, therefore, a prerequisite for the generation of a greater variety. The concept of variety used by these authors is more similar to differentiation within a product group, than to the one used in this chapter. However, their considerations are relevant here. Some of the models (e.g. Krugman) exclude differences in technology. However, even if scale economies were the only sources of trade, they would create asymmetric distribution of productive capabilities. To the extent that technological knowledge is cumulative, path dependent and specific this would contribute to create asymmetries in technological capabilities. Consequently, both asymmetric technological capabilities and increasing returns to scale will contribute to create and maintain international differences in variety.

At this point we can observe that if variety contributes to international trade, it will indirectly contribute to economic growth.

A number of implications follow for industrial and technology policies. Thus if a country i has at a given time an overall output variety V_{Qi}, and if at the same time the world output variety is V_{QW}, the overall market share of country i is likely to be related to the ratio V_{Qi}/V_{QW}. If V_{QW} were to increase, country i would need to increase V_{Qi} in order to prevent its market share falling. In other words, the ratio V_{Qi}/V_{QW} is likely to be one of the determinants of the export propensity of country i. Conversely, if a country i has $V_{Qi} \ll V_{QW}$ it is likely to have a high propensity to import.

Variety and Technological Life Cycles

A number of examples of growing variety have been given initially. However, the expected change in variety is not the same at all levels of aggregation. Recent studies in the economics of technological change have uncovered a number of similar patterns of development called dominant designs (Abernathy and Utterback, 1975, 1978), technological regimes and natural trajectories (Nelson and Winter, 1977, 1982), technological guideposts (Sahal, 1981a and b) and technological paradigms (Dosi, 1982). These concepts are different, but they all imply a pattern of maturation of a given technology, during which existing or surviving producers converge upon a common set of productive practices and product features. Thus the great variety of designs at the origin of a given technology is gradually replaced by a *dominant design* and by a common set of practices. The development of such a technological life cycle is facilitated by the presence of increasing returns to adoption (Arthur, 1983, 1988, 1989a).

The implications of these concepts for this chapter are that the variety of given technologies is expected to fall during their maturation. If this happened simultaneously for all the technologies and industries in a given economy it would make it impossible for overall variety to grow. In reality, however, this trend towards falling variety observed at a given level of aggregation is complementary with respect to the trend towards growing variety observed at a higher level of aggregation. The convergence towards common practices and product features contributes to the growth in productivity of exisiting technologies which, in turn, free the resources required to generate completely new technologies and, therefore, to raise the overall variety of the system. In summary then, we can expect variety to grow at the highest level of aggregation of an economic system or at some slightly lower levels of aggregation (e.g. that of a macrotechnology), but not necessarily at lower levels of aggregation (those of a specific technology or industry). In fact the fall in variety at a lower level of aggregation is complementary with respect to the growth in variety at higher levels of aggregation.

The relationship between microdiversity and macrodiversity can be understood better by referring to a model by Metcalfe and Gibbons (1989). They call variety the variance of the distribution of each population characteristic. Their use of the term variety is therefore different from that here. Among others they obtain the interesting result that the rate of change of average population characteristics is related to their variance. This is an economic analogue of Fisher Law, a result that Nelson and Winter (1982, p. 243) had obtained in a different way for the evolution of unit costs. The significance of these developments in the present context can be gained from the following formula (Metcalfe and Gibbons, 1989):

$$\frac{dh}{dt} = \frac{\delta \times f}{f \times \delta} \times \left[V_0 \times C(h, \alpha) - V(h) \right] \qquad (5.1)$$

where h = unit cost, $C(h, \alpha)$ is the covariance of unit cost and product quality α, $V(h)$ is the variance in unit cost, V_0 is a constant relating quality adjusted price to product quality, and δ and f are parameters describing the environment in which firms operate and the type of competition. In the particularly simple case in which all products are of the same quality, (5.1) reduces to (5.2):

$$\frac{dh}{dt} = \frac{\delta \times f}{f \times \delta} \times V(h) \qquad (5.2)$$

which means that average practice unit cost declines at a rate proportional to the variance of unit costs within the technology set (Metcalfe and Gibbons, 1987, p. 27; Nelson and Winter 1982, p. 243).

Similar results can be obtained for other characteristics of the population. If one assumes that the variance of unit cost (or of another population characteristic) is higher during the initial phases of the evolution of a technology and declines as the technology matures, it follows that the rate of fall of unit costs will decline during the evolution of the technology. This would lead to a pattern of development in which mature technologies would have, for example, a lower rate of productivity growth than new technologies. This type of evolution is compatible with the changes which can be expected to take place within a paradigm. Thus the pattern of convergence on a dominant design is likely to be accompanied by a gradual increase in industrial concentration. Such an increase is particularly fast in the case of industries characterized by high technological opportunity (Nelson and Winter, 1982). As the many competing designs and at least some of the competing firms which use them are eliminated by competition, the surviving firms are likely to have not only a higher average productivity but a lower productivity variance. This type of evolution could sow the seeds of its own demise. It could cause a switch to a different technology and a different paradigm and away from one which had been previously dominant due to increasing returns to adoption and to the consequent path dependence (Arthur, 1988). In particular, for what concerns the relationship between individual technologies and the whole economic system, the decline in variance of population characteristics and consequently in the rate of change of their average values by leading to switches to new paradigms and technologies can significantly affect the output variety of the whole system. This can happen in two ways: first, the increasing efficiency internal to each technology/sector, which allows the accumulation of the resources required for the introduction of new technologies/sectors and, second, the slowdown in productivity growth internal to each technology/paradigm as it matures can induce a switch to a new technology/paradigm. In other words, even within a population perspective the trends toward declining output variety and falling rate of productivity growth at a sectoral level can be compatible, and indeed complementary, with respect to the trend toward increasing output variety at the level of aggregation of the whole system.

SUMMARY AND CONCLUSIONS

This chapter has tried to analyse a number of aspects and implications of variety. The analysis here is by no means complete, and it is more suggestive than exhaustive. While the details of the relationship of variety to other economic phenomena have still to be worked out, the main aim here is to stress that variety is a concept/variable of general relevance, useful in the analysis of many economic phenomena. Thus variety, as defined here, is a determinant of economic growth, it is related to innovation mechanisms, it influences organizational and industrial structures, patterns of information usage and international trade. Another important area of economics which is influenced by variety but which has not been discussed here is demand.

In summary, innovations, which for Schumpeter are the mainspring of long-term economic development, lead to qualitative change in the composition of the economic system and this qualitative change is reflected in a growing variety. Variety is then a variable which can be used to map the development of the system and its changing composition, but, as seen before, it is also related to many other economic phenomena. It is, therefore, an important variable in the construction of an analytical model of Schumpeterian economic development.

6.   A model of technological evolution based on replicator dynamics

INTRODUCTION

In this chapter the explicit characteristics and population representation of product technologies (as discussed in Chapter 4) and the concept of variety are applied to the development of a model of technological evolution. According to the explicit representation of Chapter 4, qualitative change can be created either by the emergence of completely new technological populations or by the differentiation and specialization of pre-existing ones, while quantitative change is here represented by the change in the number of members of each technological population. Quantitative change is measured by the change in the level (number of members) of technological populations, while qualitative change is measured by the change in variety of the system, where variety is defined by the number of distinguishable species/populations (as discussed in Chapter 5). Such qualitative change will be at least partly endogenized because inducements to the emergence of completely new technological populations or to the specialization of pre-existing ones depend on the nature of competition. Following on from the model of competition developed in Chapter 4, it will be assumed that the inducement for participating producers to establish themselves in a niche will increase the greater the population density in characteristics space. This and other hypotheses will be based either on the results of innovation studies or on the inferences and generalizations which can be based on the explicit representation of Chapter 4. In this sense the model presented in this chapter corresponds to the need for realism and for a greater role of induction outlined in Chapter 2.

Technological and economic evolution are seen as discontinuous processes, similar to the punctuated equilibrium models in biological evolution (Eldredge and Gould, 1972, 1988; see Mokyr, 1990a and b for an adaptation to technological evolution). The processes which determine the emergence of new species/technologies fall within the two types of variation and selection. In this chapter there is generally a greater emphasis on variation than on selection. However, some selection mechanisms are present as well. For example, the rate of growth of a technological population depends on its fitness. In turn, fitness, defined as the degree of adaptation to a given external environment, is influenced by incremental innovation. The technological population having the highest fitness will grow more rapidly than others and increase its economic weight.

The model presented here is based on replicator dynamics, a technique widely used in the study of evolutionary problems, such as the primordial molecular evolution (Eigen and Schuster, 1979), ecological and genetic evolution (Hofbauer and Sigmund, 1988), and social systems (Bruckner, Ebeling and Scharnorst, 1989). A related approach has been used by Allen and McGlade(1987a and b). However, as already stated in Chapter 3, biological models can only be used as an inspiration and to ask questions, not to provide answers for economic problems. The particular version of replicator dynamics presented here is consequently adapted to the nature of the economic and technological problems discussed.

The particular version of replicator dynamics used in this chapter is based on two sets of equations. The first set is of the Lotka Volterra type, and it gives a more general and more aggregate representation of technological evolution. The second set is similar to those used by Bruckner, Ebeling and Scharnorst (1989). In turn their model is similar to one initially developed by Eigen and Schuster (1979) for prebiological macromolecules. The second type of equations, henceforth called SM, gives a much more specific and microeconomic representation of the systems studied.

The SM-type equations presented describe five basic processes, which can in principle be used to represent the evolution of any technological population. These five basic processes can be broken down into a greater number of more elementary ones, which are much more specific to each technology.

The model of technological evolution based on replicator dynamics presented in this chapter is very general in a number of senses: it is in principle applicable to any technological population that can be represented by characteristics and it can capture a number of aspects of the behaviour of such populations. The model is now formulated by means of differential equations, but it can be implemented by means of other techniques, such as evolutionary games or computationally based techniques (genetic algorithms, cellular automata, etc.). The general features of this structure of the model are presented here together with the application to a particular problem, the conditions required for variety to grow. In turn, such problems lead us to consider the relationship between variety and competition.

CONCEPTUAL BACKGROUND

Product Technology in Characteristics Space

The model presented here is based on a twin characteristics representation of product technology (Saviotti and Metcalfe, 1984; Saviotti, 1991b). Each product model is represented by two sets of characteristics, corresponding to the internal structure of the technology (technical characteristics) and to the services performed for its users (service characteristics). These two sets of characteristics are related by a pattern of correspondence or imaging.

In a population approach, each technology is represented by a collection of models having similar, but not identical, characteristics values or levels. The models of a given technological population are thus concentrated in a region of characteristics space (a cloud). In the course of time a technological population can change position, density, and fragment into two or more distinguishable technological populations (Saviotti, 1991b). The last phenomenon is equivalent to specialization.

Variety

Variety, defined as the number of distinguishable actors, activities and objects required to characterize an economic system, is an important variable to represent analytically the qualitative change taking place in an economic system (see Chapter 5). The variety of our economic system has considerably increased, at least since the beginning of the Industrial Revolution. Such growth in variety is not only an accidental outcome of the process of economic development, but it is one of its fundamental components. Variety growth is both a necessary requirement for the continuation of long-term economic development and a complementary tendency with respect to efficiency growth in traditional sectors (Saviotti, 1994a).

The nature of competition is here analysed according to the characteristics and population representation (see Chapter 4). Changes in the density of technological populations indicate either a growing product differentiation (falling density) or a move towards perfect competition (growing density). The emergence of completely new technologies creates new dimensions in characteristics space. Intra-technology competition (within the same technological population) can then be distinguished from inter-technology competition (between two different technologies supplying similar services). The concept of competition used here is closely related to the biological one.

The present model of technological evolution starts from the conceptual background described in this section: its characters are product models presented in characteristics space and it uses a population approach. Furthermore, the particular application of the model that is investigated in this chapter is the conditions required for variety growth, which will turn out to depend on the relationship between variety and competition.

The Concept of Fitness in Technological Evolution

A general definiton of fitness that can be used here is the degree of adaptation of a technology to its external environment. Using a characteristics representation, fitness could then be measured as the index of similarity between the service characteristics of a technology and the characteristics of the external environment. Such a definition of fitness is very general, but it is very difficult to apply because the characteristics of the external environment are rarely known. An approximate definition of fitness which is easier to use can be developed by considering that the technologies which have a higher fitness will adapt better and will increase their share of the total population. In turn, other technologies will change their characteristics in order to imitate the more successful ones. In this way fitness will be measured by the extent of change along a particular trajectory in characteristics space. Naturally such a change always occurs at a cost. The fitness of a given technology can then be defined in an approximate, but operationally more useful, way as the ratio between the extent of technical change (TC_i) and the price P_i at which the technology is sold:

$$F_i \cong TC_i/P_i \tag{6.1}$$

Such a definition of fitness can be simply interpreted as the value for money provided by a given technology.

Clearly the demand for a given technology T_i will be related to its fitness F_i. In this chapter for simplicity it is assumed that the demand for a technology T_i is directly proportional to its fitness F_i. In fact, using a constant of proportionality of one, the demand for the technology T_i will be assumed equal to its fitness. In this sense fitness represents the process of selection within this model of technological evolution.

THE DISAGGREGATED MODEL

Basic Processes

The SM equations as implemented in this chapter include five basic processes, which give rise to either quantitative or qualitative change in the populations represented. The five basic processes, which can be broken down into more elementary ones, are:

1. *Birth*: includes all the processes which increase the population level, that is, the number of members of the population. This process does not directly affect the characteristics of the members of the population, and it leads only to quantitative change.
2. *Death*: includes all the processes which reduce the population level. Like birth, it does not affect the characteristics of the population members and it leads only to quantitative change.

3. *Incremental innovation*: it changes the characteristics of the population members, therefore leading to qualitative change. Directly it does not affect the level of population, but, since it changes the performance of some members of the population relative to others, it leads to changes in the composition of the population and in the population fitness, which influences the rate of growth of the population.
4. *Technology transfer and diffusion*: these include all the processes that lead to the diffusion of new technological knowledge. It must be noted here that only some of the phenomena traditionally included under diffusion fall under 4. Thus the diffusion of product technology is already included in this model either by the growth of a new technological population or by a change in the characteristics of the members. In this model, technology transfer and diffusion include changes in technological knowledge.
5. *Emergence of new technological populations*: it includes all the processes which create populations having characteristics qualitatively different from the previous ones, or located in regions of characteristics space completely separable from the previously existing ones. The former type of change consists of the emergence of completely new products, and the latter of the specialization within existing technological populations. Such specialization leads to the fragmentation of the existing technological populations and to an increase in their number.

It is worth noting that in the equation describing this process (6.4) the probability of specialization is proportional to both the density of a technological population and to the range of services performed by the technology. This hypothesis can be understood by reference to the previous discussion on competition. As the density of the population increases, competition becomes more intense and there is an increasing motivation for the existing members of the technological population to reduce competition by establishing themselves in a different region of characteristics space (niche). Also, niche theory (Roughgarden, 1979; May, 1973; Maynard Smith, 1974) tells us that in the presence of moderate to small environmental fluctuations only one species/technology is stable in each niche. This theory implies that a greater range of services will provide a greater number of niches and, therefore, a greater potential variety arising from specialization.

The SM Equations

Only four of the basic processes will be used for the moment. Technology transfer and diffusion will be added later. The evolution of a technological system, consisting of a number of of interacting populations, is then represented by three equations (6.2–6.4):

$$\frac{dN_i}{dt} = \left(A_i^{(0)} - D_i^{(0)}\right)N_i + \left(A_i^{(1)} - D_i^{(0)}\right)N_i^2 - \Sigma\left(D_{ij}^{(2)} - A_{ij}^{(1)}\right)N_iN_j \quad (6.2)$$

$$\frac{dF_i}{dt} = B_i^{(0)} \times S_i^e \times N_i \Sigma\, B_{ij}^{(1)} \times S_j^e \times N_i \times N_j + B_i^{(3)} \times I_i^p \times N_i$$
$$+ \Sigma\,_{ij}B_{ij}^{(4)} \times I_j^p \times N_i \times N_j \quad (6.3)$$

$$\frac{dn}{dt} = \phi_i + E_i^{(2)} \times S_i^e \times N_i + \Sigma\,_j E_{ij}^{(3)} \times S_j^e \times N_iN_j \quad (6.4)$$

Table 6.1   *Meaning of the symbols used in equations (6.2)–(6.4)*

Symbols	Definition
N_i	Number of members/models of the ith technological population, T_i
N_j	Number of members/models of the jth technological population, T_i
$A_i^{(0)}$	Intrinsic growth rate of the population
$A_{ij}^{(2)}$	Rate constant of population growth due to complementary technologies
$D_i^{(0)}$	Rate constant for physical obsolescence
$D_i^{(1)}$	Rate constant for decay induced by environmental saturation
$D_{ij}^{(2)}$	Rate constant for decay induced by competing T_i
$B_i^{(0)}$	Rate of return from search activities carried out by T_i
$B_i^{(1)}$	Rate of return from purchase of intellectual property rights
$B_{ij}^{(2)}$	Rate of return to T_i from search activities by T_j (see* below)
$B_{ij}^{(3)}$	Rate of return to T_i from purchase of intellectual property rights from T_j
I_i^p	Purchase of intellectual property rights of T_i
$E_i^{(1)}$	Constant
$E_i^{(2)}$	Constant
F_i	Fitness of the ith technological population
$F_i^{(0)}$	Threshold fitness for specialization
S_i^e	Average search effort in T_i
$R_i^{(n)}$	Radius of sphere enclosing the technological population of T_i in characteristics space

*$B_{ij}^{(2)}$ is in general a function of the Euclidean distance in characteristics space and can be modelled as $\varepsilon_{ij}[1 - \exp(-D_{ij})]$, where D_{ij} is the centroid distance betweeen T_i and T_j, and ε_{ij} is a constant relating to the rate of return from a very closely similar technology.

The meaning of the symbols used in equations (6.2) to (6.4) are explained in Table 6.1. Equation (6.2) represents the combined effect of birth and death, that is the net rate of change in the level of a technological population i. Therefore, equation (6.2) represents the quantitative change occurring in the system. Equation (6.3) represents incremental innovation, and equation (6.4) the emergence of completely new technological populations.

The Equations for the Net Growth of the Technological Population

The growth equation (6.2) can be separated into two equations, one showing the rate of increase through birth (dN_i^b/dt) and the other the rate of decrease through death (dN_i^d/dt):

$$\frac{dN_i^b}{dt} = A_i^{(0)}N_i + A_i^{(1)}N_i^2 + \sum_{j,(i \neq j)} A_{ij}^{(2)}N_iN_j \qquad (i,j = 1,2,...,k) \qquad (6.5)$$

$$\frac{dN_i^d}{dt} = -D_i^{(0)}N_i - D_i^{(1)}N_i^2 - \sum_{j,(i \neq j)} D_{ij}^{(2)}N_iN_j \qquad (6.6)$$

The three terms in equation (6.5) have the following interpretation – phenomena which contribute to birth (equation 6.5) are:

$$+ A_i (1) N_i^2 + \sum_j A_{ij} (1) N_i N_j$$

(a) *Replication* of the members of the technological population with unchanged characteristics (coeffecient $A_i^{(0)}$). The rate of replication increases with increasing investment (K_i), with increasing fitness of the technology (F_i), and with increasing consumers'/users' income (Y). The trade-off between increasing investment in the existing vintage of process technology and investing in search activities (S_i^e) is represented by the difference $K_i - S_i^e$. Also, in the course of time, search activities can reduce unit costs and lead to a higher rate of replication. Such a reduction in unit costs is represented by the following expression:

$$\frac{1}{U_i^c(0) \times \exp\left(-a_iS_i^e t\right)}$$

Thus the intrinsic growth rate of $A_i^{(0)}$ in equations (6.2) and (6.5) can be written as:

$$A_i^{(0)} = a_i^{(0)} \left[\frac{F_i(t)\left(K_i - S_i^e\right)Y}{U_i^c(0)\exp\left(-a_i S_i^e t\right)} \right] \qquad (6.7)$$

where $a_i^{(0)}$ is a constant.

(b) *Learning effects*, such as learning by doing (Arrow, 1962) and learning by using (Rosenberg, 1982), which do not require investment. These learning effects accelerate the rate at which the population grows and are represented by the second term (in N_i^2). This effect is a form of autocatalysis.

(c) *Synergistic interactions* with complementary technologies, represented by the third term (in $A_{ij}^{(1)}$). Examples of complementary technologies could be roads and petrol pumps for motor cars, or airports for aircraft. This type of interaction is usually not taken into account in economic models where competition is the only type of interaction considered.

The death equation (6.6) also has three terms with the following interpretation:

(d) *Physical obsolescence*, leading to scrapping, described by the linear term $D_i^{(0)} N_i$. The rate constant $D_i^{(0)}$ for physical obsolescence is given by $D_i^{(0)} = 1/\tau_i$ where τ_i is the mean life span for the products of the technology i.

(e) *Self inhibition*, due to some form of environmental saturation is described by the second term in equation (6.2). The rate constant $D_i^{(1)}$ is given in terms of the carrying capacity of the environment for the technology i

$$D_i^{(1)} = \frac{d_i^{(1)}}{K_i^{(c)}}$$

In general the mean rate of learning or autocatalysis is smaller than the rate of self-inhibition, making the term $(A_i^{(1)} - D_i^{(1)})$ negative. This arises from the fact that the dominant feature that regulates the population from exponential growth is environmental saturation.

(f) *Obsolescence induced by competing technologies* is described by the third term in equation (6.6). The rate constant $D_{ij}^{(2)}$ is taken in the first order to be proportional to the fitness F_j of the competing technology j and inversely proportional to the fitness F_i of the technology i with $d_{ij}^{(2)}$ as the constant of proportionality

$$D_{ij}^{(2)} = d_{ij}^{(2)} \frac{F_j}{F_i}$$

Thus the growth equation (6.2) becomes:

$$\frac{dN_i}{dt} = \left\{ a_i^{(0)} \left[\frac{F_i(t)\left(K_i - S_i^e\right)Y}{U_i^c(0)\exp\left(-a_i S_i^e t\right)} \right] N_i + A_i^{(1)} N_i^2 + \sum_{j,(i \neq j)} A_{ij}^{(2)} N_i N_j \right\}$$

$$- \left\{ \frac{1}{\tau_i} N_i + \frac{d_i^{(1)}}{K_i^{(c)}} N_i^2 + \sum_{j,(i \neq j)} d_{ij}^{(2)} \frac{F_j}{F_i} N_i N_j \right\} \tag{6.8}$$

The Equation for Incremental Innovation

Incremental innovation determines the rate of change in the fitness of the technology (equation (6.3)). Incremental innovation can lead to the homogeneous displacement of the whole population or to an expansion of it, depending on the distribution of rates of innovation within the population. Very large differences in rates of innovation can produce an enlargement of the region occupied in characteristics space by the technology. The enlargment of the region occupied by the technological population could occasionally lead to a separation of one or more parts of the population, producing new technologies. This process will be discussed in the next subsection and it is not included in equation (6.3). It is to be noted that such fissioning process can produce large-scale perturbations in the rate of change of fitness. Thus equation (6.3) is only valid when $F_i < F_i^0$, where F_i^0 is the threshold value of fitness beyond which new technologies are generated through fissioning process. The main factors influencing incremental innovations as modelled in this chapter are search activities and purchase of intellectual property rights. The various terms in equation (6.3) have the following interpretation:

1. The level of search activities (*search effort*) *in the same* technology is represented by the first term on the right, equation (6.3).
2. The *search efforts in interacting* technologies will have an influence on the rate of change of fitness in technology i, and are modelled by the second term on the right in equation (6.3).
3. The third term on the right in equation (6.3) models the rate of change of fitness through the *purchase of intellectual property rights in the same* technology.
4. The last term on the right in equation (6.3) models the rate of change of fitness through the *purchase of intellectual property rights in interacting* technologies.

The Emergence of New Technological Populations

In biology, species are defined as populations that do not mate with members of other species or if in rare cases, they do mate, they produce no viable offsprings. Thus biological species are isolated through mating. Here we use a definition of technological species as corresponding to a distinguishable population, well separated from other regions, in characteristics space. This definition of technological species, like its counterpart in biology, is not unique, but here it will be used as an operational definition.

Biologists generally believe that geographical isolation followed by mutations is the primary mode for generating mating incompatibility, leading to speciation. This mechanism is called *allopatric* speciation. Naturally we cannot expect the same mechanisms to apply to the emergence of new technological species. As pointed out in Chapter 3, biological analogies can suggest interesting problems, but not necessarily provide economic answers. Saviotti and Mani (1995) propose that technological speciation is analogous to *sympatric* speciation, another mechanism existing also in biology, although less common than allopatric speciation, and not requiring geographical isolation. In fact the processes leading to the emergence of new technological species imply interactions, sometimes strong, between the members of the pre-existing technological populations. Thus it will be seen that the probability of specialization and that of the emergence of completely new technological species are proportional to the density of the technological population. Moreover, new species can be formed through the expansion of the population in characteristics space brought about by incremental innovation, with the region separating into two or more non-overlapping regions.

The phenomena contributing to the emergence of new technological populations and described in equation (6.4) are:

1. *Serendipity*. According to this mechanism the technology arises from search efforts coming from activities having completely different goals. This process can be considered analogous to mutation in biological systems. It is a stochastic process that could be modelled by a Poisson distribution. Serendipity is denoted in the model by the function ϕ_i.

2. *Search efforts,* in the same technology i, described by the second term in equation (6.4), and in interacting technologies j, described by the third term in equation (6.4). These search efforts can be of a very different nature, corresponding either to basic or to applied research or to development. The balance of these different types of search efforts will determine whether competition amongst existing members of the technological population will lead to specialization of the existing technological population or to the emergence of completely new technological populations.

3.   *Specialization and the emergence of completely new products.* The frag-
      mentation of the existing technological population can occur in two ways.
      First, as a consequence of the increasing density of the technological
      population, competition can become so intense to provide the motivation
      for some producers to exit the core of the technology and to establish
      themselves in niches. When these niches are in the same dimensions of
      characteristics space occupied by previous technologies the fragmentation
      leads product differentiation/specialization, which is equivalent to *character
      displacement* in an ecological context. Alternatively, when the niches are
      in completely new dimensions the fragmentation leads to the emergence
      of completely new products/Schumpeterian competition. Fragmentation
      of the initial technological population can occur not only as a result of high
      population density/intense competition. While this is a necessary condition
      it may not be sufficient. A technological population must be sufficiently
      internally diversified in order to be able to fragment. Such internal diver-
      sification, which is measured by the volume of the technological population,
      indicates the range of services provided by the technology. It seems logical
      that only a technology that provides a wide range of services can fragment
      into niches, and that the number of niches is proportional to such range of
      services. Second, when the fitness of T_i exceeds a given threshold, frag-
      mentation into smaller, more specialized units can occur. The first mechanism
      is represented by the second term and the second mechanism by the third
      term in equation (6.4).

Search Activities

Search activities play an extremely important role in economic and technological development. They are the main source of variation and of qualitative
change in the economic system. A detailed treatment of the nature of search
activities would require a separate chapter. Only some general considerations
will be provided here.

   The search activities as represented in equations (6.1) to (6.5) are apparently
exogenously set. In reality, such exogeneity is largely due to the need to keep
notation simple by not indicating the possible functional dependencies and
relationships of search activities and of other relevant variables. In fact, search
activities are related in a number of ways to other variables of the model. First,
a trade-off already exists between expenditures on capital equipment and search
effort (the expenditure on search activities). Second, search efforts are often set
as a percentage of turnover. In the present case this could be modelled by
setting search efforts proportional to existing population levels. This would have

the effect of making the first term in equation (6.3) non-linear (i.e. proportional to N_i^2). Although a linear dependence of S_i^e from N_i cannot always be expected, we can in general expect S_i^e to be a function of N_i. Third, as will be discussed in a more extended way in section 5, there is a relationship between the intensity of competition in existing technological populations and the inducements to create new technological populations either by specialization or by radical innovation. Consequently, search efforts are likely to be related to the intensity of competition in existing technological populations. All these mechanisms imply a considerable degree of endogenization of search activities. Such functional dependencies are, however, not explicitly indicated for notational simplicity.

The utilization of search efforts and of intellectual property rights generated in other technologies depends on the existing knowledge base of firms. In turn, such knowledge base depends on the search activities previously carried out by recipient firms. As pointed out by Cohen and Levinthal (1989, 1990; see also Foray, 1991) R&D contributes to the absorptive capacity of a firm. In addition to providing a further mechanism for the endogenization of search activities, their absorptive function leads to path dependency.

It can be noted that both incremental innovation (equation (6.3)) and the emergence of completely new technological populations depend on the level of search activities. Of course, not all search activities are equally relevant for both basic processes. For example, basic research is likely to be more relevant for the emergence of new technological populations, while more applied search is likely to be more relevant for incremental innovation. Rather than using different labels for basic or applied search, in a previous version of this chapter (Saviotti and Mani, 1993) it was argued that all search activities differ for the range of search – wide for basic and narrow for applied search activities – and for the probability of finding the intended outcome – higher for applied than for basic search activities. The treatment of this problem is incompatible with the length of this chapter. Here we will limit ourselves to state that search activities are more likely to contribute to the emergence of new technological populations or to incremental innovation depending on whether they scan a wide or narrow range of phenomena respectively.

This differentiation of search activities implies a particular intertemporal development pattern. Search starting in a completely new technological area/region of characteristics space is likely to cover a wide range and to have a low probability of success. When some interesting results are obtained, subsequent search is likely to focus on them. The range of search will consequently narrow and the probability of success grow. In other words, one can hypothesize a life cycle for search activities, related to the life cycle of the technology that will be produced.

THE AGGREGATE MODEL

The model presented above (equations (6.1)–(6.8)) is very general, in the sense of being potentially applicable to a large number of systems. However, it gives a very detailed description of such systems because it is expressed in terms of microeconomic variables. A more aggregate model describing many types of populations (biological, technological, etc.) is given by the Lotka Volterra equations. Comparison of the two models allows us to pose questions such as:

1. Under what conditions can the system have a stable pattern of development, and how many technologies can stably exist in it?
2. How does the stability of the system depend on the extent of search activities?
3. How is technological diversity dependent on competition?
4. Can the system enter into long-term chaotic dynamics under extreme conditions?

The Lotka Volterra Equations

The Lotka Volterra (LV) equations describe the rate of change of a population i in presence of competing species j (Roughgarden, 1979, p. 521):

$$
\begin{aligned}
\frac{dN_i}{dt} &= r_i N_i \left(1 - \frac{N_i \alpha_{ij}}{K_i^1} - \sum_{i \neq j} \frac{\alpha_{ij} N_j}{K_i^1} \right) \\
&= r_i N_i \left(1 - \frac{\sum \alpha_{ij} N_j}{KA_i} \right) \\
&= r_i N_i \left(1 - \frac{N_i \alpha_{ij}}{KA_i} - \frac{\sum \alpha_{ij} N_j}{KA_i} \right)
\end{aligned}
\tag{6.9}
$$

where r_i is the rate constant for the unlimited exponential growth of the population, K_i^1 is the carrying capacity of the environment, and α_{ij} is an element of the alpha matrix whose diagonal elements are one. The off-diagonal elements of the alpha matrix give the ratio between the inter- and intra-technology competition for the technologies i and j. When $\alpha_{ij} > 1$ inter-technology/species competition predominates and intra-species competition is larger when $\alpha_{ij} < 1$. In the limit, when $\alpha_{ij} = 0$ there is no inter-species competition. If $\alpha_{ij} < 0$ ($i \neq j$) then there is cooperation between species i and j, that is mutualistic interaction. In biological contexts (α) is taken to be symmetric.

LV equations are very general and can be applied to biological, technological, and to many other types of populations. The rate of change in the population level in equation (6.9) must be the same as that in the SM equations (equation (6.2)). By equating (6.2) and (6.9) it is possible to interpret the macrodynamics provided by the LV equations in terms of the microdynamics of the SM equations.

By equating the right-hand sides of SM and LV we obtain:

$$R_i = A_i^{(0)} \tag{6.10}$$

$$K_i^1 = \frac{R_i}{D_i^{(1)} - A_i^{(1)}} \tag{6.11}$$

$$\alpha_{ij} = \frac{1}{D_i^{(1)} - A_i^{(1)}} \left(d_{ij}^{(2)} \frac{F_j}{F_i} - A_{ij}^{(2)} \right) \tag{6.12}$$

It should be noted from equation (6.12) that α_{ij} need not be symmetric. The meaning of equations (6.10) to (6.12) is very important. To understand it better we have to analyse the terms $d_{ji}^{(2)}$, $D_i^{(1)} - A_i^{(1)}$ and $A_{ij}^{(2)}$, which describe the different types of inter- and intra-technology interactions. For the moment we neglect the term $A_{ij}^{(2)}$, which measures synergistic interactions between complementary technologies. In these conditions α_{ij} becomes:

$$\alpha_{ij} = \frac{d_{ij}^{(2)}}{D_i^{(1)} - A_i^{(1)}} \frac{F_j}{F_i} \tag{6.13}$$

where $d_{ij}^{(2)}$ measures the intensity of inter-technology competition between i and j, and $D_i^{(1)} - A_i^{(1)}$ is the net rate constant for intra-technology interactions resulting from the difference between autocatalysis due to learning effects ($A_i^{(1)}$) and self-inhibition ($D_i^{(1)}$). Thus $d_{ij}^{(2)}/(D_i^{(1)} - A_i^{(1)})$ measures the ratio between inter- and intra-technology interactions. Then there are essentially two conditions in which $\alpha_{ij} < 1$ and variety will increase: first, when inter-technology competition between i and j is very weak with respect to the interactions internal to i, and, second, when:

$$d_{ij}^{(2)}/(D_i^{(1)} - A_i^{(1)}) \approx 1$$

and

$$\alpha_{ij} \approx F_j/F_j \qquad (6.14)$$

Then:

$$\alpha_{ij} < 1 \Rightarrow F_j < F_i \qquad (6.15)$$

Variety will grow either when inter-technology interactions are very weak relative to intra-technology interactions or, when the two interactions are of the same order of magnitude, when the fitness of the entrant technology as experienced by the incumbent is lower than the fitness of the incumbent itself. The second condition has a particularly interesting interpretation. It seems logical that an incumbent technology will not compete very strongly against an entrant with a fitness lower than its own. However, two things must be noted: first, even if the entrant has a lower fitness in the region of characteristics space occupied by the incumbent it may have a higher fitness in other regions of X space; second, if α_{ij} is asymmetric when $\alpha_{ij} < 1$, $\alpha_{ji} > 1$. In the latter case there will be an asymmetric pattern of competition with the incumbent not reacting very strongly against the entrant, but with the entrant competing as intensely as it can against the incumbent.

Results from the Simulation of the Aggregate Model

In this section some results from the simulation of the aggregate model (equation (6.9)) are presented. As already pointed out, such results are drawn from Saviotti and Mani (1995). Equation (6.9) is a differential equation and does not exhibit chaotic dynamics for any set of values of the parameters. To study the effect of chaotic dynamics the following equivalent difference equation, equivalent to (6.9), has been simulated:

$$\frac{N_i(t + \Delta t) - N_i(t)}{\Delta t} = R_i N_i(t)\left[1 - \frac{N_i(t)\alpha_{ii}}{K_i^1} - \sum_{i \neq j} \frac{\alpha_{ij}N_j(t)}{K_i^1}\right] \qquad (6.16)$$

where t represents time. Taking the unit of time to be Δt, equation (6.16) can be written as:

$$N_i(t+1) - N_i(t) = R_i N_i(t)\left[1 - \frac{N_i(t)\alpha_{ii}}{K_i^1} - \sum_{i \neq j} \frac{\alpha_{ij}N_j(t)}{K_i^1}\right] \qquad (6.17)$$

In the absence of inter-technology interactions, ($\alpha_{ii} = 1$, $\alpha_{ij} = 0$, $i \neq j$), R_i has to be within the range $(-1,3)$ for N_i to be positive. When $R_i < 0$, N_i would always go to extinction. The trajectories exhibit chaotic dynamics for $R_i > R_0$, where $R_0 \approx 2.6$. When inter-technology interactions are non-zero, for some values of α_{ij}, the population could go negative. These constraints on the values of R_i and of α_{ij} make it difficult to compare the results of the difference and differential equations. The following exponential form for the non-linear term of the difference equation, which avoids these constraints, has been used:

$$N_i(t+1) = N_i(t) \exp\left[R_i \left(1 - \frac{N_i(t)\alpha_{ii}}{K_i^l} - \sum_{i \neq j} \frac{\alpha_{ij} N_j(t)}{K_i^l} \right) \right] \qquad (6.18)$$

Expanding the exponential in equation (6.18) to the first two terms yields equation (6.17). As in equation (6.17) the population would go to extinction if $R_i < 0$ and the chaotic region would start for the same value of R_0. Furthermore, our simulations of equations (6.17) and (6.18) yield, for $0 < R_i < 3$, which is the range required by equation (6.17), essentially the same results.

The parameters R_i, K_i^l and α_{ij} are chosen from a uniform distribution within given appropriate intervals. The simulations were carried out for both symmetric and asymmetric (α) matrices. In equations (6.9) to (6.12), the emergence of new technology, giving rise to variety growth, is not explicitly included, but it is simulated by the introduction of new species into the system at different rates. The following four models, A, B, C and D, were considered:

1. *Model A*: the differential equation (6.9) is used. Starting with a single technology, new technologies are introduced randomly following a Poisson distribution with mean λ, where λ represents the probability of a new technology being introduced per unit time. Both symmetric as well as asymmetric (α) matrices were used in the simulations.
2. *Model B*: this is based on the differential equation (6.9). We start with 200 technologies and assume that there is no emergence of new technologies.
3. *Model C*: this is the same model as A, but using the difference equation (6.18)
4. *Model D*: this is the same model as B, but using the difference equation (6.18)

The off diagonal matrix elements of the (α) matrix were chosen randomly from a uniform distribution in the three intervals (0, 0.5), (0, 1) and (0, 2) for three sets of simulations. Four sets of simulations were carried out using the values 0.005, 0.05, 0.10 and 0.20 for λ, the mean of the Poisson distribution

A model of technological evolution

for the emergence of new technologies. The values of K_i and R_i were drawn from a random uniform distribution in the intervals (50, 100) and (0, 10) respectively. The differential equations were solved using fourth order Runge-Kutta method with step size $H = 0.01$ which we define as a time unit. The difference equations were solved by successive iterations, each iteration defining a time unit. The simulations were carried out for 5000 time units.

Table 6.2   *Results of simulations of the differential evolutionary equations. Column 1 gives the values of λ, the mean number of species introduced per generation. When $\lambda = 0$ no new species are introduced. The total number of species introduced in 5000 time units is given in brackets. When $\lambda = 0$ all species are introduced in the first generation. Column 2 gives the upper limit for the range of α_{ij} ($i \div j$), the lower limit being 0 in all cases. Columns 3 to 10 give the number of surviving species, and the values of R_{ij}, K_i^l and α_{ij} averaged over the last 100 time units and over 10 replicates*

λ	α_{ij}	Symmetric (α)				Asymmetric (α)			
		$\langle S \rangle$	$\langle R \rangle$	$\langle K \rangle$	$\langle \alpha \rangle$	$\langle S \rangle$	$\langle R \rangle$	$\langle K \rangle$	$\langle \alpha \rangle$
Model	0.5	10.2	4.7	238	0.11	12.1	4.6	232	0.12
A	1.0	5.7	5.2	247	0.15	6.9	4.3	245	0.24
0.005	2.0	3.1	4.4	248	0.15	3.1	4.7	240	0.42
(25)									
Model	0.5	21.3	4.4	264	0.10	40.5	4.5	265	0.12
A	1.0	9.6	4.3	256	0.14	16.3	3.9	257	0.23
0.050	2.0	6.1	4.9	244	0.20	8.2	4.4	237	0.45
(250)									
Model	0.5	26.5	3.8	265	0.10	49.4	4.2	272	0.12
A	1.0	12.4	4.4	254	0.16	21.2	3.9	260	0.24
0.100	2.0	6.8	4.4	257	0.24	10.1	3.9	243	0.47
(500)									
Model	0.5	29.6	4.1	263	0.10	70.8	3.9	271	0.12
A	1.0	14.2	4.2	255	0.18	33.9	3.2	259	0.24
0.200	2.0	8.5	3.9	244	0.30	17.9	3.3	242	0.48
(1000)									
Model	0.5	15.6	4.6	271	0.09	28.1	4.1	269	0.11
B	1.0	7.4	4.7	274	0.11	12.0	3.3	268	0.20
0.000	2.0	4.6	3.7	274	0.13	4.5	1.7	262	0.28
(200)									

Table 6.3 Results of simulations of the difference evolutionary equations. Column 1 gives the values of λ, the mean number of species introduced per generation. When λ = 0 no new species are introduced. The total number of species introduced in 5000 time units is given in brackets. When λ = 0 all species are introduced in the first generation. Column 2 gives the upper limit for the range of α_{ij}, (i ÷ j), the lower limit being 0 in all cases. Columns 4 to 10 give the number of surviving species, and the values of R_{ij}, K_i^I and α_{ij} averaged over the last 100 time units and over 10 replicates.

λ	α_{ij}	Symmetric (α)				Asymmetric (α)			
		$\langle S \rangle$	$\langle R \rangle$	$\langle K \rangle$	$\langle \alpha \rangle$	$\langle S \rangle$	$\langle R \rangle$	$\langle K \rangle$	$\langle \alpha \rangle$
Model	0.5	4.5	1.5	229	0.10	3.9	1.5	236	0.11
C	1.0	2.9	1.7	259	0.15	2.0	0.9	215	0.07
0.005	2.0	2.0	2.0	245	0.13	1.6	1.4	209	0.12
(25)									
Model	0.5	10.6	1.6	264	0.09	13.2	1.7	253	0.12
C	1.0	5.4	1.6	266	0.13	4.3	1.7	220	0.18
0.050	2.0	3.0	1.2	250	0.10	1.8	1.2	196	0.19
(250)									
Model	0.5	13.0	1.9	271	0.09	17.7	1.9	269	0.12
C	1.0	6.0	1.6	262	0.10	6.5	1.3	258	0.21
0.100	2.0	3.8	1.9	260	0.15	1.3	1.1	173	0.19
(500)									
Model	0.5	14.2	1.9	273	0.08	21.6	1.9	270	0.12
C	1.0	6.2	1.7	267	0.09	6.7	1.7	257	0.23
0.200	2.0	4.9	1.8	258	0.12	2.0	1.5	193	0.28
(1000)									
Model	0.5	8.5	0.9	250	0.10	12.1	0.8	259	0.11
D	1.0	3.0	0.3	234	0.15	4.3	0.3	244	0.19
0.000	2.0	1.7	1.0	192	0.14	1.6	0.1	238	0.18
(200)									

The results of the simulations are given in Tables 6.2 (differential equations) and 6.3 (difference equations). The first column in these tables gives the values of λ used and then the total number of new technologies that are expected to occur in 5000 time units. The second column gives the range of α_{ij}. Columns 3 to 6 give the mean values of the number of technologies, and of R_i, K_i and α_{ij}, (i ≠ j) for symmetric and columns 7 to 10 for asymmetric (α) matrices. These mean values are the averages over the last 100 time units and over 10 replicates.

The results of these simulations display a number of interesting features:

1. The number of surviving technologies, that is the net variety of the system, increases with increasing rate of introduction of new technologies, as expected. However, the rate of increase of variety decreases with increasing λ. That is, the marginal rate of variety growth falls with increasing rate of introduction of new technologies. Let us use as an example the case of the differential equation (model A, Table 6.2). When $\lambda = 0.005$, on the average 25 new technologies emerged in the time scale of 5000 units and only around 10 technologies, that is the 40th best condition for competition ($0 \leq \alpha_{ij} \leq 0.5$), at the end of the time scale. When λ increased to 0.05, 0.10, and 0.20, this fraction of survivors decreased to 0.085, 0.053, and 0.030 respectively. Thus the net variety seems to depend on the intensity of competition, since this is related to the rate of introduction of new technologies. This is further confirmed through the simulations over 1000 time units. In this case, though the absolute values are different since the total number of technologies introduced in the time period are different, the trend is the same as above.

2. Asymmetric (α) matrices for all models (A–D) produce a greater variety than the corresponding symmetric case. In the case of model A, for all values of $\lambda \geq 0.05$, the asymmetric model can sustain twice as many technologies compared to the symmetric model.

3. Variety increases only when intra-specific competition dominates. As the range of α_{ij} values used for the simulation increases from $(0, 0.5)$ to $(0, 2.0)$, there is always a dramatic decrease in the number of species. Also, the mean value, (α), ranges from 0.1 to 0.5 and is around 0.1 for all cases where variety is large.

4. The difference equations, (models C–D), yield a value for the number of technologies which is always smaller than the corresponding differential equations model, being less than half in most cases. Though the asymmetric (α) matrices, in general, produce a large variety, the difference between the symmetric and the asymmetric case is not as pronounced as in models A and B. The mean alpha values range from 0.1 to 0.3. Again, unlike the differential equation models, the mean alpha values are not very different between the symmetric and the asymmetric case.

5. The most striking difference between models A,B and C,D is in the mean value of R_i, $\langle R \rangle$. For the former two models, the value is in general between 4 and 5 (with a few exceptions) as one would expect since the α_{ij} values are chosen from a uniform random distribution in the range $(0, 10)$. In model C, $\langle R \rangle$ is in general between 1 and 2 while in model D it can be as low as 0.1 ($\alpha_{ij} \in (0, 2)$, Table 6.3). This difference stems from the fact that the difference equation models C and D can produce chaotic trajectories when R_i exceeds ≈ 2.6, and this is further enhanced as the range of

α_{ij} is increased beyond 1. In general, the selective pressure through fitness and competition prevents the system from entering the chaotic region in evolutionary time. Technologies exhibiting chaotic motion do not survive for long. (See Mani, 1980, pp. 256–63 and 1089 for a similar discussion in the case of biological evolution.)

In the case of model C, since new technologies are continuously introduced, at any time there could exist shortlived technologies whose trajectories are chaotic. In the case of model D, since all technologies are introduced at the origin of time and no further technologies are allowed, the transient chaotic technologies disappear rapidly and only technologies with values of $R_i < 2.6$ survive.

This feature is demonstrated in Figures 6.1 and 6.2. They show the distribution of R_i values of technologies that have survived in the last 100 time units and for ten replicates. Figure 6.1 shows the distribution of the differential equation models A and B, and Figure 6.2 for the difference equation models C and D. In these figures the histograms marked SM and AM are are for symmetric and asymmetric (α) matrices for model A or model C, and ST and AT for model B and model D respectively. The value of $\lambda = 0.05$ was chosen since it gives approx-

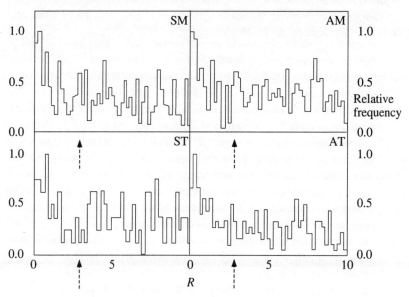

Figure 6.1 Distribution of R_i *values. SM and AM are the results for the symmetric and asymmetric (α) matrices for model A, and ST and AT for model B. The arrows indicate the onset of chaos in models C and D*

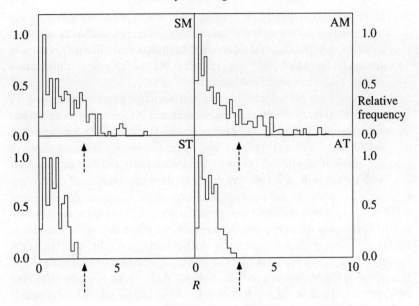

Figure 6.2 Distribution of R$_i$ values. SM and AM are the results for the symmetric and asymmetric (α) matrices for model C, and ST and AT for model D. The arrows indicate the onset of chaos

imately the same *total* number of species introduced during the time interval in all models. The values of $\alpha_{ij} \in (0, 0.5)$. In these figures the arrow indicates the position beyond which the chaotic dynamics appear in the case of models C and D. As seen from Figure 6.1, the values of R_i are distributed throughout the range $(0, 10)$, though there is an increase near $R_i = 0$. This increase in the frequency of R_i values gets more pronounced as the range of α_{ij} is increased, showing the effect of inter-technology competition. In contrast, Figure 6.2 shows that the values of R_i are concentrated below R_0, the threshold for onset of chaos. Both SM and AM curves do show that some technologies have $R_i > R_0$, and these are the transients that occur due to the introduction of new technologies. For the ST and AT curves $R_i < R_0$. When the range of α_{ij} is extended, the histograms are pushed more towards the origin giving a very low value for $\langle R \rangle$.

VARIETY AND THE NATURE OF COMPETITION

The results of the simulations previously described show that when inter-technology competition is too intense, technologies/species are selected out of the system at a rate at least as fast as that at which they are created. Net variety can only increase if the members of each technological population compete more strongly amongst themselves than with members of other technological populations.

A further and related interpretation comes from the SM equations (6.2) to (6.4). In these equations it is possible to classify the intensity of inter-technology interactions as high, medium or low. Intra-technology competition predominates in two situations, namely when inter-technology interactions are generally of low intensity $[d_{ij}^2/(A_i^1 - D_i^1) < 1]$ or when inter-technology interactions are of medium intensity $[d_{ij}^2/(A_i^1 - D_i^1) \approx 1]$, and the fitness of the entrant as experienced by the incumbent is lower than that of the incumbent itself. As long as this situation exists, the incumbent technology will concentrate on competing with itself and it will leave the entrant technologies relatively free to develop. This development, however, is more likely to occur in a region of characteristics space different from the one where the incumbent is established. Since the fitness of each technology is a function of the position in characteristics space, the entrant could start in a niche where its own fitness is higher than that of the incumbent (niche entry strategy). By using the approximate definition of fitness $(F_i \approx TC_i/P_i)$ we can see that a niche entry strategy can be either a low price or a high quality one.

These results, together with the role of variety in influencing economic development imply that the long-term economic development following from technological evolution will be greater when inter-technology competition is relatively low. For high inter-technology competition too many technologies would be selected out, variety would not increase and economic development would stagnate.

From a related point of view we can remember that in characteristics space competition becomes more intense and more similar to perfect when the density of the technological population increases. According to equations (6.2) to (6.4) variety increases partly due to specialization, and partly due to the emergence of completely new products. The probability of these two processes increases both with the density of the population and with the range of services provided by the technology. Net variety will be greater when the members of a given technological population, rather than competing more and more strongly amongst themselves, try to reduce competition by establishing themselves in a niche. Also, as already seen, the new technological populations established in niches have a greater chance of surviving if inter-technology competition is less intense than intra-technology competition. In both cases, then, there is an optimum value of competition which leads to the maximum generation of variety.

The picture that emerges from this model has both Chamberlinian and Schumpeterian features. On the one hand, as in the case of product differentiation, the members of a given technological population tend to reduce competition by branching out into one or more niches. What is given greater emphasis in this chapter with respect to the literature on product differentiation is the fact that the technological populations thus created can become completely separate from the initial ones. In other words, the link between the generation of variety and economic development is given here an emphasis which is completely absent in the literature on product differentiation. This leads us to the Schumpeterian features of the model. Variety, created by innovators, is the main determinant of long-term economic development. The optimum conditions for the creation of variety do not correspond to the maximum possible intensity of competition. There is an optimum intensity of competition above which the generation of variety decreases.

This picture reproposes the tension between static and dynamic efficiency familiar to students of industrial organization. Within a given technological population there will be a member whose position corresponds to the maximum performance of the technology. If the population did not fragment, through competition that member should be the only one to survive. If, on the other hand, specialization occurs, a growing variety may be obtained at the expense of a reduced performance of the original technology.

SUMMARY AND CONCLUSIONS

The approach described in this chapter is based on two different but related versions of replicator dynamics, the first represented by the micro equations (6.2) to (6.4), which in turn derive from those of Eigen and Schuster, and the second by the 'aggregate' or 'macro' equations based on the classic Lotka Volterra equations for competition. The former allows one to model processes of technological evolution with a considerable degree of specificity and to incorporate a number of findings of innovation studies. The latter gives a much more synthetic and aggregate, or 'macro', view of the evolutionary process, in terms of parameters which can be used for any type of evolving population, such as the intrinsic growth rate, the carrying capacity of the environment, and the ratio inter- to intra-species competition. We can think of these two systems of equations as providing a 'micro' and a 'macro' description of our system respectively.

The comparison of the two equations allows us to obtain an interesting analytical result, that is to specify the relative extent of inter- and intra-technology competition as experienced by an incumbent and by an entrant technology respectively. We assume, first, that there is no complementarity between technologies i and j, and, second, that the intensity of competition between i and j is relatively low. In these conditions the incumbent will experience a low inter-technology competition (and a high intra-technology competition) when the fitness of the entrant is lower than its own, as is likely to happen in a large number of cases. In the same conditions the entrant will experience a high inter-technology competition. The behaviour of the incumbent and of the entrant technologies will be determined by these perceived inter-technology interactions. At the beginning the incumbent will compete mostly with itself, possibly delaying its reaction, while the entrant will compete mostly with the incumbent, allocating most of its resources to this task. If the intensity of interaction of technologies i and j is very high, the entrant's fitness will have to be much lower in order to keep competition predominantly intra-technology. Conversely, if the intensity of interaction of technologies i and j is very low, competition will remain predominantly intra-technology even when the entrant's fitness is of the same order of magnitude as that of the incumbent. In summary, the higher the intensity of interaction of the technologies, the lower the fitness of the entrant will have to be relative to that of the incumbent in order to keep competition predominantly intra-technology and to allow variety to grow.

A number of entry strategies can also be defined by equating fitness to the ratio of normalized Euclidean distance (a measure of technological change in output) to the price. This ratio can be considered a measure of the quality per unit of price, or of value for money, provided by the technology. An entrant technology can raise its fitness relative to that of the incumbent by choosing a particular niche in characteristics space where the fitness of the incumbent is not very high; by choosing a low price or a high-quality entry strategy into the core of the technology. Examples of all these entry strategies are found in the empirical and marketing literature. However, their existence can only be predicted by means of an explicit approach to product technology.

The results of the simulations based on the LV equation show that the ratio inter- to intra- technology competition seems to be particularly important in determining the stability and the variety of the replicator system. For high values of this ratio ($\alpha_{ij} > 1$) the system tends to become unstable and to lead to a lower number of surviving technologies, no matter how many new ones are introduced into the system. If $\alpha_{ij} < 1$ the system tends to be more stable, and it may lead to a growing variety. When the LV equations are implemented by means of difference equations a chaotic region occurs for very high intrinsic growth rates of the population. In this region the number of surviving technologies/species is more limited whatever the value of α_{ij}.

These results, taken together with the conclusion based on the LV–SM comparison, have very important implications for competition and for economic development. As we have seen above, the asymmetric nature of α_{ij} means that as an entrant technology j appears, the incumbent technology i is likely to perceive the competition from j as less important than its own internal competition, while the entrant perceives inter-technology competition as the most important. It is in these conditions that, according to the results of the LV equation, the variety of the system can grow. It could be argued that this asymmetry, and the consequent predominance of intra-technology competition as perceived by the incumbent technology, is a necessary condition for the success of the entrant, and, therefore, for a growth in variety: the entrant would be almost invariably eliminated if all the resources of the incumbent were allocated to inter-technology competition. The asymmetric nature of inter-technology competition would then at least facilitate the growth in variety of the macrotechnological system. If such a growth in variety is a necessary requirement for the continuation of long-term economic development then the asymmetric nature of inter-technology competition is an important component of this process. In any case it can be said that the predominance of inter- over intra-technology competition would at least create more favourable conditions (than the opposite situation) for the process of economic development in the long run.

These same phenomena can be interpreted in terms of more conventional economic ideas. The processes of specialization and of the emergence of completely new products correspond to a Chamberlinian or to a Schumpeterian view of competition (Chamberlin, 1933; Schumpeter, 1912, 1942). Both of them reduce the intensity of competition and give the technologies considered a certain degree of monopoly. From the previous simulations and analytical results such reduction in competition, and the degree of monopoly achieved, may be a necessary requirement for a growth in variety of the system. Given the link with long-term economic development mentioned before, monopolistic competition is likely to be important not only in static product differentiation, but also for long-term economic development.

Particularly important is also the distinction between intra- and inter-technology competition. The former is the only type of competition traditionally considered by economists. Thus a monopolist is free from intra- but not from inter-technology competition. The presence of inter-technology competition reduces the degree of monopoly and contributes to the contestability of markets. On the other hand, the best conditions for variety growth, and thus for economic development, require inter-technology competition to be less intense than intra-technology.

The results and conclusions so far described are only some of those that can be extracted from this model. A number of other elaborations are possible. For example, the complementarity between the technologies in the SM equations (coefficient A_{ij}^2) can lead to different types of interactions between them, including predator–prey relationship and mutualism. These phenomena can have very important implications which will be worked out. Furthermore, from the general type of analysis performed by means of the LV equations, it is possible to determine the specific conditions under which a particular replicator system would evolve by means of the SM equations. It is then necessary to determine under what conditions a technological system can lead to a growing variety.

The approach described in this chapter should have a considerable generality. It can be used for different types of replicator systems (e.g. biological populations, firms, etc.), and it can be implemented by means of a number of techniques (differential or difference equations, genetic algorithms, etc.). In principle it should be applicable to a wide range of problems and systems.

PART 3

Technological Evolution, Variety and the Economy

INTRODUCTION

The need to develop an explicit representation of technological change gave rise in the first part of this book to a particular representation of product technologies. The characters of technological evolution considered were technological artefacts. These were not all the possible characters of technological evolution. Other important characters are the individuals and organizations which create and use technologies, and in particular the knowledge required to do so. As has already been anticipated in Chapter 2, scientific knowledge is not the only type of knowledge used by enterprises, and probably not the most frequent one. Technological knowledge as used in enterprises and organizations is different. It is a collective form of knowledge, because it depends not only on the individual elements of knowledge 'contained' in individuals with their training and qualifications, but also on their interactions. In turn, such interactions depend on the strategy and on the organizational structure of the firm.

In the second part of the book a number of topics were covered, starting from the use of information in organizations, to inter-firm collaborative agreements to the national system of innovation. There is thus an apparent discontinuity between the second and the third part, in the sense that the first part is concerned with artefacts while the second part is concerned with knowledge in organizations. There are, however, at least two threads of continuity: first, the problems in the third as in the second part are always approached in terms of evolutionary theories; second, knowledge, information and organizational structures contribute to qualitative change and to the generation of variety. New products and new processes can only be produced by means of the previous creation of new knowledge.

Using a slightly different teminology, attention was focused in Part 2 on the revealed technological performance (RTP) of firms. However, the production of RTP is carried out by firms having strategies, organizational structures, competences and capabilities. The production of RTP takes place starting from the knowledge base of firms. In this context it is important to remember the distinction between knowledge and information introduced in Chapter 2. Information is here interpreted as something of a factual nature, while knowledge provides generalizations and intellectual categories. Such a distinction is not based on a complete definition of knowledge and information, but it has the advantage of allowing us to compare regimes of incremental technical change and of radical technical change. New information is generated in both cases, but the retrieval of such information has very different requirements for firms. Within a regime of incremental technical change the new information generated does not require new intellectual categories to be retrieved. On the contrary, in the presence of radical technical change new information cannot be interpreted by means of the old knowledge base of firms, a situation which is called competence disrupting by Tushman and Anderson (1986). When a paradigm change takes place, a radical restructuring of the knowledge base of firms is required. Not all firms will change at once and the distribution of knowledge amongst firms will undergo radical changes. It is at this stage that coordination problems will become more acute in the economy.

A more extended treatment of the knowledge base of the firm will be given in Chapter 8. For the moment it is enough to to establish the difference between knowledge and information.

In Part 3 of the book a number of implications of the considerations of Parts 1 and 2 for knowledge bases, organizational structures and institutions will be developed. In Chapter 7 attention will be focused exclusively on information. The consequences of variety growth for the way firms use information will be discussed. This type of analysis will tell us what would happen if we were in a world where variety grows and where firms use information, labour and material inputs to produce this increased variety. Knowledge and coordination problems will thus be neglected in Chapter 7, but they will be reintroduced in Chapter 8. There, different organizational structures will be discussed with particular emphasis on inter-institutional collaborative agreements (IICAs). In Chapter 8, knowledge will be discussed both for what could be called its internal features and in relation to the external environment of the firm, of which it is one of the most important components. Also, coordination problems and the way they are influenced by radical changes in technological knowledge are given a central place. In Chapter 9 the problem of institutions will be approached at a higher level of aggregation, that of the national system of innovation (NSI). There the theoretical justification of the concept of NSI will be discussed in terms of evolutionary theories. Moreover, the implications of trends towards internationalization of the world economy and of variety growth for the NSI will be discussed.

7. Variety, organizations and information

INTRODUCTION

The concept of variety has been introduced in Chapter 5 as a variable which captures the effects of qualitative change on economic development. Furthermore, the hypotheses that variety growth is (a) a necessary condition for the continuation of long-term economic development and (b) complementary with respect to efficiency growth in established sectors were introduced. Whatever the effects of variety on economic growth, to produce a greater output variety implies greater costs. For example, the existence of a trade-off between variety and scale economies is an established theme in the literature on product differentiation (see, for example, Lancaster 1979). The particular costs which will be the object of study in this chapter are information costs.

As already pointed out in Chapter 2 and in the introduction to Part 3, information is different from knowledge. The analysis in this chapter will concentrate only on information. It will, therefore, be equivalent to asking what would happen in a world in which firms use labour, material inputs and information to produce their output. To start with, the greater the variety of an economic system the greater is the amount of information, and therefore the information costs required to describe it. These greater information costs have an impact on at least two types of costs in the economic system. First, firms which increase their product range and their output variety face greater information costs. Second, consumers benefit from this process in two ways: they can afford both larger quantities of existing goods and a greater variety of goods and services. However, this greater variety has also some associated costs, for example search costs. We can expect that there will be a tendency to reduce information costs, both at the level of production and at that of use of the greater variety created by economic development. The problem of information costs in organizations is treated first and in a more detailed way.

VARIETY AND COMPLEXITY

Before turning to the implications of increasing variety for economic development it is important to mention that variety and complexity are two different concepts. In order to appreciate this difference a more rigorous definition of variety has to be introduced (Ashby, 1956, p. 124). If an economic system is considered a set of elements then the variety of this set will increase when the number of distinguishable elements of the set increases. Consequently, one could use various measures of the number of distinguishable elements, the most immediate one being the number itself. In information theory the variety of a set is defined as the logarithm in base 2 of the number of distinguishable elements in the set.

$$V = \log_2 n \tag{7.1}$$

where V = variety and n = number of distinguishable elements in the set. Given the behaviour of the log function this particular definition implies that the marginal contribution to variety made by new and distinguishable products/activities will decline with an increasing number of products/activities already present in the system, a behaviour actually found for the model of technological evolution based on replicator dynamics (see Chapter 6). Different definitions of variety will have different implications but they all entail an increase in variety when the number of distinguishable elements of the system increases. The usefulness of this concept of variety in the case of an economic system depends on how easily distinguishable product, services, etc., are. Without getting into a detailed discussion of this problem here we can observe that there are enough cases of distinguishable products, services, etc., to make this treatment worthwhile (for a more extended discussion of this point, see Saviotti, 1988a). Complexity, on the other hand, can be defined in two different ways (Nicolis, 1987, p. 163). Structural complexity increases with the number of interacting sub-units; the percentage of mutual connectedness among them (dyadic or plural fashion) and the variance of the probability density function of the strengths of interaction between the individual sub-units. On a functional level, complexity increases with the minimum length of the (most compressed) algorithm from which one can retrieve the full behaviour of the system.

Given the previous definitions, the structural complexity of a system could change considerably by changing the interactions between sub-units and their distribution function while maintaining the number of sub-units, and therefore the variety of the system, constant. Variety is consequently a component of complexity but it is not equivalent to it. Changes in complexity itself can have important implications for economic development but in this chapter the discussion will be limited to the effects of variety.

INFORMATION, VARIETY AND ORGANIZATIONAL STRUCTURES

A system characterized by a greater variety of constituent elements is also a system which requires a greater amount of information to be described. The total cost required to describe such a system can be expected to increase with the variety of the system itself, although not linearly with it. Assuming that a growing variety of the economic system leads to positive welfare implications and to the possibility of a continued process of economic growth, this same process will only continue if information costs do not grow as rapidly as the benefits produced by the increasing variety of goods and services supplied to consumers. In other words, one can expect that both producers and consumers will tend to reduce the information costs required to generate an economic system of increasing variety. This section is devoted to analysing a number of ways in which producers can try to reduce their information costs.

Such information costs depend on a number of factors. First, new goods and services will in general require new processes. Hence a greater variety of final goods and services will be accompanied by a greater variety of the processes used to produce them. It is useful at this point to recall the distinction between output variety (V_q) and process variety (V_p) (Chapter 5). In the course of economic development one could expect producers to tend to reduce the costs that they face to produce a given output variety. These information costs can be reduced in two ways: first, by increasing the efficiency with which the information required to describe the system is stored and processed; second, by changing process organization in such a way that one has to store and process a smaller quantity of information to achieve the same output variety. For example, let us imagine a given productive process in which information about stock of parts, salaries, etc., is stored and processed manually. If without changing process organization, and therefore without changing the quantity of information required to describe it, the storage and processing of information is computerized, the information costs of the process are likely to fall. If process organization changes in such a way that a smaller quantity of information is required to describe the process a further reduction in information costs will be achieved. In the first case a change in technology would have been introduced without any change in process organization, while the opposite would be true in the second case. Naturally in real life situations, changes in organization and changes in technology are often introduced simultaneously and they are often complementary. The previous considerations were only aimed at separating them conceptually so that their roles and their interactions can be subsequently analysed. The considerations that now follow are mostly aimed at analysing the implications of changes in process organization for the information costs required to generate a given output variety V_q. In order to do that a few more concepts need to be introduced.

Information, Entropy and Variety

In order to compare the information requirements of different organizational structures we have to find a way to quantify information. Such a way is going to be provided by informational entropy, a concept introduced by Shannon and Weaver (1949; see also Saviotti, 1988a) to which the reader is referred for a more detailed analysis. Entropy is generally used to measure the randomness or uncertainty of a given set of elements (Gatlin, 1972, p. 28). Entropy is higher when the elements are placed randomly with respect to one another and falls when the elements are in an ordered configuration. For example, the entropy of a system constituted by a set of billiard balls of different colours is higher in a random configuration and higher when all the balls of the same colour are grouped together. Each different configuration of billiard balls represents a microstate of the system. The system can have many different microstates. Most of these microstates are random and very few are ordered, for example those that have all the billiard balls of the same colour together. Hence the probability of an ordered microstate, given by the number of such microstates, will in general be lower than that of a disordered microstate. If the elements of the system were in continuous motion then the system itself would continuously change between microstates. The system would then spend the majority of its time in disordered/random microstates and an average of the states of the system (a macrostate) would resemble more disordered states. Since entropy is supposed to measure the disorder of the system and since disordered states have a higher probability of existence, entropy is related to the probability of finding this system in a given state by the equation:

$$S = K \log W \tag{7.2}$$

where S is entropy, K is a constant and W is the probability of finding the system in that state, which is given by the corresponding number of microstates. The previous considerations apply to the case in which the microstates of the system are equiprobable. In this case, and when the microstates are independent, equation (7.2) can be rewritten as:

$$S = K \log (1/p_i) = - K \log p_i \tag{7.3}$$

where p_i is the probability of an individual microstate. However, if the microstates of the system are not equiprobable equation (7.3) has to be modified and it becomes:

$$S = -K p_i \log p_i \tag{7.4}$$

This equation was introduced by Shannon and Weaver (1949) in order to deal with the information content of messages. This case is particularly relevant for social systems because their microstates are not necessarily equiprobable. For example, it is clear that not all the microstates of an organization, obtained by mixing at random the members of the organization, are equivalent. It is possible to demonstrate (Gatlin, 1972, p. 36) that a given set of elements has its maximum entropy when all its microstates are independent and equiprobable. An example of this can be given by an organization in which initially all the members have the same skills, functions and power. In this case it would be possible to mix at random all the members of the organization without changing its performance. In this hypothetical case each microstate of the system would be equiprobable. If, subsequently, all the members of the organization were retrained and given completely different skills, in such a way that they could now perform different functions and occupy hierarchically different positions, a random mixing of the members of the organization would not produce equiprobable microstates. In the final state the system is more ordered and structured and has a lower entropy. The concept of entropy has been introduced here for its relationship to that of information. Information in this context has to be used in the same way in which it is used in communications theory (Shannon and Weaver, 1949, p. 8). In this sense information is not measuring knowledge or meaning, but refers only to the freedom of choice when one selects a message. For example, one unit of information is required to choose between two messages a and b. When the number of messages increases, both the information required to make a choice amongst them and the uncertainty of the system increase. Such a more uncertain system is also more disordered and, therefore, has a higher entropy. Consequently, a system with a higher entropy will require a greater quantity of information to be described. More specifically, the quantity of information required to choose one message out of a set of n messages increases with the entropy of the set of messages. It is therefore understandable that entropy has been used as a measure of information in communications theory.

Summarizing the previous discussion one could say that the greater the uncertainty or randomness of a set of messages (and consequently the greater the entropy of the set) the greater the information required to choose one out of a series of messages. If one moves from the context of communications to that of organizations, the analogue of the information required to choose one out of a set of messages becomes the information required by the top management of the organization to choose one employee or a subunit out of the n employees/subunits which constitute the organization. In even simpler terms the information which is measured by entropy is the information which is required by top management (or by anyone else who needs it) to 'know' the organization.

Within the kind of information which has been described above we can distinguish several types. For exmple, a communications engineer is interested in the capacity to transmit information. As Shannon and Weaver (1949) put it: '... this word "information" in communications theory relates not so much to what you do say as to what you could say'. This capacity is called by Gatlin (1972) *potential* information. Therefore potential information, which increases with messages variety and with freedom of choice, is measured by entropy.

It is not true, however, that as entropy increases information always increases. Let us take a simple example. A library contains information stored in the form of linear symbols ordered according to the constraints of a language. The sequences are contained in books and periodicals which are classified and neatly catalogued in shelves. This is obviously a state of very high order. If we were to take each page of each book or periodical, cut them into single letter pieces and mix them at random, the entropy of the system would increase but the information stored in the library would decrease to virtually zero. However, starting from this disordered state, many more meaningful combinations of letters could be formed than the one that was destroyed by cutting the books and periodicals into single letter pieces. Hence, while the actual information contained in the library decreased to virtually zero the information that it could contain increased. A difference has therefore to be made between *potential* information and *stored* information. In simpler terms, a greater uncertainty or randomness of the system tends to increase its potential information while a greater order and constraint tend to increase its stored information.

Another interesting distinction could be introduced between the *internal* and *external* information required by an organization. The purpose of an organization is to transform some kinds of inputs, not necessarily material, into some kinds of outputs. In so doing, the organization must have information about the type of inputs required, the process to transform them into outputs and the users of these outputs or, in general, about the external environment in which it operates. Alternatively, the organization must also have information about its internal structure and the internal resources that it can use to transform inputs into outputs. According to Duncan and Weiss (1979, p. 205):

> The objective of the kind of organisation structure that is implemented is twofold: (1) to generate information for decision making that reduces uncertainty, and (2) to generate information that will help to co-ordinate the diverse parts of the organisation

where the uncertainty reducing information (1) can be considered mainly information about the external environment. The roles of these two types of information can be better understood by comparing them to what happens in a computer. Particular types of information are stored in a computer at given locations. In order to retrieve this information the addresses of the location at which it is stored have to be known. The addresses are only part of the mechanism by which valuable information is stored. If the capacity of the computer is finite the more memory locations are used for addresses the less space there will be for the storage of valuable information. The uncertainty of the system in an organization is the analogue of the number of addresses in a computer. In both cases the quantity of valuable external information that can be stored decreases with the uncertainty of the system or the number of addresses.

We can now summarize some of the results of the previous discussion about the effect of the non-independence and non-equivalence of the microstates of the system on its entropy:

(a)   the larger the number of non-distinguishable elements of the system, and consequently the greater its variety, the larger the amount of information required to describe the system.

(b)   The greater the degree of non-independence and of non-equiprobability of the microstates of the system, the lower its entropy (Gatlin, 1972, p. 36) and consequently the lower the amount of information required to describe the system.

(c)   A lower entropy of the system, due to non-independence and non-equiprobability of its microstates, is also associated with a greater capacity of the system to store information.

Second, it could be said the concept of information as used in this chapter does not describe all the types of information that an organization uses in its decision-making processes. Types of information which would fall within the definition used here are, for example, that required to choose a particular spare part from a store, to choose the employee who is knowledgeable about a particular topic or to calculate the wages of a group of workers. In other words, it is information of the type which is commonly described as factual. As already indicated, information is not meant to be equivalent to meaning or knowledge. However, the quantity of information of this type that has to be manipulated by organizations is so large that changes in organizational methods and technologies which decrease the costs of processing and transmitting this type of information are bound to have an important economic effect.

It could be said that this paper analyses the implications of this type of information only for organizational arrangements or that, in other words, it tries to find what would be the preferred organizational structures in a world in which information of the factual type was the only factor determining such structures. Naturally, real life organizations are influenced by other factors as well. Whether real organizational structures resemble those which could be predicted on the basis of information alone will depend on the relative importance of information and of these other factors. However, it is not always true that a lower entropy is an advantage. This can be understood by returning to the previous example of the dictionary. The state in which the dictionary is normally sold has obviously a lower entropy than the state obtained by mixing at random all its letters. Consequently, the information storage capacity of the dictionary in its normal state is much higher than that in its disordered state. However, starting from the disordered state it is possible to reorder the letters in many ways, the original state of the dictionary being only one of them. Many types of meanings can therefore be created starting from the disordered state. In this sense, the disordered state of a library has been described before as having a lower stored information but a higher potential information than the ordered state. The disordered state has a greater flexibility than any of the completely ordered states. In the case of organizational changes this implies that an organization of lower entropy will be able to store a larger amount of specialized information which allows it to adapt well to a constant environment. On the other hand, an organization of higher entropy will be more easily adaptable to changes in its external environment which are required to store a different type of information. Normally we choose to store particular items of information in order to use them repeatedly. This is an effective strategy if the environment in which the information storing organization operates is stable. Thus highly structured organizations are likely to be effective when a constant set of routines is appropriate. But if the environment changes quickly, highly structured organizations are likely to experience difficulties. This could explain the observation that organizations operating in more dynamic environments tend to have 'organic' structures while organizations operating in more static and structured environments are more likely to have 'mechanistic' structures (Burns and Stalker, 1961). The information already in them blocks the channels through which new information might come: storing information reduces access to potential information. Alternatively, we could say that organic structures have a lower stored information but a higher potential information than mechanistic ones. In a related way one can expect that when the environment changes suddenly and radically the organization will have to upgrade its external information more rapidly than its internal information. In this sense external information is going to be used relatively more in the formulation of strategies while internal information is likely to be more closely related to organizational structures. If strategy precedes structure (Chandler, 1962, 1977) then it is logical to expect that external information should change in response to environmental changes and ahead of internal information.

Third, the economic value of the same quantity of different types of information may be very different. Marschak (1958) has argued that there is no relation between the number of bits conveyed and the gross value of the information. Thus, for example, knowledge of the colour and style of a bride's dress (at least two bits of information) is unlikely to be twice as valuable as the knowledge of the future value of one's stocks (at least one bit of information). It is therefore impossible to compare the value of two qualitatively different pieces of information using the concepts of information theory. It is, however, possible to compare the quantity of information that two different organizational arrangements require to produce the same output. In this case the types of information will be the same for both organizational arrangements but the uncertainty of one arrangement will be greater and correspondingly its capacity to store information lower. Of course the comparison of the information requirements of two different organizational arrangements are valid only to the extent that no other changes take place simultaneously (e.g. changes in technology, strategy, skills, etc.). Some examples of how the information requirements of a given process are influenced by changes in process organization will now be discussed.

EXAMPLES

Example 1 – Division of Labour

In this example two different organizational arrangements for the same manufacturing process are going to be compared. In one the process is carried out without division of labour and in the other the maximum division of labour is used. The process consists of a number of operations which are performed by different people. For simplicity in both cases the number n of operations will be considered equal to the number of people performing them.

Case 1

Each person carries out the n operations in a sequence, therefore producing the final product. Each person works independently of any other person involved in the process. In this system, therefore, there is no division of labour. In a formal sense this system does not constitute an organization, rather each person carrying out the complete process constitutes a unit of production and organization. This productive system constitutes a simplified model of a real system in which individual artisans produce finished products working independently of one another. The total entropy of this process (equation (7.2)) can be estimated by calculating the probabilities of the individual microstates of the system. We can imagine deriving each microstate of the system by drawing in sequence one person and one operation from two separate boxes and coupling them. A microstate of the system has been generated after n people and n operations have been drawn from separate boxes and coupled. A different microstate can be originated by putting back the people and operations in their separate boxes and drawing in a different sequence n people and n operations and coupling them one to one. In this way all the possible microstates of the system can be originated. Each microstate of the system can be considered as a snapshot in which each person is 'frozen' while performing one of the n operations. In a subsequent snapshot (microstate) each person will be found performing an operation different from that of the previous microstate. In each microstate an operation is associated with each person. The following two are examples of microstates:

$$X_1O_1, X_2O_2, ..., X_nO_n \qquad (7.5)$$

$$X_1O_3, X_2O_6, ..., X_nO_m \qquad (7.6)$$

where $X_1, ..., X_n$ represent the workers and $O_1, ..., O_n$ the operations. The probability of each of them are given by:

$$P_a = P(X_1O_1, X_2O_2, ..., X_nO_n) \qquad (7.7)$$

$$P_b = P(X_1O_3, X_2O_6, ..., X_nO_m] \qquad (7.8)$$

Since each person works independently, P_a can be expressed as the product of the probabilities of each event $X_1O_1, X_2O_2, ...$

$$P_a = P(X_1O_1)*P(X_2O_2)* ... .*P(X_nO_n) \qquad (7.9)$$

Given that there is no specialization and that consequently each person can perform equally well any of the n operations

$$P(X_1O_1) = P(X_1O_2) = ... = P(X_1O_n) = P(X_2O_1)$$
$$= P(X_2O_2) = ... = P(X_2O_n) = P(X_nO_n) \qquad (7.10)$$

Consequently:

$$P_a = P_b = \text{probability of any other microstate } P_i \qquad (7.11)$$

All the microstates of the system are therefore equiprobable. Since the sum of the probabilities of the microstates must be equal to 1 then:

$$P_i = 1/n \qquad (7.12)$$

where n is the number of microstates of the system. Consequently, the entropy of the system will be

$$H = -\sum 1/n \log 1/n = +\sum 1/n \log n = n\, 1/n \log n = \log n \qquad (7.13)$$

Here, and in what follows, equation (7.2) is used without the constant K because what is important is to estimate the change in entropy between two different situations and not its absolute value. Since the microstates of the system are independent and equiprobable this type of organizational arrangement corresponds to the maximum possible entropy of the system of n workers and n operations.

Case 2
In this case the n operations which constitute the process remain constant but specialization and division of labour are introduced in their most extreme form. Each person will then be able to perform only one of the n operations. The same microstates of the system can be originated except that now they are no longer equiprobable. In particular, one microstate, that in which each person is performing the operation that he/she has been trained to perform, has a non-zero probability and this probability is actually equal to 1. Shannon's expression (7.4) for the entropy of the system is then reduced to a single term:

$$H = 1 \log 1 = 0 \qquad (7.14)$$

In other words, passing from a system in which there was no division of labour and specialization to one with the maximum possible specialization and division of labour the entropy of the system has decreased from log n to zero. Since entropy can be considered a measure of the information which is required to describe the system, this example shows that the introduction of specialization and division of labour decreases the information required to describe the process. Hence, the information that the organization has to store to know itself and to coordinate its own internal processes, what was previously called internal information, decreases with increasing division of labour. Correspondingly, the information that the organization can store about the environment in which it is operating and about the technologies it is using (external information) increases. This is understandable if we think that information has to be stored or 'embodied' in the human skills of an organization. In the absence of specialization every person in the organization would have to store the same types of information. On the other hand, with division of labour every member of the organization has to store only a very limited range of types of information and consequently can store a greater quantity of these types. Collectively the organization can store more information.

The two cases previously analysed are extreme cases. They are important, however, because any real process is likely to have a degree of division of labour included between these two. The entropy and the information requirements of any real process are therefore going to decrease as the process moves away from the extreme without any division of labour and toward that with the maximum division of labour.

The situation does not change substantially if the number of operations $n(O)$ is different from the number of people $n(x)$. Both for $n(O) > n(x)$ and $n(O) < n(x)$ the entropy of the system will be above its minimum that corresponds to the situation in which each person performs only one operation.

The representation of the division of labour which was given in this section is clearly rather abstract and oversimplified. In a system with a high degree of division of labour the output of the operation performed by each individual worker has to be transferred to the next worker in the sequence of operations. In other words, a transaction occurs betwen each pair of workers in subsequent operations. A process with n operations will contain $(n-1)$ transactions. To obtain the benefits of the division of labour some coordination is required in terms of time, position, etc. This coordination requires additional information and causes additional costs. In the presence of coordination costs, actual information requirements would be determined by the balance between operation costs and coordination costs. The case previously illustrated is therefore an idealized one in which coordination costs can be considered negligible with respect to operation costs. Coordination costs will be introduced in Chapter 8.

At a higher level of aggregation, that of an industrial sector or of a national economy, the division of labour in production is equivalent to arm's length transactions between independent firms. In this case as well the most extreme form of division of labour and independent transactions would be the organizational structure with the lowest entropy, and therefore with the lowest information requirements, only when transaction costs are negligible with respect to production costs. This situation is similar to that described by Williamson (1975, 1979, 1981) in the transaction cost approach.

Example 2 – Hierarchical Organizations

In this example two different structures of the same organization will be compared, one with no departmental boundaries and one in which the organization is constituted by a series of departments. Following Simon's terminology (1981) the first case would be an example of a 'flat' system with only one hierarchical level and with a 'span' of control equal to the number of employees of the organization (see Chapter 2 for a different use of the concept of span). By introducing departments the number of hierarchical levels would have to increase to at least two, because now if all the departments but one were at the same hierarchical level the department in charge of overall coordination and planning would have to occupy a higher hierarchical level. Furthermore, the span of control would now be restricted to the employees of each department. Finally, the degree of non-equivalence would increase by introducing departments because workers in each department would have skills specific to that department and not interchangeable with those of other departments. As in the previous example, we will compare the informational entropy of two different organizational structures, the flat, departmentless organization and the hierarchical organization.

Case 1

The organization is constituted by *n* workers performing *n* operations. The lack of hierarchical structures implies that the operations performed by different people are sufficiently similar that the various workers can be interchanged amongst them. In a first approximation we can assume that these operations are identical and that the workers are completely interchangeable amongst them. This is obviously an oversimplified situation but it is useful to compare this case, in which people can freely move amongst all the operations in the organization, and case 2, in which people can only be exchanged amongst the operations contained in one department. This situation and the implications for information are clearly different from the effects of the division of labour. The difference can be understood if one imagines to start from *n* people and *n* equivalent operations and to generate a real life organization containing different departments in a number of stages. In the first stage the *n* people are put together under one institutional roof and assigned in a random fashion to the *n* equivalent operations. In the second stage the departmental boundaries are introduced and now people can only be interchanged amongst the operations internal to the department. In the third stage the operations in each department are differentiated and division of labour is introduced.

As will be proved in this section, the introduction of departmental boundaries reduces the information requirements of the organization. The calculations here will be based on the assumption that all workers within each department are equivalent and, therefore, interchangeable. Clearly this is not a very realistic assumption. A high degree of division of labour normally exists in each department. The reasoning in this section can be understood as follows. If we compare the flat structureless organization and the department-based hierarchical one, we see that the latter has lower information requirements than the former even in the case in which all the workers in a department are equivalent. As we have seen before, division of labour leads to a further fall in information requirements. Therefore, a hierarchical organization could have higher information requirements than a flat one only in the very unlikely case in which the latter had a division of labour so much greater than the former that it could compensate the effect of the introduction of departmental boundaries.

Since in this case people can be interchanged amongst a set of *n* equivalent operations all the microstates of the organization are equiprobable. Consequently the entropy of the system has its maximum possible value, given by the logarithm of the number of microstates of the system, which in this case is equal to the factorial of the number of people:

$$H = \log n! \tag{7.15}$$

When the microstates are equiprobable the entropy of the system is given by equation (7.2), which again turns out to be equal to its maximum possible value.

Case 2

When departmental boundaries are introduced, only microstates of the system obtained by moving people around within each department are possible. A lower number of microstates can therefore be obtained with respect to the previous case. However, even in this case the microstates of the system are equiprobable, since the operations in departments are equivalent. The change in entropy between case 1 and case 2 is given by:

$$\Delta S(1 \rightarrow 2) = S(2) - S(1) = R \log p(2) - R \log p(1) = R \log p(2)/p(1) \quad (7.16)$$

where $p(2)$ and $p(1)$ represent the numbers of microstates of the organization in case 2 and case 1 respectively. In this case, in order to prove that the information requirements of the hierarchical organization are lower than those of the flat one, we have only to prove that $\Delta S(1 \rightarrow 2) < 0$.

If $n(1), n(2), ..., n(k)$ are the numbers of people employed in each department in case 2 and n the number of people employed in the organization as a whole then:

$$p(2) = N_1! * N_2! * \ ... \ * N_k! \quad (7.17)$$

where $N_1!, N_2! \ ... \ N_k!$ are the factorials of $n(1), n(2), \ ... \ n(k)$.
Consequently:

$$\Delta S(1 \rightarrow 2) = \frac{N_1! * N_2! * ... * N_k!}{N!} \quad (7.18)$$

It can be proved that $\Delta S(1 \rightarrow 2)$ is less than zero. If we expand all the factorials:

$$\Delta S(1 \rightarrow 2) = \frac{1*2*3*...*n(1)*1*2*3*...n(2)*1*2*3*...n(k)}{1*2*3*...*n} \quad (7.19)$$

If we assume that factorials are ordered in the following way:

$$N_1! < N_2! < N_3! \ ... \ < N_k! \quad (7.20)$$

and if we simplify the factors corresponding to the smallest factorial, we find:

$$\Delta S(1 \rightarrow 2) = R \log \frac{1*2*3*...*n(2)*...1*2*3*...*n(k)}{(n(1)+1)*(n(1)+2)*...*n(2)*...*n} \quad (7.21)$$

To each factor contributing to the second factorial in the numerator will correspond a larger factor in the denominator. Thus, for example, $n(1) + 1$ will correspond to 1, $n(1) + 2$ will correspond to 2 etc. The same will occur for each of the subsequent factorials. Consequently the denominator will always be greater than the numerator and $\Delta S(1 \rightarrow 2)$ will always be smaller than zero.

This will occur as a consequence of the introduction of departments into the organization. With this change the uncertainty of the system is limited by reducing the freedom of motion and of communication of the employees within the organization. From what was said before, it follows that increasing the number of departments leads to a fall in the entropy of the system, and therefore in the quantity of information required to know and coordinate the members of the organization. Intuitively this change can be interpreted as a decrease in the number of information paths possible within the organization. When there are no departments and all members of the organization are equivalent, communication may be required between all possible pairs of members. On the other hand, communications between members of different departments are much more selective and lower in number.

As previously pointed out, the information saving effect of the introduction of departmental boundaries is different from that due to the division of labour, discussed in the previous example. The information costs of the organization would be further reduced if after introducing departments division of labour was introduced as well. In other words, the types of organizational change illustrated in examples 1 and 2 can both lead to reductions in the entropy of a system and these reductions are cumulative.

According to Simon (1981), hierarchical organizations tend to be more stable than unstructured organizations and therefore they have a higher probability of survival in an evolutionary process. The improved chances of survival may be partly due to the fall in information requirements discussed in case 2.

Example 3 – U and M Form Organizations

This is a further and more detailed application of the case described in example 2. Even in this case we compare the information requirements of the two types of organizational structures by calculating their informational entropies. A schematic representation of the two types of organization is given in Figures 7.1 and 7.2. The entropy for the transition from a U to an M form organization can be calculated in the same way as in example 2:

$$= R \log p(M) - R \log p(U) = R \log \frac{p(M)}{p(U)} \qquad (7.22)$$

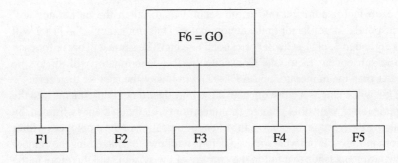

Figure 7.1 Multidivisional or U form. F_6 = GO = general office; F_1, F_2, F_3, F_4, F_5 = functional departments

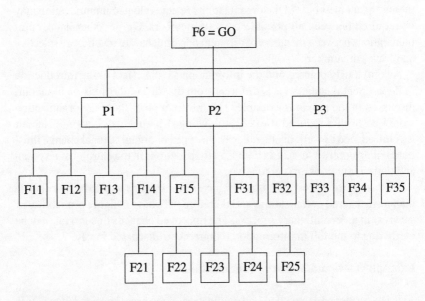

Figure 7.2 Multidivisional or M form. F_6 = GO = general office; P_1, P_2, P_3 = divisional offices; F_{11}, F_{12}, F_{13} ..., F_{34}, F_{35} = functional departments

In order to calculate $p(M)$ and $p(U)$ some simplifying assumptions have to be made. First we can assume that total employment N_T remains constant during the transition $U \rightarrow M$. Second we can assume that in both cases employment is evenly distributed amongst different departments, divisions, etc. Therefore if we introduce the following notations:

State U

$n_1, n_2, n_3, n_4, n_5, n_6$ = numbers of people employed in functions F_1, F_2, F_3, F_4, F_5 and F_6 respectively, where F_6 coincides with the general office.

State M

$n_{11}, n_{12}, n_{13}, \ldots, n_{21}, n_{22}, \ldots, n_{31}, \ldots, n_{35}$, = numbers of people employed in functions $F_{11}, F_{12}, \ldots$; n_1, n_2, n_3, = numbers of people employed in divisional offices 1, 2 and 3; n_6 = number of people employed in the general office.

The previous assumptions can be stated as:

$$N_T = n_1 + n_2 + n_3 + n_4 + n_5 + n_6 = n_6 + n_1 + n_{11} + n_{12} +$$
$$\ldots, + n_2 + n_{21} + n_{22} + \ldots + n_3 + n_{31} + \ldots + n_{35} \qquad (7.23)$$

$$N_T = N_D(U)\, n_U = N_D(M)\, n_M \qquad (7.24)$$

$$n_1 = n_2 = n_3 = n_4 = n_5 = n_6 = n_U = N_T/N_D(U) \qquad (7.25)$$

$$n_6 = n_1 = n_{11} = n_{12} = \ldots = n_{35} = N_T/N_D(M) \qquad (7.26)$$

where $N_D(U)$ and $N_D(M)$ are the total numbers of subunits (departments, etc.) in cases U and M, n_U and n_M are the numbers of people employed in each subunit in cases U and M. We can then proceed in a way similar to that of example 2 to calculate the probabilities of the two states U and M.

$$P_M = n_1!*n_{11}!* \ldots * n_2!* \ldots *n_{21}!* \ldots *n_6! \qquad (7.27)$$

Given the previous assumptions:

$$n_1! = n_{11}! = \ldots n_3! = \ldots n_6! = n_m! \qquad (7.28)$$

Consequently:

$$P_M = N_D(M)* n_M! \qquad (7.29)$$

Similarly:

$$P_U = n_1!*n_2!*n_3!*n_4!*n_5!*n_6! \qquad (7.30)$$

but:

$$n_1! = n_2! = n_3! = n_4! = n_5! = n_6! = n_U! \qquad (7.31)$$

and

$$P_U = N_D(U)*n_U! \qquad (7.32)$$

Thus:

$$\Delta S(U \to M) = \frac{N_D(M) * n_M!}{N_{D(U)} * n_U!} \qquad (7.33)$$

$$\Delta S(U \to M) < 0 \, IF = \frac{N_D(M) * N_M!}{N_D(U) * N_U!} \qquad (7.34)$$

But:

$$\frac{n_U}{n_M} = \frac{\dfrac{N_T}{N_D(U)}}{\dfrac{N_T}{N_D(M)}} = \frac{N_D(M)}{N_D(U)} \qquad (7.35)$$

and:

$$\frac{N_D(M)}{n_D(U)} = \frac{n_U}{n_M} < \frac{n_U!}{n_M!} \qquad (7.36)$$

This condition (equation (7.36)) is always satisfied for $n_U > n_M$. Consequently the transition (U→M) will always lead to a fall in the entropy of the organization, and, therefore, to a fall in information costs per unit of output variety, provided that employment in each subunit of the M state is smaller than employment in each subunit of the U state. This is always going to be the case if total employment in the organization is kept constant. Of course this does not imply that employment cannot change. The calculations here prove only that at constant employment an M form organization has lower information requirements than a U form one. If employment increases this will imply an increase in information requirements in both cases, but at the final level of employment information requirements will still be lower for the M form.

PROCESSES OF TECHNOLOGICAL DEVELOPMENT

The previous section dealt with organizational forms and organizational changes that could be used to reduce the information costs that firms face in generating an increase in the variety of products and services that they produce (output variety). This section will be concerned with a different level of aggregation, namely that of a technology or an industry.

Reference has already been made to the fact that dominant designs, technological trajectories, technological paradigms, etc. can have implications for variety (see pp. 108–10). For example, the emergence of a dominant design is likely to limit the output variety of the technology by reducing the number of distinguishable products. In a similar way, according to product life-cycle theories of international trade (Vernon 1966), a technology has to mature and become standardized before it diffuses internationally. In a similar way these processes would have implications for the information requirements of changes in variety. For example, the adoption of a dominant design/regime, trajectory/ paradigm/guidepost would inhibit wide-ranging exploration of a rich field of potential information. By limiting the search in this way the paradigm would create a relatively stable environment in which highly structured organizations which store information efficiently would perform particularly well. Alternatively, a radical change in technology or some other important environmental change would invalidate much of the previous stored information and, therefore, put highly structured organizations at a disadvantage. In these conditions organic structures with their greater flexibility and higher potential information would perform better (Burns and Stalker, 1961). By decreasing input variety and process information requirements one would expect these trends in technology to lead to a fall in process entropy and possibly even in output entropy. These processes function at a level of aggregation higher than that of individual firms/organizations and lower than that of the whole economic system. The problem then arises of the compatibility of these changes in variety, process information requirements and entropy with those at the lower and higher levels of aggregation.

For what concerns individual firms and organizations these trends in technology will impose 'common' constraints which will make firms' technological behaviour quite similar, although not identical in a number of respects. Therefore, one could expect that as a paradigm becomes established the variance in output quality and (even if perhaps to a lesser extent) in firm behaviour to decrease. Convergence would take place towards common practices and conceptual structures.

From what was said before, the output variety of the whole system is expected to grow over sufficiently large periods of time while the output variety of individual technologies and industrial sectors in many cases is expected to fall. If the number of technologies and industrial sectors in the whole economic system were constant this could not happen. However, there are two ways in which these patterns of evolution at different levels of aggregation of the system can be compatible. First, the decreasing output variety of each technology could lead to savings in process information costs and in other dimensions. In a way similar to what followed from Pasinetti's model, savings in individual technologies could allow the accumulation of the resources required to generate new products and services and, therefore, to increase the output variety of the whole system. In this sense paradigms would play a role similar to that of the organizational changes at the level of the firm discussed in the previous sections. Second, it would be possible for a paradigm to define a number of common practices upon which all the firms using the technology would converge but making a 'modular' use of the common practices. For example, a large variety of models could be produced making use of common parts and of standardized process equipment and practices. In this way it would be possible for process variety and process information costs to fall while simultaneously output variety increased at the level of the individual technology. There are examples of both types of behaviour, with aircraft and helicopters following the former type (Saviotti, 1988b; Saviotti and Trickett, 1992) and motor cars and agricultural tractors the second type (Coombs *et al.*, 1978; Saviotti *et al.*, 1980).

Reference has already been made to the relationship between the fall in the variance of productivity growth within a given sector/technology (Metcalfe and Gibbons, 1989) and the growth in overall variety. Without repeating the reasoning in an extended form here we can summarize the conclusions as follows:

(a) Productivity growth within each sector/technology is obtained partly by converging upon a dominant design, a standard set of practices, etc. In addition to other types of savings, information requirements are reduced by means of these trends. In this process the internal variety of the sector may fall, but even in this case productivity growth allows the accumulation of resources required for search activities and for the generation of new technologies. In this way overall variety can increase.

(b) The fall in the variance of productivity growth is accompanied by a fall in the rate of growth of output, which could create inducements for the exit from the sector/technology and for the creation of completely new technologies.

ROUTINES

Nelson and Winter (1982) give a sophisticated discussion of the term routine and of its implications for what concerns organizations. They define routines as a general term for all regular and predictable behavioural patterns of firms (ibid., p. 14). Such a definition includes a very large number of routines at very different hierarchical levels within organizations and with very different levels of complexity. Elaborating slightly on their definition one could say that routines are constant patterns of internal activities of firms undertaken in response to environmental stimuli occurring within a predetermined range. Some of the negative meanings associated with the term routine and with bureaucrats as routine implementers can be understood in this sense. Thus people (external to organizations) sometimes wonder why their problem, which they consider novel and different, is handled by means of existing routines, designed for different problems (different range of external stimuli).

Routines could, therefore, be redefined as the union of a set of environmental stimuli with a set of internal organizational responses. The main feature of routines is that the set of internal organizational responses can cope with a large number of external stimuli. This may mean either a relatively constant type of stimulus occurring very frequently or a relatively large range of different types of stimuli. Naturally, routines of different flexibility would be required to cope with these two situations. However flexible routines are they tend to have a considerable intertemporal invariance with respect to stimuli coming from their environment, otherwise they would not be routines.

Nelson and Winter (1982) discuss a large number of aspects of routines. Routines can be the memory of an organization, its skills, a truce among different groups in the organization or its genes. Also, they discuss the relationship of routines to innovation. The two concepts are not opposites, as it is commonly implied: first, the application of prevailing routines can create puzzles which lead to innovation; second, many innovations are, at least partly, constituted by different combinations of existing routines, in a way that Nelson and Winter find reminiscent of Schumpeter's new combinations of means of prodution by the entrepreneur (1912, pp. 65–6). Furthermore they interpret heuristics and changes in technological paradigms as the analogue of routines. Routines, heuristics and the technological trends discussed in the previous section can, therefore, be interpreted as examples of the stable patterns of behaviour which is followed by organizations.

In a way it may seem surprising that what one could consider as a particular feature of organizations (routines) or of technologies (technological trajectories, paradigms) share some general characteristics. In reality if one considers organizations and technologies as complex systems these regular patterns of behaviour are nothing else than examples of self-regulation and constitute the analogue of what for biological systems is homoeostasis (Saviotti, 1986). Such patterned behaviour is the logical requirement for the stability of complex systems. A system whose internal structure fluctuated wildly in response to environmental stimuli would have no coherence and no stability.

Thus the concept of routines is of quite general applicability and has many important implications for the behaviour of organizations. For the more restricted purposes of this chapter it is important to try and analyse the implications of routines for the information requirements of organizations. In order to do this we start from a definition of heuristics as 'any principle or device that contributes to the reduction in the average search to solution' (Newell, Shaw and Simon, 1962, p. 85). In a similar way routines, by sticking to a predetermined course of behaviour in response to a set of environmental stimuli, reduce the search required to 'process' the stimulus. If we imagine an organization without routines we can realize that the search, and, therefore, the information required to process a given stimulus, would be much wider in the absence of routines. We can, therefore, argue that one of the functions of routines, although not the only one, is to contribute, together with other organizational devices, to information saving.

Naturally this is only one of the functions of routines. To the extent that they contribute to the observed behaviour of organizations they do so based on all their functions. What can be done in this chapter is to isolate the implications of the need to economize the information required in given productive processes. One could, therefore, say that if to use information efficiently was the only goal of organizations, routines and heuristics would exist anyway. Naturally one could not infer from this that they would have the same form that they have in real life organizations.

In principle one can expect routines to change depending on the functions that they have to perform. For example, we can expect different routines when they function as truce and when they function as information savers. The real routine would be a compromise between the two. However, it is difficult to imagine a prevailing routine as being highly information inefficient whoever are the groups jostling for power within the organization. If that were to happen it would always be possible for one of the groups to propose a change to a more information efficient routine and to improve its power position in the subsequent truce. This is to say that there is not necessarily a conflict between the best routines which satisfy different functions.

ELEMENTARY MECHANISMS IN TECHNOLOGICAL EVOLUTION

The definition of elementary mechanisms in technological evolution and their representation by means of a twin characteristics approach have been discussed in Chapter 4. The implications of such elementary mechanisms for variety growth have been discussed in Chapter 5. For example, pure substitution does not change at all the variety of the economic system while the emergence of completely new products makes the maximum possible contribution to variety growth (see Chapter 5, Table 5.1). Correspondingly, such elementary mechanisms create different information requirements. Thus the emergence of completely new products will lead to greater information requirements than pure substitution or specialization. However, the degree of novelty of the technology will not only create requirements for new information, but also for new knowledge required to interpret the new information This takes us out of the subject matter of this chapter. Problems of knowledge generation and absorption will be dealt with in Chapter 8.

VARIETY AND THE DEMAND FOR GOODS AND SERVICES

The previous part of this chapter dealt with the implications of a growing output variety of the whole economic system for information requirements, organizational structures and the evolution of technologies. In other words, so far the text has been concerned only with the supply side. Some preliminary considerations about the implications of a growing output variety for demand will now be introduced. The purpose of these considerations will be simply to show that the same type of analysis can be used for demand as it has been used for supply. The analysis itself, however, will not be complete by any means.

From the beginning of Chapter 5 it has been assumed that a growing output variety would be beneficial to consumers. To be able to use a wider range of products and services can be considered an advantage. However, it is not necessarily an unmixed benefit. To be able to choose only one product limits the satisfaction or utility that one obtains from purchases, but it has associated with it very limited uncertainty and, therefore, very limited information requirements. In other words, a consumer faces information costs (see, for example, Stigler, 1961) to scan what the market offers, to analyse product characteristics and to compare them to his/her demands. These information costs are likely to rise with output variety, although not necessarily linearly with it (Saviotti, 1988a). One can expect mechanisms to be developed to decrease the information costs required to enjoy the services of a unit of output variety. Better education, specialist publications and advertising supply consumers with an increased flow of information about the goods and services that they are supposed to choose. On the other hand, trade marks, brand names and even the reputation of particular chains of shops and supermarkets function as information savers because they replace the information that consumers would use to evaluate the quality of the goods and services under consideration. A user could simply choose the output of a known trade mark instead of all the goods produced by different manufacturers. In this way the user would not need to have a detailed knowledge of the internal structure of the product or even of its services in order to make a choice. The advertising, trade mark, etc., would function as a source of expert knowledge reducing the quantity of information needed to make a choice while enjoying the services of a greater variety of goods.

SUMMMARY AND CONCLUSIONS

In this chapter the implications for organizational·structures and for information requirements of the trend towards increasing variety (Chapters 5 and 6)
have been discussed. Variety growth leads to an increase in information requirements and, therefore, costs. We can expect that in the process of economic
evolution there will be tendencies to reduce information costs both on the
supply and on the demand side. Changes in information costs of these types
can be better analysed by using together the concept of entropy. On the supply
side, information costs can be reduced either by changing organizational
structures, thus intrinsically reducing the quantity of information to be processed,
or by leaving the quantity of information to be processed unchanged but by
adopting more efficient technologies to process it. The latter option is clearly
the one that is exploited by information technology. In general it is to be
expected that the two options will be used simultaneously and interactively.
However, it is still useful to separate them for analytical purposes. This chapter
has been mainly concerned with changes of the former type.

Using the concept of entropy it has been demonstrated that in the absence of
coordination problems division of labour will decrease the information requirements of a given process. Similarly, a change in organizational structure in which
subunits of some type are introduced into a homogeneous organization leads
to a reduction in information requirements. In particular it was shown that an
M form/multidivisional organization has lower information requirements than
a U form/multifunctional one.

Processes of technological development have important implications for
variety and information. Variety may fall in a technology/sector during its life
cycle. However, this fall is accompanied by a reduction in costs in general and
information costs in particular. Such increased efficiency can contribute to the
accumulation of resources required for search activities and for the generation
of new sectors.

Amongst elementary mechanisms of technological development some (pure
substitution) do not contribute to overall variety while others (specialization,
product diversification, emergence of new products) contribute to different
extents. In order for the overall variety of the system to increase, variety
increasing processes must predominate over substitution. However, the elementary
mechanisms which make the greatest contribution to variety growth, such as
the emergence of completely new products, create not only new information,
but new knowledge. Firms and organizations have to acquire the new knowledge
in order to interpret the new information.

Finally, the examples which have been considered show that in many cases
the tendency to economize information in given productive processes, technologies
and organizational practices, leads to organizational structures and patterns of

development which are very similar to those observed in real life examples. In other words, one could say that if the tendency to economize information as defined in this chapter was the only factor determining the structure of organizations, such structure would be very similar to the one we can observe in real organizations. This means that either information is one of the most important factors determining organizational structures or that the other factors which could influence them tend to produce the same type of organizational structure. Naturally it is impossible to give an answer to these questions here because the other factors would have to be taken into account. However, the analysis of one of the factors constitutes a beginning and helps to formulate the problem.

8. Knowledge, the environment and organizational structures

INTRODUCTION

To the extent that economic theories have been concerned with technological change they have been concerned with artefacts. The concept of different vintages of capital, embodying different levels and types of knowledge, has been one of the main ways in which economists have tried to model technological change. Disembodied technological progress was already assumed in Solow's (1956, 1957) theory of economic growth, but his concept of technological progress was completely unarticulated. In recent theories of economic growth (Romer, 1987, 1990) and of international trade (Grossman and Helpman, 1989, 1991) knowledge has been given a more prominent role. These theories represent important improvements towards the goal of incorporating knowledge creation and utilization into economic theories. However, they have an approach towards knowledge which is both aggregate and implicit, that is, which stresses far more the consequences of knowledge for known economic variables than the mechanisms of generation and utilization of knowledge. This chapter will concentrate more on those which could be called intrinsic features of knowledge and on their implications for organizational structures.

To begin with, the distinction between knowledge and information established in Chapter 7 will be restated. While early papers on R&D (Nelson, 1959; Arrow, 1962) treated it as an information generating activity it is now clear that R&D does more than that (Foray, 1991). Although a complete differentiation of the two terms is not attempted, it is enough to establish that knowledge provides generalizations and relations while information is of a factual nature. Information is stored in some media (papers, individuals, equipment, etc.) but it can only be retrieved by means of the intellectual categories supplied by knowledge. When new knowledge emerges in the external environment it also leads to new information Saviotti, 1994b). However, both firms and organizations cannot absorb the new knowledge without the interpretive categories provided by the new knowledge. In periods of radical technical change firms' knowledge has to be substantially updated if they are to be able to adapt to their external environment.

The considerations in Chapter 7 referred exclusively to situations in which firms use information of a factual nature to produce their output. Such a situation could occur in a regime of incremental technical change in which the new information which is created can be interpreted by means of the existing knowledge of the firm. This chapter will analyse some of the consequences of changes in knowledge for organizational structures. It will begin with some general considerations about the nature of technological knowledge, it will elaborate the concept of the external environment of the firm/organization, and it will then proceed to discuss the relative stability of different organizational structures as determined by the conditions of the environment, of which knowledge is one of the most important components.

TECHNOLOGICAL KNOWLEDGE

Evidence of the growing importance of technological knowledge for economic development is given by the rise in R&D intensity of the main industrialized economies after the Second World War (see, for example, Mytelka, 1991a; Dasgupta and David, 1992; David and Foray, 1994). At least as important has been the growing integration of processes of knowledge generation with other, more conventional, economic activities. The clearest example of such integration is the institutionalization of industrial R&D. Such a phenomenon, which began to develop at the end of the 19th century in Germany and in the United States, has been judged by Freeman (1982) as one of the most important social innovations of this century. R&D was not seen any more by firms as something which could potentially be useful and whose production could be left to outside institutions (e.g. universities, specialist research laboratories, etc.), but as a valuable component of the production process of the enterprise that had to be closely integrated with the other components of such a production process. Knowledge becomes then a central actor in the process of knowledge generation. Understanding knowledge generation and use becomes a central problem for economics.

Technological knowledge has some general features which can be discussed independently of the institutional context in which it is generated and diffused; on the other hand knowledge is produced and used by organizations as a result of the interactions and flows taking place in such organizations.

PROPERTIES OF TECHNOLOGICAL KNOWLEDGE

The knowledge which is crucial in determining the commercial success of innovations is not the same as that which can be generated in the laboratories of universities or basic research institutions, although the two are related.

Without attempting to give a general definition of such a knowledge it is worth establishing some characteristics of technological and organizational knowledge. We can take as our starting point a model of technology in which all knowledge is created by science, and technology simply applies it. Such a model was very common amongst historians of science and technology and, in particular amongst other social scientists (Layton, 1974). From the economist's point of view, such a model was compatible with the exogenous nature of technology and of inventive activity. Layton stressed how technology was itself a form of knowledge, albeit different from scientific knowledge.

Recently, concepts such as competencies (McKelvey, 1982), the knowledge base of a firm/organization (Metcalfe and Gibbons, 1989; Metcalfe and Boden, 1992) and corporate capability (Teece, Pisano and Shuen, 1990) have introduced more explicitly the role of knowledge in organizations and in technological change. Such knowledge is not only different from scientific knowledge, but it has a collective character. It is quite possible to have different organizations containing individuals of exactly the same qualifications and yet producing different outputs. What is important, in addition to individual skills and knowledge, are the mechanisms of interaction between individual elements of knowledge. In other words, the knowledge possessed by an organization/firm is a collective form of knowledge, and it is more than the sum of the individual elements of knowledge contained in the organization itself. Whatever their differences, technological and scientific knowledge are often used jointly. It is then important to have available some typologies of knowledge which encompass both scientific knowledge and the more practical types of knowledge used by organizations.

To begin with, both theories and more applied pieces of knowledge are correlational structures, that is, they establish correlations between the different variables describing their observation space (see Chapter 2). The span of the theory is a measure of the size of such observation space (for example, the number and range of variables over which the theory allows us to establish correlations). Such concept of span is very similar to that of span of control of organizations (Simon, 1981). However large, the span of a piece of knowledge is finite. This leads to other relevant characteristics of knowledge, that is its local character and its degree of specificity.

Critics of the production function have pointed out that the range of techniques available to a firm was not as wide as that implied by the function itself (Atkinson and Stiglitz, 1969; David, 1975). Nelson and Winter (1982) have considered that firms' knowledge is local, in the sense that they would search in the vicinity of their previous technology. Thus, if we could represent their technology by means of a K/L (capital/labour) ratio, firms' search would have a higher probability of success in a range of K/L ratios closer to their previous one.

In order to understand this point we can recall that one of the main goals of theories is to correlate the variables underlying events and phenomena. For simplicity of presentation we can imagine placing all such variables along a given dimension and ordering them. Variables corresponding to similar events will tend in general to be closer than variables corresponding to very different events. The most powerful theory would correlate all the existing variables, that is, express relationships between any pair/set of variables. Less powerful theories would allow us to correlate only smaller subsets of variables. The smaller the span of the theory, the more local the theory is. Intuitively to say that a theory is local means that it can explain and correlate events of a given type, but that it becomes progressively less effective as we start considering events which differ more and more from those that the theory was initially designed to explain. Thus, if we had previous knowledge of the properties of molecules of low molecular weight we are likely to be able to extend such knowledge to other molecules of slightly higher molecular weight, but not necessarily to high molecular weight polymers. Similarly, if we had knowledge of the properties of metallic materials, it is likely that we can understand more easily the properties of other metallic materials than those of composites, made from polymers. The same considerations can be placed in a slightly different form in terms of learning, the activity by means of which firms' knowledge is augmented. We can define learning as the internalization of knowledge external to the firm. The local character of knowledge then implies that the probability of learning is inversely proportional to the distance/difference between the firm's internal (pre-existing) knowledge and the external knowledge to be acquired (Saviotti and Mani, 1994).

A number of authors have pointed out that firms' knowledge is highly specific. The concept of specificity is related to the localized nature of knowledge but it is not identical to it. The more practical types of knowledge created and used by industrial firms and organizations have both similarities and differences with respect to scientific theories. Industrial knowledge is intended to allow firms to operate on particular subsets of the external environment (e.g. chemical compounds, materials, pieces of information, etc.). The modification of the external environment requires knowledge of the relationships of the variables defining the subsets. However, as already pointed out, industrial and techno-logical knowledge are not purely the application of scientific theories. The knowledge provided by scientific theories is more general, that is, it covers a greater span, or equivalently, it is less local, but it is also less specific. The real life systems on which industrial firms operate are far more complex than the simplified models studied by scientific theories. A theory is always based on a simplified representation of reality, that is, it excludes some/several constituents of the systems studied in order to be able to generalize. The theory will thus give us an approximate representation of the behaviour of particular systems. For example, it will predict only the range in which the possible values of a particular property of the system will fall but not its exact value. However, a given value of particular properties might be crucial for the commercial success of a product. Even minimal differences in performance of the systems on which they operate can give firms a decisive competitive advantage. Industrial researchers will not limit themselves to use theories, but they will complement them with more *ad hoc* approaches. The more *ad hoc* character of this knowledge implies that it is usable only for a given system or for other systems which are closely related to it. In other words, firms' knowledge will be very highly specific. A classification of knowledge which encompasses both scientific theories and practical knowledge can be based on their degree of generality/localization on the one hand, and on their degree of depth/specificity on the other. Scientific theories are more general and less specific, while industrial knowledge is more local and more specific.

A second important general characteristic common to theories and to practical knowledge is that they are retrieval/interpretive structures. New theories create new information, but such information can only be retrieved and understood by the agents 'possessing' the new knowledge. Moreover, extensions of new paradigms can only be understood by the agents knowing the fundamental concepts and tools of the new paradigm.

Such a characteristic limits the learning possibilities of firms and organizations. As we have already seen, the probability of learning increases with the similarity (the inverse of the distance) of the internal (pre-existing) and external knowledge of the firm. This implies that the correlational and the retrieval/interpretive functions of knowledge are not completely independent. These characteristics of knowledge have important implications due to the discontinuities existing in both scientific and technological evolution.

Knowledge is often a public good, that is, it can be used without being consumed, and access to it by non-paying users cannot be restricted. In reality a knowledge which is a public good in this sense is an extreme case. Although it is true that knowledge is not consumed by being used, the value of old pieces of knowledge falls as new ones appear. Access to new pieces of knowledge, on the other hand, is not necessarily easy or costless. An important distinction which tells us how easily communicable or retrievable different pieces of knowledge are is that between tacit and codified knowledge (Polanyi, 1962; Teece, 1981; Nelson and Winter, 1982). Tacit is the knowledge that can be used by individuals and organizations to achieve some practical purposes, but which cannot be easily explained or communicated. Codified, on the other hand, is knowledge which can be expressed more formally, according to a code, and can be easily/costlessly communicated. Clearly, tacit knowledge will resemble more a private good while codified knowledge will resemble more a public good.

The meaning of the previous dichotomy must not be exaggerated. Codified knowledge is easy to transfer only to those users who have acquired the code. The acquisition of codes often involves long and costly scientific training. When the cost of acquisition of the codes is included in the costs of communication the difference in ease of communication between tacit and codified knowledge is less extreme than one would think. Also, the 'market' for tacit knowledge will be, at best, a very peculiar one. Tacit knowledge is, by definition, embodied in particular individuals and can be transferred only by transferring them. The newer and the more scarce such knowledge is, the more imperfect the relevant markets will be, and the greater the incentives for firms to internalize the generation and use of such knowledge. The aim of these observations is to point out that the knowledge used by enteprises is rarely a completely public or private good: most types of knowledge will sit somewhere in between the two extremes of a private and a public good, with tacit knowledge being closer to the private extreme and codified knowledge to the public one.

The characteristics of knowledge so far introduced are not independent. We can hypothesize that the more local and specific knowledge is the more tacit and private it will be. Conversely, more general and less specific knowledge will tend to be more codified and public. We can extend these considerations to the usual classification of research activities: basic research will tend to be more codified, more public, more general and less specific, while development will be more tacit, more private, less general and more specific. The situation is illustrated in Figure 8.1.

Another important property of technological knowledge is its cumulative character. The learning of newer pieces of knowledge requires a knowledge of the previous ones. By performing R&D or other search activities on particular systems, industrial firms and other research organizations increase their knowledge of such systems. The value of the knowledge created increases with the amount of search. This creates barriers to entry because firms coming into a new technological area have to start learning from scratch. Different learning mechanisms can operate here, starting from learning by doing (Arrow 1962; David, 1975), learning by using (Rosenberg, 1982), learning by searching

Figure 8.1 Range of variation of types of knowledge having industrial applications

(Malerba, 1992; Dodgson, 1993), etc. Previously accumulated knowledge about given systems will make it easier to acquire further knowledge about them. It is easier for a firm to acquire new external knowledge the more similar it is to the firm's pre-existing internal knowledge. It is in this sense that R&D contributes to the absorptive capacity of firms (Cohen and Levinthal, 1989, 1990). As long as there are no radical changes in external technological knowledge, firms' knowledge is likely to be cumulative and to display increasing returns to adoption. This implies that firms wanting to enter a particular technological area would face a knowledge barrier. Conversely, firms having accumulated knowledge in a technological area will tend to be locked in that area. Furthermore, if there are multiple options to the development of a technology, after a firm has opted for one of these it becomes extremely difficult to switch to a different one. In other words, in a number of cases technological knowledge can show increasing returns to adoption and, therefore, display irreversibility and path dependence in its development (see Arthur, 1983, 1988, 1989a).

Irreversibility and path dependence are not unlimited. The emergence of a radically new technology renders the previous internal knowledge of the firm useless, a situation that Tushman and Anderson (1986) call competence destroying. The cumulative and path dependent character is lost and, to the extent that there is no similarity between the old internal and the new external knowledge, all firms are in an equivalent position. Such a conclusion is implied also by the local character of knowledge. As long as a firm operates within an old paradigm it can keep using the same conceptual structures that it already knows, that is, it can gravitate around its old knowledge base. Putting it differently, its ability to retrieve knowledge or information will remain high, give the firm an advantage over new entrants and lock it into its previous knowledge path. The emergence of a new paradigm will destroy the value of these accumulated competences, and eliminate the path dependence. As the new paradigm starts to develop and mature the process of accumulation and the creation of path dependence will start again. Therefore, the early stages of emergence of a new paradigm provide favourable conditions for the entry of firms based on new technologies.

At this point we have to remember that formal R&D is not the only type of knowledge generating activity in an industrial environment. The concept of search activities, that is of those activities which scan the external environment of firms, provides a more general analogue of R&D, including, for example, parts of marketing and of engineering design. By means of search activities firms scan the external environment looking for alternatives to their current routines and decision rules. As we have already seen, such routines and decision rules provide a mechanism for the transmission of variety (Chapter 3) while being simultaneously information saving devices. Search activities provide a means to augment the firm knowledge base and to develop new routines and decision rules when they are required. Given the nature of routines and decision rules such changes will be rather infrequent, while the contribution of search activities to the accumulation of knowledge within a regime of incremental innovation will be continuous. In this sense we can divide all the activities of firms into routines and search activities. We can interpret the hypothesis about the complementarity of variety growth and efficiency growth (Chapter 5) as implying that routines have to become gradually more efficient in order to generate the resources required for search activities, which, in turn, will lead to greater variety. An adequate discussion of search activities requires a more detailed treatment of the external environment of organizations.

KNOWLEDGE AND THE EXTERNAL ENVIRONMENT OF FIRMS

The external environment of the firm is the subset of what is outside the boundaries of the firm but which influences the behaviour and performance of the firm itself. For the purposes of this chapter two problems are important: first, what are the most relevant aspects of the external environment; second, what relationship is there between the structure of the external environment and its changes on the one hand, and the nature of the organizations operating in it on the other. The second problem can be better understood if we think that the main goal of firms, and of other organizations, is to adapt to the external environment in which they operate. This process of adaptation includes both adaptation to a given environment and the modification of the environment in order to suit the firm's goals. It seems logical that firms have to adopt strategic goals and organizational structures that improve the adaptation to the external environment. Moreover, the process of adaptation is not automatic, but requires learning, and it is limited by inertia (Hannan and Freeman, 1977), that is particular structures developed to adapt to given environments may survive even when the conditions of the environment change.

Organization theorists have developed typologies of organizational environments. Such typologies reflect the complexity of these environments. Different typologies are broadly similar, but there is no agreed model. For example, there is general agreement that environments may be viewed as having two components, climate and texture (see, for example, Terreberry, 1968; Jurkovitch, 1969; Aldrich, 1979; McKelvey, 1982). Climate is the general non-purposeful milieu surrounding the texture of all organizations in a particular environment. Texture is the set of all interactions amongst the (myopically) purposeful organizations operating in the environment. There is no agreed set of attributes of the climate, although the lists provided by different authors are broadly similar (see McKelvey, 1982, p. 122). A description of texture which is still widely used was provided by Emery and Trist (1965). They identified four types of texture: type I, placid randomized; type II, placid – clustered; type III, disturbed – reactive; type IV, turbulent field. Types I and IV differ for their rate of change and for the intensity of interaction of the participating organizations.

For the purposes of this chapter, a simplified version of these typologies will be useful. Amongst the attributes of the external environment there are both impersonal elements (e.g. location and prices of raw materials), and organizations other than those on which the analysis is focusing. The most important of such other organizations are:

(a)   competitors
(b)   users/customers
(c)   suppliers of inputs, equipment, knowledge, human capital
(d)   regulating institutions.

Amongst the various attributes of the environment, those which seem to be common to most typologies are:

(a)   complexity/diversity
(b)   interactivity
(c)   rate of change (quantitative/qualitative).

Environmental typologies are not useful *per se*, but because organizations are expected to develop strategic goals and organizational structures adapted to their external environments. Empirical evidence of this adaptation has been gathered starting from the 1960s (see, for example, Burns and Stalker (1961); Woodward (1965); Lawrence and Lorsch (1967)). These and other authors found evidence of a relationship between external environments, production technologies and organizational structures. Mintzberg (1979) obtained the following generalizations from a number of empirical studies.

1.   The more dynamic the environment, the more organic the structure.
2.   The greater the complexity of the environment, the more decentralized the structure.
3.   The more diversified the organization's markets, the greater the propensity to split into specialized divisions, given favourable economies of scale.
4.   Extreme hostility in its environment drives any organization to centralize its structure temporarily.
5.   A high environmental heterogeneity encourages organizations to adopt different types of structure for different subsets of the environment.

A number of comments are relevant in order to focus the results of organization theories on the goals of this chapter. First, the previous theories focus predominantly on the effect of environmental characteristics and changes on the structure of organizations, rather than on their boundary. The boundary, except possibly for its locations, is taken as given. Second, technological knowledge is an increasingly important component of the external environment of organizations. That is reflected in an increasing importance of the knowledge base of organizations in determining their performance on the one hand, and of the suppliers of equipment, knowledge and human capital with respect to those of human capital on the other. Third, the adaptation of organizations to their external environment is a slow process which requires learning. Furthermore, even after a particular organizational structure is developed in order to improve adaptation to the external environment, such structure can acquire a stability which will confer to it a considerable degree of inertia in the presence of environmental changes. In other words, there can be hysteresis in the process of adaptation of organizations to their external environment. Likewise, as already mentioned, adaptation does not occur to a static and unchanging environment. In a number of cases firms and other organizations try to modify their external environment to suit their goals. The knowledge created by a particular firm or organization can become a necessary component of the knowledge bases of all comparable firms/organizations. Thus the invention of the transistor by Bell Labs created a new knowledge area that other electronics firms could not neglect. It is then better to describe this situation as a co-evolution of organizations and of their environment.

Knowledge is, therefore, one of the components of the external environment and one of the most relevant aspects of firm structure and behaviour. Firms scan the external environment in order to detect any possible pieces of external knowledge which are useful for their productive purposes. When they find such useful pieces of knowledge they have to internalize them. As we have seen in the previous section the capacity of firms to learn and internalize knowledge depends on the firm's previous knowledge.

Such a path dependence, however, is not infinite. As long as knowledge changes incrementally, it will also be cumulative. In these conditions, to have already performed search activities in a given area of knowledge will confer a competitive advantage to a firm in nearby areas. However radically new knowledge which requires completely new intellectual categories appears, the pre-existing form of knowledge may not be very useful. Competitive advantage coming from the accumulation of old knowledge is reduced or destroyed by the emergence of radically new knowledge, corresponding to what Tushman and Anderson (1986) call competence destroying technological change. At the moment of transition, when the radically new knowledge appears, path dependency is likely to fall and the distribution of competitive advantage is going to change drastically.

Recently, economists have started developing a more complex characterization of the external environment of firms. Nelson and Winter (1977, 1982) proposed a 'selection environment', which could be a generalized analogue of the market for the most different types of organizations such as firms, schools, hospitals, prisons, etc. Their selection environment can be specified by means of four elements:

1. the definition of worth or profit for the firms in the sector;
2. the manner in which consumers and regulatory institutions influence what is profitable;
3. investment processes;
4. imitation processes.

Metcalfe and Gibbons (1989) have developed a characterization of the selection environment for the analysis of economic growth and competition which emphasizes its capacity to evaluate different product and process technologies, its rate of growth and its homogeneity.

THE KNOWLEDGE BASE OF AN ORGANIZATION

Up to this point a number of features of knowledge have been described without reference to the institutional structures in which they are embedded. However, it is clear that the knowledge created and used by organizations is not simply the sum of the pieces of knowledge embodied in the individual members of the organization. Individual human resources are combined or aggregated to produce the output(s) of the organization. The combination of individual human resources involves interaction and coordination. In turn such processes of interaction and coordination depend on the strategy and on the structure of the firm. The strategy determines broadly the type of human resources to be employed and the organizational structure the patterns of communication and interaction. Both strategy and structure correspond to higher-level decision rules (Nelson and Winter, 1982) and have a certain inter-temporal stability. Within a given strategy and structure, incremental modifications in lower-level routines are possible but basic mechanisms of knowledge accumulation are set. This tends to increase the path dependence of organizational knowledge.

The collective knowledge used by an organization, which depends on both the individual human resources and on the mechanisms of interaction within the organization, is called its knowledge base (KB). The KB of the firm can be distinguished from its revealed technological performance (RTP), that is the nature of its output. Such output can be an artefact or even a service. The KB and RTP of a firm are related, in the sense that the KB has to precede RTP in time. KB represents a potential that is later embodied in RTP. Each firm's KB will differ for its location, that is the areas of knowledge where the firm has capabilities, and for the degree of accumulation of knowledge in these areas. We can apply here the characterizations of knowledge previously described. Different firms' KBs will differ for their location, span, specificity and accumulated knowledge. The more specific each KB the more appropriable it will be. The degree of accumulation can be estimated based on the total volume of search activities in the area. It is in principle possible to estimate a degree of similarity (or equivalently a distance) between the KB of an organization and the external knowledge to be learned.

The previous considerations can then be reformulated as follows: the probability of learning a given type of external knowledge is inversely proportional to the distance (or directly proportional to the similarity) between the organization's KB and the external knowledge. The difficulties that a firm experiences in learning increase the greater the difference between the external knowledge to be learned and its pre-existing KB. Thus an existing KB can be relatively easily extended to incorporate external knowledge in the case of an incremental innovation, but a firm experiences much more severe difficulties in incorporating the external knowledge on which a radical innovation is based. In fact, as Schumpeter (1942) already foresaw, it is much more likely for a radical innovation to be introduced by new firms. The difficulty of incorporating new external knowledge corresponds also to the case of competence destroying technological change (Tushman and Anderson, 1986). However, it must be remembered that the KB of a firm is constituted by many parts, usually located in different divisions of the firm. It is quite possible for an established firm to have a KB which is weak in a new technological area (e.g. genetic engineering) but to have strong competences in what Teece (1986, 1988) calls complementary assets, such as marketing. If the new product can be marketed using old channels, new firms would be in an advantageous position in the early stages of introduction,while the KB of pre-existing firms would have some decisive advantages in the later stages of large-scale production and commercialization.

Although firms create internally large quantities of knowledge they must continuously acquire external knowledge and integrate it within their KB. As we have seen before, the probability of such integration increases with the similarity of the internal and external knowledge. The pre-existing internal knowledge of a firm is very specific. For example, the distribution over different areas of technological and organizational knowledge is unlikely to be the same for different firms. In addition to differences in this distribution, Arrow (1974) stressed that firms have different codes of communication. In turn, differences in codes of communication are related to differences in organizational structures: the membership of committees and meetings determines who talks to whom and, therefore, the patterns of interaction of the different pieces of knowledge embodied in different members or subsets of the firm. If we imagine a firm without internal divisions (e.g. departments), a very large number of communication paths are possible, because any member can communicate with any other member. On the other hand, in a hierarchical organization with rigidly defined internal divisions only selected members of each division can communicate with their counterparts. In the latter case information flows are considerably reduced with respect to the former (see Saviotti, 1988b, 1991a).

Information flows in hierarchical organizations are also more rigid than in an unstructured one and reduce the adaptability of the hierarchical organization to environmental changes. This different adaptability of organizational structures had previously been described by the dichotomy organic vs. mechanistic structures (Burns and Stalker, 1961). Furthermore, within the same type of organizational structure (e.g. hierarchical, M form, etc.) considerable differences exist for what concerns the codes of communication and patterns of interaction. Consequently, even if two firms were to start with the same KB, differences in modes of interaction and codes of communication would lead to divergent paths of accummulation of knowledge. In other words, the patterns of interaction within a firm's organizational structure would give a further contribution to the specificity and path dependency of its KB. Such specificity and path dependency would increase within an existing technological paradigm but they would largely disappear at the transition between two different paradigms.

KNOWLEDGE AND ORGANIZATIONAL STRUCTURES

The discussion in Chapters 7 and 8 implies that both changes in information and in knowledge can lead to changes in the organizational structure of firms. We can now try to work out some of these implications for actual organizational structures. Until quite recently we could imagine representing any organizational structure either as a market or a hierarchy. Which one of the two is best or most efficient in a given situation depends on the balance between production costs and transaction costs. In particular, transaction costs are heavily influenced by asset specificity, by the frequency of transactions and by the presence of opportunism (Williamson, 1975, 1985). Any organizational form that is not a market or a hierarchical organization was expected to have an infrequent or a temporary existence.

Recently a new phenomenon, that of inter-institutional collaborative agreements (IICAs), seems to have taken organization theorists by surprise. Several types of inter-firm collaboration/linkages/alliances/partnerships, often even if not always technological in nature, have become an increasingly common form of industrial organization starting from the early 1980s (Chesnais, 1988; Mytelka, 1991a; Hagedoorn and Shackenraad, 1990, 1992). Such types of inter-firm collaboration have been particularly common in information technology, biotechnology and in new materials, although they are not uniquely confined to these fields. Sometimes inter-firm collaboration and collaboration with other institutions (universities, government laboratories, etc.; see, for example, Laredo, (1991); Laredo and Mustar, 1993) developed spontaneously, and at other times it was sponsored by governments or by international organizations (see, for example, the ESPRIT programme: Mytelka, 1991b). The existence of inter-firm and of inter-institutional collaboration has important practical and theoretical implications. Firms and governments now have to consider regularly collaboration as one of their strategic options. As we have seen, theoretically the phenomenon is in need of an explanation. Two types of question were posed by the existence of inter-firm collaboration: Are they a temporary or permanent feature of industrial organization? Can they be explained by some extension of the same theories that are presently used or do they need completely new theories? The second question can be reformulated as: Is inter-firm collaboration an intermediate case between markets and hierarchies, or is it a qualitatively different phenomenon?

As pointed out at the beginning, different names have been used for the phenomenon that here will be called inter-firm collaboration. There are other differences amongst the authors that have studied it. For example, not everyone agrees on what types of collaboration to include. However, there is substantial agreement on the fact that the new type of inter-firm collaboration which has emerged, starting from the 1980s, is qualitatively different from the pre-existing ones in both motivation and methods. The new types of inter-firm collaboration are generally concentrated in few, high-technology fields (Hagedoorn and Shackenraad, 1990, 1992); they are virtually always between firms in western Europe, North America and Japan, while the previous collaborations were usually betwen partners in developed and developing countries; they are generally intended to give firms new capabilities rather than to provide a substitute for direct investment; also, the new forms of collaboration are very often between actual or potential competitors in many markets, but, nevertheless they involve a much greater degree of collaboration than was typically the case with traditional alliances.

Essentially the same phenomenon has been analysed in terms of networks (de Bresson and Amesse, 1991; Freeman, 1991). Networks theories (see, for example, Callon, 1992, 1993) can in principle provide a means of structuring and interpreting studies of collaboration. However, so far their application has produced results which are largely parallel to those of studies of inter-firm collaboration. In other words, networks theories and methaphores have a considerable potential usefulness in the study of inter-firm collaboration, but such potential has not been realized so far. Network theories will be analysed in greater detail in Chapter 9.

Once the novelty of the phenomenon of inter-firm collaboration has been accepted, the problem arises of explaining why it only began in the 1980s, and of providing a theoretical explanation of this phenomenon. Up to the 1980s it was accepted that markets and hierarchical organizations were the only stable governance structures (Williamson, 1975, 1985). It was considered normal that, as firms grew in size and complexity, they would integrate vertically and internalize all the functions that are of difficult appropriability (Chandler, 1962, 1977). Inter-firm collaboration of the traditional type as considered at best an inferior substitute for direct investment and for the internalization of functions. Such a theoretical position has been challenged by the new types of inter-firm collaboration. The problem is not only to explain this new phenomenon, but to provide a theoretical structure which encompasses inter-firm collaboration as well as markets and hierarchies.

Scholars studying this phenomenon differ in a number of ways, but they generally stress the knowledge intensity and the strategic significance of the new types of inter-firm collaboration on the one hand, and the increased uncertainty characterizing the external environment in which these collaborations take place on the other. Changing systems of production, new technologies and innovation, for example resulting in new technoeconomic paradigms (Freeman and Perez, 1988), changing economic and competitive relations (Porter and Fuller, 1986), and organizational learning (Dodgson, 1993) have all been proposed as causes for inter-firm collaboration. What all these potential causes have in common is that they lead to a much higher uncertainty in the external environment in which firms operate. In summary, we can say that a potentially new governance structure has emerged in the 1980s, and that this has occurred in the presence of an increased uncertainty in the external environment.

The problem could then be reformulated as follows: Has the increased uncertainty in the external environment led to the emergence of the new types of inter-firm collaboration, and will the new types of inter-firm collaboration disappear if and when the uncertainty of the environment falls back to previous levels?

DIVISION OF LABOUR AND COORDINATION

Since Adam Smith (1776, 1982), division of labour has been considered one of the determinants of economic growth and development. Increasing the extent of division of labour can increase productivity and, therefore, lead to a growth in total output. However, one might ask the questions: Can the division of labour be increased indefinitely? and, Will this increasing division of labour produce constant or falling marginal increases in productivity? An answer given to these questions in the past has been that the division of labour is limited by the extent of the market (Stigler, 1951). The answer tentatively given in this chapter will be that, while the extent of the market is undoubtedly a determinant of the possible extent of division of labour, it is not the only determinant. The problem of division of labour will be placed here in the context of knowledge-intensive production processes, taking into account the structure of the external environment in which firms operate, and the role played by knowledge generation in environmental change.

We can in principle think to divide the production processes taking place in an economy into the maximum possible number of stages. Each stage, consisting of the transformation of an input into an output, is performed by an individual. In this sense the economy would then be constituted by a collection of individuals performing elementary stages and trading their output by market transactions. Quite clearly no economy is or ever was organized in this way. Instead of a collection of individual workers producing and trading output in elementary stages, we have collections of groups of workers, each group separated from other groups by means of an institutional interface. The location of such institutional interfaces was considered given before transaction cost analysis. In order to analyse the phenomenon of inter-firm collaboration we can use the following properties of the institutional interface:

1. Location – what factors will determine the location of the institutional interface between a firm and other firms, and markets?
2. Discreteness or diffuseness/fuzziness with respect to flows of information or capital (human, physical) – is the institutional interface clearly defined, in the sense that we can always tell of what organization each individual is a member, or is it diffuse as when individuals are members of two/several organizations?
3. Intertemporal stability – is the institutional interface stable or does it change frequently?

At least three types of change taking place in an economic system can influence division of labour: the market can expand (growth in total output); the structure of the output can change, for example leading to completely new types of output, or to the specialization of existing types of output; and new processes can be introduced to produce new or old types of output. The latter two types of change are what is called product or process innovation. All these types of change will lead to new forms of division of labour.

In principle we can think of separating the different forms of division of labour induced by each of these three changes. Thus we could think that an expansion in the size of the market, with unchanged production processes and output structure, will allow an increase in the number of steps into which a production process is divided. However, such a greater divisibility will provide the opportunity of replacing some of the operations performed by human beings with capital equipment. In turn, this will change the nature of the process and the knowledge required to operate and modify it. Alternatively, if new knowledge were to allow the introduction of a new production process, at unchanged market size, such a production process would be more efficient and thus potentially lead to a market expansion. Without getting into further details we can say that these phenomena (market expansion, product and process innovation) interact and lead to different forms of division of labour. That is, as structural change leads to a qualitative change in the composition of the economy, division of labour has to be continuously readjusted. In particular, if the variety of the economic system grows in the course of economic development, the total number of stages into which labour can be divided in an economy will increase.

The changes in division of labour described in the previous paragraph are determined by (a) greater output, (b) a different output structure, and (c) a different way of producing output. Moreover, knowledge can be an important factor giving rise to changes in the division of labour. Changes in knowledge are closely related to coordination costs. According to Becker and Murphy (1992), division of labour is not only limited by the extent of the market, but also by knowledge and by coordination costs. Increased knowledge allows a greater specialization to take place by reducing coordination costs. However, how greater knowledge can reduce coordination costs is by no means made clear by these authors. While their hypothesis seems plausible it may not necessarily apply to all conditions, that is particular types of knowledge changes may not necessarily lead to an increased division of labour. The analysis of this relationship is now discussed.

COORDINATION

The problem of coordination can be represented in the following way. A production process is divided into N stages. In each stage a worker receives an output from the previous stage, transforms it into something different, and then passes the new output to the worker in the following stage. A number of coordination problems can arise:

1. if the worker in stage (k+1) (L_{k+1}) is not ready to receive the output q_k from worker k, delays occur which raise the cost of the process;
2. if L_{k+1} does not know exactly what to do with q_k then delays occur.

We can call these different aspects time coordination and knowledge coordination. The first type of coordination problem can be largely eliminated by a type of process organization which involves storage buffers between each pair of stages, in which L_k leaves q_k in the buffer and L_{k+1} picks it up whenever it is suitable for him/her.

The second type of coordination problem (knowledge coordination) is particularly important when changes occur in a production process. A new type of production process will involve a new set of specifications for what each worker L_i has to do, including what operations to perform on q_k. Some considerations about the nature of knowledge are very important here.

First, at least some production processes follow a life-cycle development (Abernathy and Utterback, 1975, 1978). Such processes begin with low-volume production, a flexible organization, using general purpose machine tools, a multiplicity of product designs, emphasizing product performance and product innovation. As the product matures and as production volumes increase, more rigid organizational structures, based on specialized equipment, and a dominant design emerge. Product innovation is replaced by process innovation. Increased production volumes are likely to lead to an increased division of labour. Second, as the technology matures and a new paradigm becomes established (Dosi, 1982), changes in knowledge and the greater availability of the new vintages of human capital will also allow a greater division of labour. In production processes characterized by such patterns of development we can expect division of labour to increase systematically as the market expands and the technology matures.

It is important to note that such a process evolution is only likely in the presence of a stable external environment. The large-scale, rigid and dedicated organizational structure emphasizes efficiency with respect to adaptability. If rapid and radical changes were to take place in the external environment, small and flexible organizations, adopting an organic style (Burns and Stalker, 1961), would have a greater survival ability than large, rigid, mechnistic ones. A constant external environment allows a high degree of process standardization and it is likely to increase not only the divisibility of labour, but also to reduce both time and coordination problems. To summarize this section, we can say that changes in knowledge and in process organization, which are related to environmental changes, have a profound influence on both division of labour and coordination.

TRANSACTION COST ANALYSIS

The problem of coordination costs is underlying transaction cost analysis (Williamson, 1975, 1985) as discussed in the previous section. Production processes can be divided into a number of stages connected in an input–output fashion. The passage of the output of stage k to stage (k+1), where it becomes the input, is a transaction. It is precisely in transactions that problems of coordination occur. The more difficult the coordination, the higher the transaction cost. Transaction costs are essentially coordination costs. The definition of coordination here has to be used in a sufficiently broad way, to include, for example, transport costs. Then, following Williamson, the particular governance structure used, and therefore the boundaries of the firm, will depend on the balance between production costs (the costs of the production stages) and transaction costs. For very low transaction costs, markets will be the best governance structure, and for very high transaction costs (relative to productions costs), hierarchical organizations will be the best governance structure. That is, the balance between production and transaction costs determines the location of institutional boundaries/interfaces.

Two problems arise at this point. First, markets and hierarchical organizations can be conceived at the extremes of a range of possible situations, with intermediate cases falling in between. A relevant question which emerges is then whether inter-firm collaboration is an intermediate case between the two extremes (de Bresson and Amesse, 1991). Second, transaction cost analysis tends to address the problem of the location of inter-firm boundaries, but not those of the nature and of the permanence of such boundaries. The problem is in part linked to the absence in transaction cost analysis of the external environment of the firm. It is this type of analysis which has been introduced in this chapter.

ORGANIZATIONAL BOUNDARIES AND ENVIRONMENTAL CHANGE

The boundary of an organization separates its internal and external environments. Such a boundary can be considered as constituted by all the members of the organization who communicate with other organizations. This boundary can be very diffuse, as when many members of the organization communicate, or very sharp, as when one/few members of the organization communicate. Organizational boundaries are themselves part of the process of adaptation, and change together with organizational structures, following changes in the external environment.

As discussed previously, changes in knowledge are amongst the most important changes in the external environment. Such changes are likely to require a new division of labour and to give rise to greater coordination problems. One of the advantages of the division of labour is that it reduces the quantity of information required by each worker (Saviotti, 1988b, 1991a). In a very static environment and for very well-known processes the worker in stage (k+1) only needs to know what to do with the output of stage k, and not how such an output had been obtained through the sequence of the previous k stages. In these conditions, coordination of the subsequent productive stages is easy. Coordination costs are very low with respect to production costs. The division of labour is limited only by the extent of the market (Smith, 1776, 1982; Stigler, 1951; Becker and Murphy, 1993). However, if we imagine a production process which changes continuously as it is carried out, then coordination problems will become very significant. The output of each productive stage will have to be accompanied by very detailed instructions specifying what to do with it. Alternatively, each worker must know what the other workers are doing in order to be able to perform his/her operations. The knowledge of each worker must overlap with that of other workers.

A change in knowledge also has consequences for the division of labour between organizations. For static and well-known processes each organization can purchase inputs (materials, equipment, knowledge) in an embodied form, where knowledge would be embodied in texts. Knowledge has to be retrieved and decoded by the appropriate vintages and types of human capital in the organization. Radical changes in technological knowledge will require both a redefinition of the division of labour within the organization (see previous paragraph), and will make the old vintages of human capital in the organization redundant. At the beginning of a new technological paradigm, new vintages of human capital will be in scarce supply, given the delays of teaching institutions. No firm will be able to purchase all the new human capital required to retrieve and decode the new knowledge. Inter-firm collaboration will then allow the reaching of the critical mass of human capital required to use the new knowledge. In these conditions the knowledge base of each firm, intended as the collective knowledge that the firm uses for its productive purposes, will overlap different institutional boundaries, including individuals who are members of different organizations.

A period of paradigmatic change is characterized by high uncertainty. The expectation of further radical changes as the new paradigm moves towards normalization/standardization are likely to limit the commitment of each firm to new productive processes and new outputs. Inter-firm collaboration would allow firms to enter new fields with a minimum commitment and to increase the reversibility of entry by minimizing exit costs. Thus both risk limitation and the scarcity of the new vintages of human capital would tend to favour inter-firm collaboration with respect to more stable arrangements.

Summarizing, one could say that radical changes in knowledge will lead to (a) a redefinition of intra-organizational division of labour, with a greater degree of overlap of the knowledge of individual workers, and (b) the knowledge bases of different firms will overlap, and institutional boundaries will become fuzzier.

As a new technology matures and becomes more standardized the shortage of human capital will decrease and coordination problems will be reduced. We can then expect that the overlap of the knowledge of individual workers and of organizations will be reduced, as well as the need for inter-firm collaboration.

SUMMARY AND CONCLUSIONS

Markets, hierarchical organizations and inter-firm collaboration, are different governance structures and can be thought of as different combinations of division of labour and coordination. Each of these combinations performs better than the others depending on the conditions in the external environment in which the firm/organization operates. Static and predictable environments do not lead to any serious coordination problems. In these conditions the economics of processes is dominated by production costs. Rapid, qualitative and quantitative changes in knowledge require new forms of division of labour and raise coordination costs more than production costs. If the new knowledge is radically different from the old one a new vintage of human capital will be required to retrieve and develop it. Moreover, the greater uncertainty created by radically new knowledge will limit the commitment of firms to new productive processes and outputs. Static environments with limited organization complexity and low intensity of interactions between their components tend to give rise to market transactions. Environments characterized by slow and predictable change, with a higher degree of complexity and interactivity between their components, tend to give rise to hierarchical organizations. More dynamic and uncertain environments characterized by complex and sophisticated knowledge (technological and organizational) give rise to inter-firm collaboration.

We can now return to some of the fundamental questions raised at the beginning. Following the previous considerations we can say that market relations, hierarchical organizations and inter-firm collaboration differ along at least three dimensions: rate of change, complexity and interactivity. We could say that inter-firm collaboration is an intermediate case between market relations and hierarchical organizations if the three governance structures could be placed along a single dimension. Markets and hierarchies being the extremes of a range and inter-firm collaborations falling in between. The three governance structures cannot be placed along a single dimension because they differ along at least three. Furthermore, inter-firm collaborations arise for rates of change and degrees of complexity greater than those at which markets and hierarchies are found and are therefore, outside their range. Lastly, inter-firm collaboration and networks requires the existence of a certain quantity of trust (de Bresson and Amesse, 1991), while the existence of hierarchical organization is justified by the presence of opportunism in inter-individual transactions. To represent inter-firm collaboration as an intermediate case between markets and hierarchies does not seem to be completely accurate.

The other important question raised by the emergence of inter-firm collaboration is whether such a governance structure is only a temporary phenomenon or whether it will become a normal type of industrial organization in addition to the more traditional markets and hierarchies. Following the previous reasoning, inter-firm collaboration arises in the presence of environmental conditions different from those leading to either markets or hierarchies. The problem then becomes that of the permanence of the environmental conditions which give rise to inter-firm collaboration. Such environmental conditions are a greater rate of change, greater uncertainty and complexity than those leading to hierarchical organizations. Such conditions are particularly common in the transition to a new technological paradigm and in its early stages. Rate of change, complexity and uncertainty fall during the normalization phase of a paradigm and the maturation of a technology. It would then be possible for new technologies to be introduced by networks of collaborating firms and for hierarchical organizations to take over these same technologies when they mature. The concentration of inter-firm collaboration in the economic system, as opposed to that of market relations and hierarchies, will be determined by the percentage of new technologies in use and by their pervasiveness. To the extent that this approach is correct we can expect the economic weight of inter-firm collaboration to be proportional to the extent and rate of radical, knowledge-intensive change in the economic system. Such change must have been greater and more knowledge intensive in the 1970s and 1980s than even in recent history. We can reasonably expect knowledge intensity to increase in future. In this case inter-firm collaboration would have an assured place amongst the prevailing forms of industrial organization.

9. The concept of national system of innovation

THE NATURE OF THE CONCEPT

The concept of national system of innovation (NSI) owes its origin to the intertemporal advantages that a number of firms or industrial sectors, based in particular countries, have in the course of time, and in the high degree of institutional specificity displayed by innovating countries at equivalent levels of economic development. Economic and technological development are characterized by a number of general trends. For example, the percentage of the labour force employed in agriculture declines with industrialization, which is accompanied by growing incomes per head. Also, and more recently, R&D expenditures as a percentage of GDP have tended to increase as the income per head of the country increases. Likewise, the ratio of R&D expenditures to TBP (technological balance of payments) increases with income per head. While these and other tendencies are common to most countries, a number of features are quite specific to each country as a producer. Areas of strength in technology and in trade are often quite country specific.

Innovating firms are not distributed uniformly over the world economic system at a given point in time. The firms and industrial sectors introducing successful innovations and profiting from them are located in a small number of countries. Furthermore, the number of such countries can increase, but only very slowly. The only substantial addition to the group of innovating countries after the Second World War has been that of Japan (Dosi, Pavitt and Soete, 1990). Even those countries that are innovative do not produce the most successful technological and industrial innovations in all sectors at a given time. Each innovating country has some sectors of greater competitive advantage, such as chemicals, luxury cars and machine tools in Germany; computers, aerospace and software in the USA; electronic and photographic equipment in Japan; clothing, footware and ceramic tiles in Italy, etc. (see, for example, Porter, 1990).

In other words, there is a strikingly localized and asymmetric distribution of innovative performance in the world economic system. Such distribution is not only asymmetric at a given time, but the subsequent development of innovative activities/firms tends to cluster in those that were already innovating countries and firms. Existing configurations of successful innovators in the world economic system tend to show a considerable stability and to change only infrequently, whether by the addition of a new innovating country or by the decline of an older one. This specificity cannot be explained by factor endowments, but it is more likely to be caused by specific institutional configurations and by the cumulative, local and specific character of the knowledge that the institutions possess.

Countries differ not only for their innovative performance, usually embodied in goods or services, that is in their revealed technological performance, but perhaps even more strikingly in their internal arrangements or configurations. Germany may be successful in chemicals or in luxury cars, but other countries produce, even if less successfully, comparable goods. However, the role of capital markets, the institutions which generate and diffuse basic knowledge, the role of the state, are strikingly different amongst countries at equivalent levels of economic development. Examples of these differences could be the relative roles of banks and of the stock market in Germany, Sweden, Switzerland and Japan on the one hand, in the USA and in Britain on the other (Porter, 1990); or the role of the strong user–producer and user–supplier interactions in the Scandinavian innovation systems (Lundvall, 1988; Carlsson, 1992); or the role of knowledge-creating institutions in the USA (Nelson, 1990).

In other words, there are persistent asymmetries amongst countries at the level of their performance and at that of their internal structures. It can be argued that the internal structural asymmetry could be more stable than performance asymmetry. A certain degree of convergence amongst performance of firms and countries can be expected because they compete by means of their outputs, which must show some broad international comparability and adjustment to prevailing patterns of success. However, changes in the institutions that produce those outputs, in those that regulate them, and in those that produce inputs and environmental constraints can take place without changing the basic structure of these institutions. Thus, even organizational structures which had become predominant in the USA after the Second World War, as the multifunctional or the multidivisional form, were adopted only very slowly in other industrialized countries. Likewise, the structure of financial markets is very different even amongst high-income countries.

The national character of technological 'asymmetries' means that the firms and other institutions contributing to the generation of innovations in one country do not act independently, but are linked in some kind of network. In other words, these institutions constitute a system, that some authors have called a national system of innovation (NSI) (Lundvall, 1985, 1986, 1988, 1992; Freeman, 1987,1988; Nelson, 1988, 1990; Freeman and Lundvall, 1990; Niosi *et al.*, 1992). A number of antecedents for conceptualizing production systems in systemic terms exist, especially in the French research tradition. Examples of such concepts are national production systems (Perroux, 1969; quoted in Dosi, Pavitt and Soete, 1990) and 'filieres' (Dosi, Pavitt and Soete, 1990). Also, the concept of vertically integrated sectors (Pasinetti, 1981) presents some similarities with these.

Adapting these concepts to technology policy we can say that the outputs of each NSI will need to be comparable. Each country produces at least a number of products and services which are traded internationally and chosen by users/consumers on the basis of uniform criteria. Trends in demand and in technology common to most countries function as output constraints for individual NSIs, specifying what can and cannot be successfully produced and sold. Each NSI adapts to common output constraints using its own, specific national institutional configuration. Thus new technologies are introduced by small high-technology firms in the USA, but by large firms (often multinationals) in Japan and in Germany. New output constraints are created by technological leaders and imitated by other countries. In other words, we have simultaneously one trend towards specificity and differentiation and another trend towards homogenization. Each NSI can be expected to react to output constraints by modifying incrementally existing institutions and patterns of institutional interactions. In other words, common outcomes and output constraints can be achieved by means of a multiplicity of institutional configurations/structures of NSIs. Also, such a mechanism obviously leads to path dependence.

A NSI can be defined as 'that combination of institutions which are influential in creating and implementing a country's innovation potential, and their patterns of interaction'.

The name NSI implies that the most appropriate locus for innovative specificity is the nation state. However, there are cases in which the innovation system is known to be regional or local (for example, confined within a city or town, see Porter, 1990). The implication in this case is that inter-firm and inter-institutional interactions are much easier within a short geographical distance and especially within the same cultural context. Porter (1990) stresses how the presence of more than one competitor in a nation, or, even more so, in a region or a city, is correlated with a strong export performance of the competitors. Even if the concentration of the productive and innovative activities within a country is very highly asymmetric, some of the benefits will be distributed over the whole country, and flows of information and communication will be easier in the country itself.

What is essential for the purposes of this chapter is not the distinction between national and regional innovation system (although this distinction may be a very relevant one for other purposes) but that between the local accumulation of innovative capabilities and the internationalization of the economy. Some important changes have recently taken place in the international economic environment. These changes are the growing internationalization of firms' operations and the collapse of the Soviet system. The former has been accompanied by different types of collaboration between firms, generally having a substantial technological content (see, for example, Mytelka, 1991a). The latter is accelerating pre-existing pressures on the balance between military and civilian R&D and technology (Gummett and Reppy, 1988; Gummett and Walker, 1990; Gummett, 1991).

These environmental changes have considerable implications for the concept of NSI. In a broad sense they imply a tendency to globalization, that can be interpreted as the spread of similar economic routines and pratices at a world level. If this were the case one could expect the specificity on which the concept of NSI is based to fall in the course of time. In other words, the tendencies to international convergence would lead to the irrelevance of the concept of NSI.

In this chapter an attempt will be made to examine the extent to which convergence can be expected to make the concept of NSI meaningless. In order to do this a clarification of the theoretical foundations of the concept of NSI will be attempted. The concept of NSI is considered a useful interpretive device, but at the moment it is only very broadly defined. In order to make it more useful for technology policy analysis it needs to be further developed.

In what follows, some policy implications of orthodox and of evolutionary theories of economic change which are particularly relevant for the concept of NSI are discussed.

ECONOMIC THEORIES AND THE CONCEPT OF NSI

This section begins with some broad policy implications of orthodox economic theories. Fundamental for these theories are the concept of equilibrium and the representation of technological change founded exclusively on its efficiency increasing properties. In other words, as already pointed out, qualitative change, as represented by the emergence of new entities, is neglected. Also, technology is assumed to be exogenous to the economic system. It can have economic consequences but no economic origin. In this way most of the problems related to either the sponsorship or to the control of technology are automatically excluded from this theoretical background (Coombs, Saviotti and Walsh, 1987). Equilibrium is taken to be unique and to be the most efficient state of the economy. When new technologies are exogenously generated they constitute a disturbance for the economic system, which leads to a readjustment of its equilibrium position, with the new one corresponding to a greater efficiency. At any time firms will either achieve the existing best practice or remain behind it. The position of the average firm with respect to the technological frontier will determine the resultant productivity and competitiveness in a given economy. The target to be achieved either spontaneously by the economic system or by means of government policies is to approach the equilibrium state. Such an equilibrium is considered not only the most efficient state, but also to be independent of the path followed to reach it and obtained reversibly. In summary, three important properties of equilibrium in orthodox economics are uniqueness, path independency and reversibility.

Studies of innovation and of technological change developed in the last twenty years have provided a considerable amount of evidence which cannot be easily accommodated within orthodox theories. A selection of concepts from these studies which are relevant for technology policy will be presented here. The early studies of technological innovation were articulated around the dichotomy demand pull–technology push (Mowery and Rosenberg, 1979; Freeman, 1982; Coombs, Saviotti and Walsh, 1987). Such dichotomy turned out to be an oversimplification and gave way to a richer array of concepts describing patterns of technological change, such as dominant designs (Abernathy and Utterback, 1975, 1978), natural trajectories and technological regimes (Nelson and Winter, 1977), technological guideposts (Sahal, 1981a and b, 1985), and technological paradigms (Dosi, 1982). In turn, such concepts have been incorporated into an attempt to construct an evolutionary theory of economic and technological change (Nelson and Winter, 1982; Dosi *et al.*, 1988).

Dominant designs, technological regimes and technological guideposts, imply that after a given configuration, e.g. a set of technological characteristics (Saviotti and Metcalfe, 1984), is chosen, subsequent examples of technological development will be improved variants of that configuration, sharing with it some central and defining elements. A paradigm will be constituted by these shared elements of the technology and by the knowledge possessed by engineers, designers and manufacturing firms. Routines and decision rules will be part of this paradigm (Nelson and Winter, 1982). The implication of these concepts is that progress and adaptation to demand/selection environment will take place almost continuously within established boundaries, while radical changes, leading to the replacement of the existing paradigm, will be infrequent.

The evolutionary theories which will be used here have a generally Schumpeterian flavour, but have benefited from contributions coming from a number of other disciplines and research traditions. In particular, biology, systems theory, irreversible thermodynamics and organization theory made important contributions to modern evolutionary theories of economic and technological change (Saviotti and Metcalfe, 1991).

From a Schumpeterian matrix we shall use the fundamental role of innovations (as opposed to routine activities) in stimulating long-term economic development, and the discontinuous nature of the introduction of innovations. From system theory and irreversible thermodynamics we borrow the concept of an open system, exchanging matter, energy and information with its environment (von Bertalanffy, 1950). Open systems may undergo discontinuous transitions to states of increasing order and complexity, as they are moved away from equilibrium. In other words, as the flow of matter, energy and information between the system and its environment increases, the system itself may undergo transitions to states of greater order and complexity. These transitions have a number of important properties. First, the number of states after the transition can be greater than that before the transition. Hence, even if one started from one steady state, the number of steady states could be greater after the transition. This property is called multistability and can be represented by means of a bifurcation diagram (Prigogine and Stengers, 1984; Allen, 1982).

Second, when in the vicinity of a transition the system undergoes stochastic fluctuations and its behaviour becomes indeterminate. In other words, it is not certain to which of the possible states the transition will lead. In proximity of a transition, when the behaviour of the system becomes indeterminate due to fluctuations, historical accidents can influence the final state of the system. According to this property, called path dependence, the outcome of a transition depends on the path followed to reach the final state. Particular applications of this general situation to processes of technological choice and of geographic location have been given by Arthur (1983, 1988, 1989a and b). He argues that in circumstances of increasing returns to adoption a technology which is not necessarily the 'best' may be chosen amongst a set of competing ones. In the period of transition from the old to the new technology, historical events (fluctuations) may steer the choice towards an inferior technology, which would then be stabilized by increasing returns. Likewise, the initial location of some firms in a place, if accompanied by economies of agglomeration, will make the subsequent location of other firms in the same place more convenient than elsewhere. In other words, as any policymaker has always known, but as economists have consistently refused to admit, history matters.

Third, the transition of open systems are irreversible, in the sense that it is not possible to return to a previous state of the system without introducing some change in the external environment.

These features of open systems have very important policy implications. First, each country, being an open system, will have steady states characterized by some degree of order and structure. Such order and structure could not exist in a system which was a random assembly of independent institutions. Order and structure necessarily imply institutional interaction. Second, radical changes in the structure of the system are likely to be infrequent. This does not exclude incremental improvements, but tends to consider radical changes in the institutions and in patterns of institutional interaction as having a low probability under most circumstances. Adaptation to environmental changes without any fundamental change in the structure of the system is an example of hysteresis or homoeostasis (Ashby, 1956). Third, multistability implies that NSIs can produce comparable outcomes, that is products and services which are traded in world markets, starting from specific institutional realities. We can translate this into terms relevant for technology policy by saying that more than one institutional configuration and set of related policies may be stable. Thus institutional imitation is not necessarily the answer to technology policy problems. The answer has to come from some criterion of coherence/synergism of the institutions. From the viewpoint of technology policy it is, therefore, particularly important to understand the relationship between common outcomes and the specific patterns of institutional interaction which characterize each NSI. Moreover, the concept of path dependency implies that the final (steady) state(s) achieved varies depending on the path followed. The socio-economic structures and policies of the past shape, address and limit those of the future.

THE NSI AND THE NATURE OF TECHNOLOGICAL KNOWLEDGE

As we have seen in Chapter 8, at least part of technological knowledge will be local, tacit, specific, and cumulative. These features imply that the state of technological knowledge of a set of institutions at a given time is path dependent. A general outcome of evolutionary theories is reinforced by considerations on the nature of technological knowledge. We can then expect that the technological knowledge of different firms, which constitutes a substantial part of their knowledge base, has a number of features which are specific to each firm. The nature of knowledge is also related to its appropriability and transferability. Tacit, specific knowledge will be easy to appropriate and difficult to transfer.

Naturally, not all technological knowledge is local, tacit and specific. The outcome of basic research is likely to be codified and to resemble a latent public good. The institutions responsible for the generation of this type of knowledge are amongst the most important in determining the performance of a country as an innovator and constitute a necessary addition to the basic Schumpeterian model of economic development (Nelson, 1988, 1990). This type of knowledge can be acquired at no cost only by those institutions which know the relevant codes. Thus, for example, to learn even the most basic types of research on biotechnology one must have the required skills. These are not necessarily available in all countries and can only be acquired at a cost. However, the process of acquisition of knowledge could in this case lead to a path independent outcome (see Chapter 8).

All the institutions involved in generating innovations will have a knowledge base which is at least partly local, tacit, specific and cumulative. These features will tend to differentiate the knowledge bases of different firms. On the other hand, advances in basic scientific and technological knowledge will constitute a common and unifying trend amongst all participating institutions.

NATIONAL SYSTEMS OF INNOVATION AND NETWORKS

Learning, knowledge generation and acquisition are amongst the most important activities leading to innovations. Such activities are not carried out only by individual firms or organizations, but depend crucially on inter-organizational interactions. In other words, the generation of innovations in a country is carried out by a network of organizations. We can then represent the NSI by means of a network (or a group of interconnected networks) of organizations, where the interactions represent links between the different nodes of the network. Networks can be of different complexity and intensity of interaction. Furthermore, a transition between different NSIs is likely to imply a radical restructuring of existing networks, determined by a change of the participating institutions and/or of the links between them.

The network concept has been used in different research traditions for various purposes. For example, both sociologists (Burt, Christman and Kilburn, 1983; Callon, 1989, 1992) and political scientists (Wright, 1988) have used the concept in different ways. The considerations that follow are not a review of these different concepts, but rely predominantly on the ideas of Callon *et al.*

We shall consider networks as having three poles – scientific, technoindustrial, and market. Given the importance of the balance between military and civilian technology we might add a defence pole. In the network, actors exchange intermediaries, which can be capital goods, disembodied information or documents of any kind, technical artefacts, trained personnel and their skills, and funds supporting innovation. Intermediaries are not independent of the particular network in which they are used. Actors may have to perform 'translations' on intermediaries to reinterpret and divert them from their intended purpose, in order to produce new texts, new instruments and new machines.

Networks of these types can be converging, disperse or integrated, and they can be short, long, or incomplete. Converging networks are characterized by close links between actors (high connectivity). An actor can at any time mobilize the skills within a strongly converging network without having to embark upon adaptations, translations or costly decodings (Callon, Laredo and Rabeharison, 1990; OECD, 1992, pp. 82–3). In dispersed networks, which have low density, translations are required, but are not yet firmly in place. It is difficult for actors to mobilize the rest of the network. Long networks span the range of activities from basic research to users uninterruptedly. Short networks cover only a part of the range, but are not incomplete. In incomplete networks one or more poles are either missing or underdeveloped.

In a slightly more economic language one could say that actors perform activities (transformation of inputs into outputs) and exchange intermediaries in order to coordinate theirs and other institutions' activities. The exchange of intermediaries constitutes an important part of the links in a network. A change in existing networks can then be a change in actors, in links and in activities.

It is also possible to interpret the existence of networks as part of the structure or morphology of the system. Such a structure and morphology are the natural outcome of the existence of open systems.

Networks by definition must have a minimum of stability, but in the middle or long run they may change, and so they must be analysed dynamically. Thus networks can be static, flexible or in the process of branching out (OECD, 1992; Imai and Baba, 1991). During network changes actors fluctuate between attachment and detachment. Static networks correspond to existing technological trajectories and competences, to procedural rationality, limited yet perfect information, predictability and incremental innovation. Flexibility, uncertainty, risk, variable factor combinations, radical innovation and market creation are likely to become more important when existing networks become unstable and there is a transition to a different type of network structure. Network stability is also a prerequisite for the development and application of quantitative analytical techniques (Callon, 1992).

A very important question arises here about the efficiency and stability of network structures. Efficiency refers to the transformation of the existing resources of a country into successful innovations. More specifically, an NSI will be efficient to the extent that it achieves its intended goal(s) with the minimum possible use of resources. Stability refers to the persistence of a given NSI in the presence of fluctuations in the external environment. The two concepts are not synonyms but nor are they entirely unconnected. A stable NSI cannot be extremely inefficient for very long, but needs not be the 'best' in order to survive for quite reasonable periods of time. The conditions leading to efficiency/stability are amongst the most important aspects of an NSI.

The previous problems can be analysed in terms of the interactions internal to the network. Each institution involved in the network produces some form of generalized output, which does not have to be conceived here in a strict economic sense. For example, output can be laws, financial packages, the outcome of an R&D project or programme, etc. The output of each institution is then used as an input by one (or more) other institutions in the network. The network can then be expected to be stable if the output of each institution constitutes an appropriate input for the other institutions. In other words, stability implies some kind of coherence or synergism between the interacting organizations and institutions.

We can note here that the stability of a network is related to the stability of the environment in which it is embedded. A very stable environment will lead to very stable networks and vice versa. We can expect successful networks to achieve an increasing degree of adaptation to the environment in which they exist. If the environment is static a finer and finer tuning of the networks to their environment will take place. Furthermore, changes in networks can take place in different ways. For example, there can be a change in actors, activities and links or in some of them only. These different types of changes may be extended to all the network or involving only a part of it. Examples of adaptation strategies to an environmental change could then be: same actors preserving the same links, but performing different activities; the same links preserved by different actors performing the same activities; new links established by new actors performing a modified version of the old activities.

Two concepts are relevant in this context. The first is that of technological system (Carlsson and Stankiewicz, 1991; Carlsson, 1992). Such a system is defined as a network of agents interacting in a specific technology area under a particular institutional infrastructure for the purpose of generating, diffusing and utilizing technological knowledge. The second is that of technoeconomic network (TEN) (Callon, Laredo and Rabeharisoa, 1990; Laredo, 1991). A TEN is defined as a coordinated set of heterogeneous actors, laboratories, technical research centres, financial organizations, users and public authorities, which participate collectively in the development and diffusion of innovations, and which organizes via numerous interactions the relationship between research and the market place.

Both of these concepts stress the interactions between the units of the economic system and are related more or less directly to the concept of network.

IMPLICATIONS OF VARIETY FOR THE NSI

In Chapter 5 the two hypotheses were made that (a) variety growth is a necessary requirement for long-term economic growth and development, and that (b) variety growth (in new sectors) and productivity growth (in pre-exisiting sectors) are complementary phenomena. Also, variety can grow by means of the creation of new products or by specialization in existing products. Furthermore, it was proved that variety can only grow if intra-technology competition is greater than inter-technology competition. These hypotheses and results have very important implications for the concept of NSI.

Following the previous considerations we can assume that the variety of the world system (V_w) will grow in the course of time. Also, we can expect that each country will achieve a certain degree of specialization, that is, it will not produce all the possible types of output. The variety produced at the country level (V_c) will, therefore, be lower than the world variety, and the ratio of the two will define the rate of participation of the country to the world variety. Such rate of participation is likely to be a determinant of the international competitiveness of the country.

The growth in variety in the course of time implies that the patterns of international specialization must be continuously redefined. At each subsequent stage new types of output will be available in the world economy, introduced by one or more leading countries. The other countries will then have the opportunity to imitate the new sectors or to remain linked to their previous sectors of production. If they were to choose the latter behaviour their rate of participation in world variety would fall. Even if their market share in the pre-existing types of output were to remain constant their share of world output would fall. Of course, it would in principle be possible for them to maintain a constant share of the world economy by increasing their share of the markets in their old types of output. However, such behaviour seems unlikely and it is going to be limited by the following considerations.

New sectors tend to have higher rates of growth and higher profit rates than older ones. Older sectors become progressively more competitive as greater numbers of firms enter them, and their profit rates decline. The labour intensity of older sectors tends to fall while new sectors employ a higher intensity of skilled labour. To maintain a constant share of world output by remaining confined to older sectors would imply increasing constantly market share in sectors which are becoming progressively more competitive. This does not seem to be a good strategy and there is hardly a country that explicitly follows it.

The previous considerations have important implications for theories of international trade. A static specialization, based on comparative advantage as determined by natural endowments, would be very unlikely to provide a country with an income level constant relative to that of other countries. Worsening terms of trade and the drive to industrialization in developing countries can be seen as an attempt to conserve a roughly constant share of world variety or to limit its fall.

It is nevertheless impossible to produce all the new goods and services and even the largest countries must specialize. Specialization takes the form of choosing a sector (inter-industrial) and of positioning themselves within a sector (intra-industrial). Several strategies are possible: creation of completely new sectors (mostly USA); specialization of existing sectors (Japan); choice of the upmarket sections of medium-technology sectors (Germany); and low-cost entry into traditional sectors (developing countries). Each form of specialization implies a different participation in world variety at a given time, and changes in strategy reflect, among other things, the need to adapt to changing world variety.The precise implications of these considerations have to be worked out analytically, but we can conclude here that changing world variety implies a need to restructure national economies in order to keep a reasonable participation in the growth of world variety.

Different implications for the balance of new/older sectors and for the production/search activities follow from the strategy chosen to adapt to growing world variety. The complementarity between variety growth (new sectors) and productivity growth (older sectors) is justified on the one hand by the fact that the resources required for search activities, leading to variety growth, can only come from growing productivity in pre-existing sectors; and, on the other, by the underutilization of resources that would follow from growing productivity and saturating demand within a constant set of activities. Subsidization of older technologies/activities is likely to slow down their productivity growth (for example, by retaining too much labour if the subsidies are motivated by the pre-occupation to avoid unemployment), and hinder the accumulation of R&D resources and the creation of new sectors. In summary, such subsidies could delay the adaptation of the country to a growing world variety. This is not a general criticism of subsidies, but only implies that subsidies must not break the virtuous circle variety growth/productivity growth. Subsidies would be far more effective if allocated to the creation of new sectors or to the specialization of some of the existing ones.

In summary, the specialization of different countries must adapt to the growing world variety. Such adaptation is better achieved by respecting the complementarity between variety growth and productivity growth.

CONVERGENCE, DIVERGENCE AND NSI

The concept of NSI implies that inter-country differences in innovative performance, procedures and structures is greater than the intra-country differences of the same variables. In turn, these differences can be related to differential barriers to the flow of information, artefacts, people, etc. between different nation states, as compared to the barriers internal to each of them. Furthermore, NSIs show varying performance (rates of economic growth, trade performance, etc.) and a very high degree of institutional specificity. We can, therefore, characterize different NSIs in terms of their asymmetries at the level of structure and of performance.

Some scholars have argued that recent trends towards internationalization and globalization could diminish the national specificity of innovation systems and, in the long run, make the same concept of NSI meaningless. However, the position taken in this chapter is that, while these trends could lead to some degree of convergence, they would not necessarily lead to a complete homogeneity of the various NSIs.

Consider, for example, the consequences of the fact that differences in performance create inducements for change for the less successful NSIs. In other words, an innovating country achieving low rates of economic growth is likely to 'observe' the structure and behaviour of the more successful NSIs and to imitate them, to a certain extent, i.e., imitation of performance is likely to induce imitation of structures. An example of such an induced diffusion of practices is the attempt to imitate in other countries Japanese procedures of quality control and 'just-in-time'. While some form of behaviour may diffuse, it is also possible to achieve similar outcomes by different means, as the concept of multistability implies, and as some of the previous examples demonstrate. Therefore, even forms of imitation and diffusion induced by differences in performance, do not necessarily lead to complete homogeneity and convergence.

More fundamentally, the degree of homogeneity/asymmetry amongst NSIs is determined by the balance between convergence and divergence in the world economic system. Imitation, diffusion, technology transfer and trade are phenomena which contribute to convergence. On the other hand, innovations do not spring up at random, but originate in particular places. The economic rewards for such innovations tend to remain, sometimes for a long time, in the country/NSI which created them. Hence, innovation creates heterogeneity/ asymmetry/divergence while imitation/technology transfer/diffusion and trade lead to convergence/homogenization. Whether the world system tends to converge or to diverge depends on the balance between these two trends, and not only on the increase of phenomena leading to convergence. For example, it is quite conceivable that an increased rate of innovation (carrying increased divergence with it) will accompany the growing internationalization that the world economy is experiencing. The outcome would be determined by the balance between the increases in the rates of convergence and divergence.

This situation can be represented in more general terms. Following Prigogine and Stengers (1984) we can classify all the phenomena taking place in an economic system as 'generalized forces' and 'fluxes' (p. 135). Generalized forces (e.g. chemical reactions, innovations, etc.) produce local outcomes and give rise to asymmetries. In this way, generalized forces create a diffusion potential, which 'causes' fluxes. The morphology of the system and its degree of heterogeneity are determined by the balance between forces and fluxes.

These considerations can be given a more concrete form by reference to the concepts of technological system and of TEN. The technological systems studied by Carlsson (1992) tend to show a high degree of technological rather than national specificity. To the extent that the productive system of an economy can be represented by a set of technological systems, one can expect internationally similar patterns of development. This would lead to a growing international convergence although national specificity would still exist at the level of institutions and policies. A similar situation exists for what concerns the use of networks in comparative policy studies (Wilks and Wright, 1987), where a greater emphasis is placed on inter-sectoral differences than on inter-country differences. On the other hand, TENs contain actors which are likely to have different degrees of national specificity. Thus industrial firms are likely to experience greater pressures towards international convergence than are universities or government research laboratories.

These two examples add some flesh to the more general considerations about convergence and divergence presented above. However, while it is possible to establish in general that growing pressures towards convergence do not necessarily lead to a greater degree of convergence, the particular mechanisms by which convergence and divergence are obtained deserve greater attention and are rich in policy implications.

The problem of the balance between convergence and divergence can be approached also by means of network concepts and of the previous considerations on variety. Let us imagine to start with a situation in which all the networks relevant for technology policy are national. Firms, government departments, universities, research laboratories, etc. will be the members of such networks. We can imagine that all the possible outcomes of the growing internationalization of markets are included between two extremes: on the one hand, completely new and international networks could be formed, not including any of the existing actors; on the other, existing networks could expand to include new links amongst actors previously unconnected and based in different countries. The former case, in a pure form, is not very probable. To the extent that the collective goals of these internationalized networks include using inputs and selling outputs in given countries, some of their links will have to remain national. While it is possible that some of the previous links are severed and replaced by new international ones, it is unlikely that all of them will. Hence it is quite likely that an increasing complexity of networks will be the outcome of the growing internationalization, but that a significant degree of national specificity will remain. Such increasing complexity would be constituted by the greater number of links in the networks and by the greater cultural heterogeneity of the actors involved. The most likely outcome of the ongoing processes of specialization/globalization is an increasing degree of interaction of the actors involved and an increasing density of the corresponding networks.

As we have seen in the previous section, variety growth leads to a number of implications for the specialization of individual countries, for their NSI and in particular for what concerns the balance convergence/divergence. First, the presence of an ever-growing output variety creates growing possibilities for the specialization and differentiation of NSIs. The number of strategic choices (i.e. choices of subsets of the set of all output types) increases with the number of output types (output variety). Hence, if the rate of growth of output variety is at least as great as that of diffusion/convergence, constant or growing asymmetries may remain amongst NSIs in the world economic system. Second, institutional variety is likely to grow following a growth in output variety. This could happen for a number of reasons. It is quite often the case that such new types of output are introduced into the market by new firms. These firms require new skills and regulations, which can be provided by educational and regulatory institutions. New actors will be required, and new links will be formed amongst them, that is new networks will be created. The number of new networks is likely to be less than the number of the new distinguishable types of output, creating the greater variety. Some of the actors entering into the new networks will be pre-existing institutions and some of the firms producing the new outputs will be multi-product firms, producing older types as well. However, it seems that coherent diversification is more likely to lead to successful firms than unrelated diversification (Teece *et al.*, 1992). If this is the case, radical innovations would be more probably produced by new firms.

In summary, a growing output variety is likely to lead to an increase in the number of actors and of networks in the economic system, even though the latter increase may be numerically smaller than that of output variety. Alternatively, the growth in institutional variety is likely to remain below that of output variety because not all the institutional configurations which are possible at the new variety level will be compatible with the existing institutional structure of the country.

In the presence of growing output and institutional variety there is no necessary reason for the convergence of NSIs. The number of both strategic and institutional choices possible at the national level increases, leading to a greater number of possible configurations for each NSI. This can occur also in the presence of the faster diffusion of international practices implied by internationalization/globalization. Furthermore, it is to be remembered that convergence, even if it were to take place, would be a slow process. At the beginning NSIs would have a very high degree of institutional asymmetry since processes of institutional change show a very considerable degree of inertia and path dependency. Thus, there is no necessary reason for the convergence of NSIs, but, if it were to take place, it would be a slow process.

In summary, the concept of NSI and some of its features follow naturally from the foundations of evolutionary theories, while they could not be foreseen on the basis of orthodox economics. Naturally, in order to be able to exploit it fully, we need to articulate more completely the concept of NSI. A more systematic analysis of NSIs using network theories and concepts could be useful in this respect. In particular, studies of the patterns of interaction of the different types of institutions which participate in the same network, in order to identify the conditions for synergism or, alternatively, for destructive interactions, and identifying at least some of the multiple institutional configurations which can give rise to similar outcomes, could also be very useful.

10. Summary and conclusions

The starting point of this book is constituted by a number of shortcomings in the economic analysis of technological change. Two of these shortcomings and the consequent need for change are particularly important. First, while traditionally economics has concentrated on the effects of technological change on known economic variables, the need to incorporate actors and mechanisms of technological change is identified. The two approaches are contrasted as implicit and explicit respectively. Second, the need to incorporate the study of qualitative change into economics is identified. This need is not confined to the analysis of technological change, but technological change is one of the main sources of qualitative change in the economic system. However, this second neglected aspect of technological change leads us to the need for a general treatment of all types of innovation (organizational, etc.). In fact, a proper dynamics of economic change must not simply contain time in its equations, but provide us with some understanding of qualitative change and of its role in economic development.

It is argued that both of these problems can be better attacked in the context of evolutionary theories. These theories in their modern form are emerging from the convergence of a number of research traditions: biology, evolutionary interpretations in economics, thermodynamics of irreversible processes, systems theory, firm and organization theories. All these traditions give us a better way of analysing qualitative change in complex systems. In particular, the biological metaphor, concerned with the origin of species, provides an appropriate starting point to perform this task. Naturally, the biological analogy or any other metaphor can only be used for heuristic purposes and not in order to supply us with preconceived answers coming from a completely different observation space. Moreover, it is argued that any metaphor/analogy can only help us over a finite range of variables. The need for theoretical pluralism follows from the local character of knowledge. A particular theory/set of theories has in general been developed for a given range of observables/variables. When it is extended to another set of variables its effectiveness is likely to fall. To overcome this problem the theory will need to be adapted to the new set of observables/variables and, even then, it might be effective only over a subset of it. The use of several metaphors to construct an evolutionary theory seems then advisable. In fact, the research traditions that contribute to the emergence of modern evolutionary theories show some degree of complementarity and of coherence, in the sense that some of them explain aspects of the others.

A number of key concepts emerge from this discussion of evolutionary theories: variation, selection, reproduction and inheritance, fitness and adaptation, a population perspective, system openness, irreversibility and path dependence, elementary interactions and external environments. Such concepts are incorporated as far as possible in the subsequent analysis.

The missing characters of technological change which are discussed in the following parts of the book are product models, knowledge and information.

An explicit model of technological evolution is presented in Part 2. Product models are represented by means of a twin characteristics and population approach. This allows us to map trends in technological evolution and to infer a number of generalizations about it. Variety is a general concept which can be used to develop an analytical treatment of qualitative change in economic development. The hypotheses that variety growth is a necessary requirement for long-term economic development and that it is complementary with respect to efficiency growth in established sectors are explored. A general model of technological evolution which uses some of the inferences obtained in Chapter 4 is then presented in Chapter 6. This model allows us to treat several aspects of technological evolution, but attention is focused here on the conditions required for variety growth. In order for this to happen inter-technology competition must be lower then intra-technology competition. It is worth emphasizing that competition is here treated by means of a model of biological inspiration capable of encompassing different situations ranging from perfect to Schumpeterian competition. A non-negligible advantage of this treatment of competition is the possibility to distinguish between intra- and inter-technology competition. Only the former is usually considered by economists. However, inter-technology competition is also very important. For example, a monopolist is only free from intra- but not from inter-technology competition. Moreover, inter-technology competition contributes to the contestability of markets.

Knowledge and information are distinguished in Part 3. The effects of both on organizational structures and institutions are examined. Firms can change organizational structures in order to reduce information costs while producing a constant or increasing output variety. However, if radical changes in knowledge take place, firms have to update their knowledge base before being able to acquire the new information. Knowledge is then both a component of the organizational structure of firms and of their external environment. All firms' activities can be reduced to division of labour and coordination, and the particular balance between the two determines the prevalent type of industrial structure. In turn, the external environment, and knowledge in particular, determines the balance between division of labour and coordination and the type of institutional interface.

Amongst the properties of technological knowledge there are specificity and path dependence. These properties contribute to the justification of the existence of the national system of innovation (NSI). A further justification comes from other aspects of evolutionary theories. Whether present trends to internationalization and globalization will make the concept of NSI irrelevant depends on the balance between diffusive fluxes (diffusion, technology transfer, trade), leading to convergence, and innovation, creating heterogeneity. A growing world variety would imply the need to adapt national variety and would allow a greater scope for national specialization.

In summary, in this book evolutionary theories have been considered a better option than neoclassical ones mainly for the possibility that the former have to incorporate qualitative change. It must be observed, however, that the two theories are not substitutes, in the sense that they have different observation spaces. Furthermore, evolutionary theories are at an early stage in their life cycle and lack the sophisticated formal structure of neoclassical economics. The purpose of the development of evolutionary theories is then twofold: first, they have to extend the observation space of neoclassical economics by incorporating the analysis of qualitative change; and, second, they can challenge a number of established assumptions of orthodox economics. The comparison betwen the two is not intended here as a military confrontation. Rather, it aims at opening up new territories and directions for economic analysis. Whether in future the prevalent label of economics will be evolutionary does not matter very much. That we make progress on the issues outlined in this book and on those discussed by evolutionary theorists is very important.

References

Abernathy, W.J. and Utterback, J.M. (1975), 'A dynamic model of process and product innovation', *Omega*, **3** (6), 639–56.

Abernathy, W.J. and Utterback, J.M. (1978), 'Patterns of industrial innovation', *Technology Review*, June/July, 41–7.

Ahmad, S. (1966), 'On the theory of induced innovation', *Economic Journal*, 76, 344–57.

Aldrich, H.E. (1979), *Organizations and Environments*, Englewood Cliff, NJ: Prentice Hall.

Allen, P.M. (1982), 'The genesis of structure in social systems: the paradigm of self organisation', in *Theory and Explanation in Archeology*, New York: Academic Press.

Allen, P.M. (1988), 'Evolution, innovation and economics', in G. Dosi *et al.* (eds), *Technical Change and Economic Theory*, London: Pinter.

Allen, P.M. and McGlade, J.M. (1987a), 'Modelling complex human systems: a fisheries example', *European Journal of Operational Research*, **30**, 147–67.

Allen, P.M. and McGlade, J.M. (1987b), 'Evolutionary drive: the effect of microscopic diversity, error making and noise', *Foundations of Physics*, **17**, 723–38.

Amendola, M. and Gaffard, J.L. (1988), *The Innovative Choice*, Oxford: Basil Blackwell.

Antonelli, C., Petit, P. and Tahar, G. (1992), *The Economics of Industrial Modernization*, London: Academic Press.

Arrow, K. (1962), 'The economic implications of learning by doing', *Review of Economic Studies*, **29** (80), 155–73.

Arrow, K. (1974), *The Limits of Organizations*, New York: Norton.

Arthur, W.B. (1983), 'Competing technologies and lock-in by historical events: the dynamics of allocation under increasing returns', International Institute for Applied Systems Analysis, paper WP-83-90, Laxenburg, Austria.

Arthur, W.B. (1988), 'Competing technologies: an overview', in: G. Dosi, *et al.* (eds), *Technical Change and Economic Theory*, London: Pinter.

Arthur, W.B. (1989a), 'Competing technologies, increasing returns, and lock-in by historical events', *The Economic Journal*, 99, 116–31.

Arthur, W.B. (1989b), '"Silicon valley" locational clusters: when do increasing returns imply monopoly?', working paper 89-007, October, Santa Fe Institute.

Ashby, W.R. (1956), *Introduction to Cybernetics*, New York: Wiley.

Atkinson, A.B. and Stiglitz, J. (1969), 'A new view of technological change', *Economic Journal*, **79** 125–53.

Barker, T. (1977), 'International trade and economic growth: an alternative to the neoclassical approach', *Cambridge Journal of Economics*, **1**, 153–72.

Basalla, G. (1988), *The Evolution of Technology*, Cambridge: Cambridge University Press.

Becker, G.S. and Murphy K.M. (1992), 'The division of labour, coordination costs and knowledge', *Quarterly Journal of Economics*, **107**, 1137–60.

Berle, A.A. and Means G.C. (1932), *The Modern Corporation and Private Property*, New York: Macmillan.

Binmore, K. and Dasgupta, P. (1989), *Economic Organizations as Games*, Oxford: Blackwell.

Binswanger, H.P., Ruttan, V.W., *et al.* (1978), *Induced Innovation: Technology, Institutions and Development*, Baltimore: The John Hopkins University Press.

Blaug, M. (1980), *The Methodology of Economics*, Cambridge: Cambridge University Press.

Boulding, K. (1978), *Ecodynamics, A New Theory of Societal Evolution*, Beverly Hills, London: Sage.

Boulding, K. (1981), *Evolutionary Economics*, Beverly Hills, London: Sage.

Bruckner, E., Ebeling, W. and Scharnorst, A. (1989), 'Stochastic dynamics of instabilities in evolutionary systems', *System Dynamics Review*, **5**, 176–91.

Burns, T. and Stalker, G.M. (1961), *The Management of Innovation*, London: Tavistock.

Burt, R.S., Christman, K.P. and Kilburn, H.C. (1983), *Applied Network Analysis*, Beverly Hills, Calif.: Sage.

Callon, M. (1989), *La Science et ses Reseaux: Genese et Circulation des Faits Scientifiques*, Paris: La Decouverte.

Callon, M. (1992), 'The dynamics of techno-economic networks', in R. Coombs, P. Saviotti and V. Walsh (eds), *Technical Change and Company Strategies*, London: Academic Press.

Callon, M. (1993), 'Variety and irreversibility in networks of technique conception and adoption', in D. Foray and C. Freeman (eds), *Technology and the Wealth of Nations*, London: Pinter.

Callon, M., Laredo, P. and Rabeharisoa V. (1990), 'The management and evaluation of technological programmes and the dynamics of techno-economic networks: the case of AFME', Paris: Centre de Sociologie de l'Innovation, Ecole des Mines.

Carlsson, B. (1992), 'Technological systems and economic development potential: four Swedish case studies', presented at the International Joseph A. Schumpeter Conference, Kyoto, 19–22 August.

Carlsson, B. and Stankiewicz, R. (1991), 'On the nature, function and composition of technological systems', *Journal of Evolutionary Economics*, **1**, 93–118.

Casti, J. (1989), *Mathematical Models of Nature and Man*, New York: Wiley Interscience.

Chamberlin, E.J. (1933), *The Theory of Monopolistic Competition*, Cambridge, Mass.: Harvard University Press.

Chandler, A.D. (1962), *Strategy and Structure*, Cambridge Mass.: MIT Press.

Chandler, A.D. (1977), *The Visible Hand*, Cambridge Mass.: Harvard University Press.

Chatfield, C. and Collins, A.J. (1981), *Introduction to Multivariate Analysis*, London: Chapman and Hall.

Chesnais, F. (1988), 'Technical cooperation agreement between independent firms, novel issues for economic analysis and the formulation of national technological policies', *STI Review*, 4, 51–120.

Clark, N. and Juma, C. (1987), *Long Run Economics: An Evolutionary Approach to Economic Growth*, London: Pinter.

Clark, N. and Juma C. (1988), 'Evolutionary theories in economic thought', in G. Dosi *et al.* (eds), *Technical Change and Economic Theory*, London: Pinter.

Coase, R. (1937), 'The nature of the firm', *Economica*, **4**, 386–405.

Cohen, M. and Levinthal, D. (1989), 'Innovating and learning: the two faces of R&D', *Economic Journal*, **99**, 569–96.

Cohen, M. and Levinthal D. (1990), 'Absorptive capacity: a new perspective on learning and innovation', *Administrative Science Quarterly*, **35**, 128–52.

Coombs, R. *et al.* (1978), 'Incremental innovation in the UK tractor industry', Manchester University, PREST.

Coombs, R., Saviotti, P.P. and Walsh, V. (1987), *Economics and Technological Change*, London: Macmillan.

Cooper, R.A. and Weekes, A.J. (1983), *Data, Models and Statistical Analysis*, Oxford: Philip Allan.

Cyert, R.M. and March, J.G. (1963), *A Behavioural Theory of the Firm*, Englewood Cliffs, NJ: Prentice Hall.

Dasgupta, P. and David P. (1992), 'Toward a new economics of science', Center for Economic Policy Research, Stanford University.

David, P.A. (1975), *Technical Choice, Innovation and Economic Growth*, Cambridge: Cambridge University Press.

David, P. and Foray D. (1994), 'Accessing and expanding the science and technology knowledge base', Paris OECD, DSTI/STP/TIP(94)4.

Davies, S. (1979), *The Diffusion of Process Innovation*, Cambridge: Cambridge University Press.

De Bresson, C. and Amesse, F. (1991), 'Networks of innovators: a review and introduction to the issue', *Research Policy*, **20**, 363–79.

Denison, E. (1962), 'United States economic growth', *Journal of Business*, **35**, 109–21.

Dixit, A.K. and Stiglitz, J.E. (1977), 'Monopolistic competition and optimum product diversity', *American Economic Review*, **67**, 297–308.

Dodgson, M. (1993), 'Learning, trust and inter-firm technological linkages: some theoretical associations', presented at the 2nd ASEAT conference, Manchester, April.

Dosi, G. (1982), 'Technological paradigms and technological trajectories: a suggested interpretation of the determinants and directions of technical change', *Research Policy*, **11**, 147–62.

Dosi, G. (1988), 'Institutions and markets in a dynamic world', *The Manchester School*, **56**, 119–46.

Dosi, G., Freeman, C., Nelson, R., Silverberg, G. and Soete. L. (eds) (1988), *Technical Change and Economic Theory*, London: Pinter.

Dosi, G. and Kaniovski, Yu (1993), 'The method of generalized urn scheme in the analysis of technological dynamics', presented at the conference 'New Developments in Technology Studies: Evolutionary Economics and Chaos Theory', Amsterdam, 6–8 May.

Dosi, G. and Nelson, R.R. (1994), 'An introduction to evolutionary theories in economics', *Journal of Evolutionary Economics*, **4**, 153–72.

Dosi, G., Pavitt, K. and Soete, L. (1990), *The Economics of Technical Change and International Trade*, Hemel Hempstead: Harvester Wheatsheaf.

Duncan, R and Weiss, A. (1979), 'Organisational learning: implications for organisational design', *Research in Organisational Behaviour*, **1**, 75–123.

Eaton, B.C. and Lipsey, R.G. (1975), 'The principle of minimum differentiation reconsidered: some new developments in the theory of spatial competition', *Review of Economic Studies*, **42**, 27–49.

Eigen, M. and Schuster, P. (1979), *The Hypercycle: a Principle of Natural Self-Organization*, Heidelberg: Springer Verlag.

Eldredge, N. and Gould, S.J. (1972), 'Punctuated equilibria: an alternative approach to phyletic gradualism', in T.J.M. Schopf (ed.), *Models in Paleobiology*, pp. 82–115, San Francisco: Freeman Cooper.

Eldredge, N. and Gould, S.J. (1988), 'Punctuated equilibrium prevails', *Nature*, **332**, 211–12.

Elster, J. (1983), *Explaining Technical Change*, Cambridge: Cambridge University Press.

Emery, F.E. (ed.) (1969), *Systems Thinking*, Harmondsworth: Penguin Books.

Emery, F.E. and Trist, E.L. (1965), 'The causal texture of organizational environments', *Human Relations*, **18**, 21–32.

Faber, M. and Proops, J.L.R. (1991), 'Evolution in biology, physics and economics: a conceptual analysis', in P.P. Saviotti and J.S. Metcalfe (eds), *Evolutionary Theories of Economic and Technological Change*, London: Harwood Publishers.

Farrel, J. and Saloner, G. (1986), 'Installed base and compatibility: innovation, product preannouncements and predation', *American Economic Review*, **76**, 940–55.

Fisher, R.A. (1958), *The Genetical Theory of Natural Selection*, New York: Drew (originally published 1929).

Foray, D. (1991), 'Towards an economic analysis of the organisations of research and development', *Revue d'Economie Politique*, **101**, 779–808.

Foray, D. and Grubler, A. (1989), 'Towards a taxonomy of technological change', Paris and Laxenburg, mimeo.

Foray, D. and Grubler, A. (1990a), 'Morphological analysis, diffusion and lock-out of technologies: ferrous casting in France and the FRG', *Research Policy*, 19, 535–50.

Foray, D. and Grubler, A. (1990b), 'Towards a taxonomy of technological change', Paris and Laxenburg, mimeo.

Foster, J. (1985), *Evolutionary Macroeconomics*, London: Allen & Unwin.

Freeman, C. (1982), *The Economics of Industrial Innovation*, London: Pinter.

Freeman, C. (1987), *Technology Policy and Economic Performance*, London: Pinter.

Freeman, C. (1988), 'Japan: a new national system of innovation?', in G. Dosi *et al.* (eds), *Technical Change and Economic Theory*, London: Pinter.

Freeman, C. (1991), 'Networks of innovators: a synthesis of research issues', *Research Policy*, **20**, 499–514.

Freeman, C., Clark, J. and Soete, L. (1982), *Unemployment and Technical Change: a Study of Long Waves in Economic Development*, London: Frances Pinter.

Freeman, C. and Lundvall, B.A. (eds) (1990), *Small Countries Facing the Technological Revolution*, London: Pinter.

Gatlin, L.L. (1972), *Information Theory and the Living System*, New York: Columbia University Press.

Georgescu Roegen, N. (1971), *The Entropy Law and the Economic Process*, Cambridge, Mass.: Harvard University Press.

Georgescu Roegen, N. (1976), *Energy and Economic Myths*, New York: Pergamon.

Georgescu Roegen, N. (1982), *Analytical Economics*, Cambridge, Mass.: Harvard University Press.

Goodwin, R.M. (1951), 'The nonlinear accelerator and the persistence of business cycles', *Econometrica*, **19**, 1–17.

Griliches, Z. (1957), 'Hybrid corn: an exploration in the economics of technical change', *Econometrica*, **25**, 501–22.

Grossman, G. and Helpman, E. (1989), 'Product development and international trade', *Journal of Political Economy*, **97**, 1261–83.

Grossman, G. and Helpman, E. (1991), 'Endogenous product cycles', *Economic Journal*, **101**, 1214–29.

Gummett, P. (ed.) (1991), *Future Relations Between Defence and Civil Science and Technology*, A Report for the (UK) Parliamentary Office of Science and Technology, London, Science Policy Support Group, Review Paper No. 2.

Gummett, P. and Reppy, J. (eds) (1988), *The Relations between Defence and Civil Technologies*, Dordrecht: Kluwer.

Gummett, P. and Walker, W. (1990), 'The industrial and technological consequences of the peace', *RUSI Journal*, **135**, 46–52.

Hagedoorn, J. (1989), *The Dynamic Analysis of Process Control*, London: Pinter.

Hagedoorn, J. and Shackenraad, J. (1990), 'Inter-firm partnerships and cooperative strategies in core technologies', in C. Freeman and L. Soete (eds), *New Explorations in the Economics of Technological Change*, London: Pinter.

Hagedoorn, J. and Shackenraad, J. (1992), 'Leading companies and networks of strategic alliances in information technologies', *Research Policy*, **21**, 163–90.

Hahn, F. (1991), 'The next hundred years', *Economic Journal*, **101**, 47–50.

Hannan, M.T. and Freeman, J. (1977), 'The population ecology of organizations', *American Journal of Sociology*, **82**, 929–64.

Hannan, M.T. and Freeman, J. (1989), *Organisational Ecology*, Cambridge, Mass.: Harvard University Press.

Hanusch, H. (ed.) (1988), *Evolutionary Economics*, Cambridge: Cambridge University Press.

Hayek, F.A. (1982), *Law, Legislation and Liberty*, 3 vols, London: Routledge and Kegan Paul.

Hayek, F.A. (1988),*The Fatal Conceit: the Errors of Socialism*, vol. 1 of *Collected Works of F.A. Hayek*, London: Routledge.

Heertje, A. (1977), *Economics and Technical Change*, London: Weidenfeld and Nicholson.

Heiner, R.A. (1983), 'The origin of predictable behaviour', *American Economic Review*, **73**, 560–95.

Heiner, R.A. (1988), 'Imperfect decisions and routinised production: implications for evolutionary modeling and inertial technical change', in G. Dosi *et al.* (eds), *Technical Change and Economic Theory*, London: Pinter.

Helpman, E. (1981), 'International trade in the presence of product differentiation, economies of scale and monopolistic competition', *Journal of
International Economics*, **11**, 305–40.

Hicks, J.R. (1932), *The Theory of Wages*, London: MacMillan.

Hodgson, G. (1988), *Economics and Institutions*, Oxford: Polity Press.

Hodgson, G. (1991), 'Evolution and intention in economic theory', in P.P.
Saviotti and J.S. Metcalfe (eds), *Evolutionary Theories of Economic and Technological Change*, London: Harwood Publishers.

Hodgson, G. (1993), *Economics and Evolution: Putting Life Back Into Economics*,
Oxford: Polity Press.

Hofbauer, J. and Sigmund, K. (1988), *The Theory of Evolution and Dynamical
Sytems*, Cambridge: Cambridge University Press.

Holland, J.H. (1986), 'Escaping brittleness: the possibilities of general purpose
machine learning algorithms applied to parallel rule-based systems', in R.
Michalski, J. Carbonell and T. Mitchell (eds), *Machine Learning: An Artificial
Intelligence Approach*, **2**, Los Altos, CA.: Kaufman.

Hotelling, H. (1929), 'Stability in competition', *Economic Journal*, **39**, 41–57.

Imai, K.J. and Baba Y. (1991), 'Systemic innovations and cross border networks:
transcending markets and hierarchies to create a new techno-economic
system', in OECD, *Technology and Productivity: the Challenges for Economic
Policy*, Paris: OECD.

Jurkovitch, R. (1969), 'A core typology of organizational environments', *Administrative Science Quarterly*, **19**, 380–94.

Kauffman, S.A. (1988), 'The evolution of economic webs', in P.W. Anderson,
K.J. Arrow and D. Pines (eds), *The Economy as an Evolving Complex System*,
Redwood City: Addison Wesley.

Kennedy, C. (1964), 'Induced bias in innovation and the theory of distribution',
Economic Journal, **74**, 541–7.

Krugman, P.R. (1979), 'Increasing returns, monopolistic competition and international trade', *Journal of International Economics*, **9**, 469–79.

Kuhn, T. (1962), *The Structure of Scientific Revolutions*, Chicago: Chicago
University Press.

Kuznets, S. (1965), *Economic Growth and Structure*, New York: Norton.

Lakatos, I. (1974), 'Falsification and the methodology of scientific research
programmes', in I. Lakatos and A. Musgrave (eds), *Criticism and the Growth
of Knowledge*, Cambridge: Cambridge University Press.

Lancaster, K.J. (1966), 'A new approach to consumer theory', *Journal of
Political Economy*, **14**, 133–56.

Lancaster, K.J. (1971), *Consumer Demand: a New Approach*, New York:
Columbia University Press.

Lancaster, K.J. (1975), 'Socially optimal product differentiation', *American
Economic Review*, **65**, 567–85.

Lancaster, K.J. (1979), *Variety, Equity and Efficiency*, New York: Columbia University Press.

Lancaster, K.J. (1990), 'The economics of product variety: a survey', *Marketing Science*, **9**, 189–206.

Langrish, J., Gibbons, M., Evans, W. and Jevons, F. (1972), *Wealth from Knowledge*, London: Macmillan.

Laredo, P. (1991), 'State intervention in innovation. The role of technological programmes in the emergence of a new composite economic agent: the techno-economic network', presented at the second international workshop 'Policies and Strategies for Technology in Industrialised Countries', Moscow, May.

Laredo, P. and Mustar P. (1993), 'The techno-economic network, a socio-economic approach to state intervention in innovation', presented at the second ASEAT Conference, Manchester, April.

Laszlo, E. (1987), *Evolution: the Grand Synthesis*, Boston, Mass.: New Science Library-Shambhala.

Lawrence, P. and Lorsch, J.L. (1967), *Organizations and Environment: Managing Differentiation and Integration*, Cambridge, Mass.: Harvard University Press.

Layton, E.T. (1974), 'Technology as knowledge', *Technology and Culture*, **15**, 31–41.

Lotka, A.J. (1956), *Elements of Mathematical Biology*, New York: Dover (originally published 1924).

Lundvall, B.A. (1985), *Product Innovation and User Producer Interaction*, Aalborg: Aalborg University Press.

Lundvall, B.A. (1986), 'Long waves and the uneven development of capitalism', paper presented at the international workshop on 'Long Term Fluctuations', Sienna.

Lundvall, B.A. (1988), 'Innovation as an interactive process: from user–producer interaction to the national system of innovation', in G. Dosi *et al.*, *Technical Change and Economic Theory*, London: Pinter.

Lundvall, B.A. (1992), *National Systems of Innovation*, London: Pinter.

McKelvey, B. (1982), *Organizational Systematics*, Berkeley: University of California Press.

McNulty, P.J. (1968), 'Economic theory and the meaning of competition', *Quarterly Journal of Economics*, **82**, 639–56.

Machlup, F. (1967), 'Theories of the firm, marginalist, managerial behaviour, *American Economic Review*, **57**, 1–33.

Malerba, F. (1992), 'Learning by firms and incremental technical change', *The Economic Journal*, **102**, 845–59.

Mani, G.S. (ed.) (1980), 'A Darwinian theory of enzyme polymorphism', in *Evolutionary Dynamics of Genetic Diversity; Lecture Notes in Biomathematics*, **53**, 242–98.

Mani, G.S. (1991), 'Is there a general theory of biological evolution?' in P.P. Saviotti and J.S. Metcalfe (eds), *Evolutionary Theories of Economic and Technological Change*, London: Harwood Publishers.

Mansfield, E. (1963), 'Intra-firm rates of diffusion of an innovation', *Review of Economics and Statistics*, **30**, 348–59.

Mansfield, E. (1969), *Industrial Research and Technological Innovation: an Econometric Analysis*, London: Longman.

Marris, R. (1964), *The Economic Theory of Managerial Capitalism*, Glencoe, Illinois: Free Press.

Marschak, J. (1958), 'Economics of inquiring, communicating, deciding', *American Economic Review*, papers and proceedings, **58**, 1–18.

Marshall, A. (1949), *Principles of Economics*, 8th ed., London: Macmillan (originally published 1890).

May, R.M. (1973), *Stability and Complexity in Model Ecosystems*, Princeton: Princeton University Press.

Maynard Smith. J. (1974), *Models in Ecology*, Cambridge: Cambridge University Press.

Metcalfe, J.S. (1981), 'Impulse and diffusion in the study of technical change', *Futures*, **13**, 347–59.

Metcalfe, J.S. (1984), 'Technological innovation and the competitive process', *Greek Economic Review*, **6**, 287–316.

Metcalfe, J.S. (1988), 'The diffusion of innovation', in G. Dosi *et al.*, *Technical Change and Economic Theory*, London: Pinter.

Metcalfe, J.S. and Gibbons, M. (1987), 'Technology, variety and organisation', mimeo, University of Manchester.

Metcalfe, J.S. and Gibbons, M. (1989), 'Technology, variety and organisation: a systematic perspective on the competitive process', *Research on Technological Innovation, Management and Policy*, **4**, 153–93.

Metcalfe, J.S. and Boden, M. (1992), 'Evolutionary epistemology and the nature of technology strategy', in R. Coombs, P. Saviotti and V. Walsh (eds), (1992), *Technological Change and Company Strategies*, London: Academic Press.

Mintzberg, H. (1979), *The Structure of Organizations*, Englewood Cliffs, NJ: Prentice Hall.

Mitchell Waldrop, M. (1992), *Complexity: The Emerging Science at the Edge of Order and Chaos*, London: Viking.

Mokyr, J. (1990a), *The Lever of Riches: Technological Creativity and Economic Progress*, New York: Oxford University Press.

Mokyr, J. (1990b), 'Punctuated equilibria and technological progress', *American Economic Review*, **80**, 350–4.

Mokyr, J. (1991), 'Evolutionary biology, technological change and economic history', *Bulletin of Economic Research*, **43**, 127–49.

Moss, S. (1981), *An Economic Theory of Business Strategy*, Oxford: Martin Robertson.

Mowery, D. and Rosenberg, N. (1979), 'Market demand and innovation', *Research Policy*, **8**, 103–53.

Mytelka, L.K. (ed.) (1991a), *Strategic Partnership and the World Economy*, London: Pinter.

Mytelka, L.K. (ed.) (1991b), 'States, strategic alliances and international oligopolies: the European ESPRIT programme', *Strategic Partnership and the World Economy*, London: Pinter.

Nelson, R. (1959), 'The simple economics of basic scientific research', *Journal of Political Economy*, 297–306.

Nelson, R. (1988), 'Institutions supporting technical change in the US', in G. Dosi *et al.*, *Technical Change and Economic Theory*, London: Pinter.

Nelson, R. (1990), 'Capitalism as an engine of progress', *Research Policy*, **19**, 193–214.

Nelson, R. (1993), 'The co-evolution of technologies and institutions', presented at the conference 'New Developments in Technology Studies: Evolutionary Economics and Chaos Theory', Amsterdam, 6-8 May.

Nelson, R. (1995), 'Recent evolutionary theorizing about economic change', *Journal of Economic Literature*, **33**, 48–90.

Nelson, R. and Winter, S. (1974), 'Neoclassical vs. evolutionary theories of economic growth: critique and prospectus', *Economic Journal*, **84**, 886–905.

Nelson, R. and Winter, S. (1977), 'In search of useful theory of innovation', *Research Policy*, **6**, 36–76.

Nelson, R. and Winter, S. (1982), *An Evolutionary Theory of Economic Change*, Cambridge, Mass.: Harvard University Press.

Newell, A., Shaw, J.C. and Simon, H.A. (1962), 'The process of creative thinking', in H.E. Gruber, G. Terrell and M. Wertheimer (eds), *Contemporary Approaches to Creative Thinking*, New York: Atherton Press.

Nicolis, J.S. (1987), 'A study program of chaotic dynamics applied to information processing', in I. Prigogine and M. Sanglier (eds), *Laws of Nature and Human Conduct*, Brussels: GORDES.

Nicolis, G. and Prigogine, I. (1989), *Exploring Complexity*, New York: Freeman.

Niosi, J.P., Bellon, B., Saviotti, P. and Crow, M. (1992), 'Les systèmes nationaux d'innovation: a la recherche d'un concept utilisable', *Revue Française d'Economie*, **7**, 215–49.

Niosi, J., Saviotti, P., Bellon, B. and Crow, M. (1993), 'National systems of innovation: in search of a workable concept', *Technology in Society*, **15**, 207–27.

OECD (1992), *Technology and the Economy: the Key Relationships*, ed. by F. Chesnais, Paris.

Pasinetti, L.L. (1981), *Structural Change and Economic Growth*, Cambridge: Cambridge University Press.

Pasinetti, L.L. (1990), 'Structural change and unemployment', *Structural Change and Economic Dynamics*, **1**, 7–14.

Pasinetti, L.L. (1993), *Structural Economic Dynamics*, Cambridge: Cambridge University Press.

Patel, P. and Pavitt, K. (1994), 'Technological competencies in the world's largest firms', SPRU, University of Sussex, mimeo.

Pavitt, K. (1984), 'Patterns of technical change: towards a taxonomy and a theory', *Research Policy*, **13**, 343–74.

Penrose, E. (1980), *The Theory of the Growth of the Firm*, Oxford: Blackwell, (originally published 1959).

Perez, C. (1983), 'Structural change and the assimilation of new technologies in the the economic system', *Futures*, **15**, 357–75.

Perroux, F. (1969), *L'Economie du XXe Siecle*, Paris: Press Universitaires de France.

Pielou, C. (1977), *Mathematical Ecology*, New York: John Wiley.

Pielou, C. (1984), *The Interpretation of Ecological Data*, New York: John Wiley.

Polanyi, M. (1962), *Personal Knowledge: Towards a Post-Critical Philosophy*, New York: Harper Torchbooks.

Porter, M. (1990), *The Competitive Advantage of Nations*, London: Macmillan.

Porter, M. and Fuller, K. (1986), 'Coalitions and corporate strategies', in M. Porter (ed.), *Competition in Global Industries*, Boston: Harvard Business School Press.

Posner, M. (1961), 'International trade and technical change', *Oxford Economic Papers*, **13**, 323–41.

Prigogine, I. (1976), 'Order through fluctuations in self-organisation and social system', in E. Jantsch and C.H. Waddington, *Evolution and Consciousness: Human Systems in Transition*, New York: Addison Wesley.

Prigogine, I. (1987), 'A new rationality?', in I. Prigogine and M. Sanglier (eds), *Laws of Nature and Human Conduct*, Brussels: GORDES.

Prigogine, I. and Stengers I. (1984), *Order out of Chaos*, London: Fontana.

Romer, P. (1987), 'Growth based on increasing returns due to specialization', *American Economic Review*, **77**, 56–62.

Romer, P. (1990), 'Endogenous technological change', *Journal of Political Economy*, **98**, S71–102.

Rosenberg, N. (1976), *Perspectives on Technology*, Cambridge: Cambridge University Press.

Rosenberg, N. (1982), *Inside the Black Box: Technology and Economics*. Cambridge: Cambridge University Press.

Rosseger, G. (1980), *The Economics of Production and Innovation: an Industrial Perspective*, Amsterdam: Elsevier.

Roughgarden, J. (1979), *Theory of Population Genetics and Evolutionary Ecology: an Introduction*, New York: Macmillan.

Sahal, D. (1981a), *Patterns of Technological Innovation*, Reading, Mass.: Addison Wesley.

Sahal, D. (1981b), 'Alternative conceptions of technology', *Research Policy*, **10**, 2–24.

Sahal, D. (1985), 'Foundations of technometrics', *Technological Forecasting and Social Change*, **27**, 1–37.

Salop, S.C. (1979), 'Monopolistic competition with outside goods', *Bell Journal of Economics*, **10**, 141–56.

Salter, W.E.G. (1962), *Productivity and Technical Change*, Cambridge: Cambridge University Press.

Saviotti, P.P. (1985), 'An approach to the measurement of technology based on the hedonic price method and on related methods', *Technological Forecasting and Social Change*, **27**, 309–34.

Saviotti, P.P. (1986), 'Systems theory and technological change', *Futures*, **18**, 773–86.

Saviotti, P.P. (1988a), 'A characteristics approach to technological evolution and competition', presented at the conference on 'Recent Trends in the Economics of Technological Change', Manchester, 21–22 March.

Saviotti, P.P. (1988b), 'Information, entropy and variety in technoeconomic development', *Research Policy*, **17**, 89–103.

Saviotti, P.P. (1991a), 'The role of variety in economic and technological development', in P.P. Saviotti and J.S. Metcalfe (eds.), *Evolutionary Theories of Economic and Technological Change: Present State and Future Prospects*, Reading: Harwood Publishers.

Saviotti, P.P. (1991b), 'Technological evolution, product characteristics, competition and variety', presented at the Colloquium Management of Technology, Paris, 27–28 May.

Saviotti, P.P. (1994a), 'Variety, economic and technological development', in Y. Shionoya and M. Perlman (eds), *Technology, Industries and Institutions: Studies in Schumpeterian Perspectives*, Ann Arbor: University of Michigan Press.

Saviotti, P.P. (1994b), 'Knowledge, information and organizational structures', presented at the 11th International Economic History Congress, Milan, 12–16 September.

Saviotti, P.P. and Bowman A. (1984), 'Indicators of output of technology', in M. Gibbons, P. Gummett and B.M. Udgaonkar (eds), *Science and Technology Policy in the 1980s and Beyond*, London: Longman.

Saviotti, P.P., Coombs, R.W., Gibbons, M. and Stubbs, P.C. (1980), *Technology and Competitiveness in the Tractor Industry,* Manchester: Manchester University PREST.

Saviotti, P.P. and Mani, G.S. (1993), 'A model of technological evolution based on replicator dynamics', presented at the conference 'New Developments in Technology Studies: Evolutionary Economics and Chaos Theory', Amsterdam, 6–8 May.

Saviotti, P.P. and Mani, G.S. (1994), 'Technological evolution, self-organization and knowledge,' presented at the 1994 EAEPE conference 'Challenges to Institutional and Evolutionary Economic Theory: Growth, Uncertainty and Change', 27–29 October.

Saviotti, P.P. and Mani, G.S. (1995), 'Competition, variety and technological evolution: a replicator dynamics model', *Journal of Evolutionary Economics.*

Saviotti, P.P. and Metcalfe, J.S. (1984), 'A theoretical approach to the construction of technological output indicators', *Research Policy,* **13**, 141–51.

Saviotti, P.P. and Metcalfe, J.S. (eds) (1991), *Evolutionary Theories of Economic and Technological Change: Present State and Future Prospects*, Reading: Harwood Publishers.

Saviotti, P. and Trickett, A. (1992), 'The evolution of helicopter technology, 1940–1986', *Economics of Innovation and New Technology,* **2**, 111–30.

Schmookler, J. (1966), *Invention and Economic Growth*, Cambridge, Mass.: Harvard University Press.

Schumpeter, J. (1912), *The Theory of Economic Development*, english translation (1934), Cambridge, Mass.: Harvard University Press.

Schumpeter, J. (1942), *Capitalism, Socialism and Democracy*, (5th ed., 1976), London: George Allen and Unwin.

Shannon, C.E. and Weaver, W. (1949), *The Mathematical Theory of Communication*, Urbana: University of Illinois Press.

Silverberg, G. (1987), 'Technical progress, capital accumulation and effective demand: a self-organization model', in D. Batten and J. Casti (eds), *Economic Evolution and Structural Adjustment*, Berlin, Heidelberg, New York, Tokyo: Springer Verlag.

Silverberg, G. (1988), 'Modelling economic dynamics and technical change', in G. Dosi *et al.*, *Technical Change and Economic Theory*, London: Pinter.

Silverberg, J., Dosi, G. and Orsenigo, L. (1988), 'Innovation, diversity and diffusion: a self-organisation model', *Economic Journal*, **98**, 1032–54.

Simon, H.A. (1947), *Administrative Behavior*, New York: Free Press.

Simon, H.A. (1957), *Models of Man: Social and Rational*, New York: Wiley.

Simon, H.A. (1962), 'The architecture of complexity', *Proceedings of the American Philosophical Society*, **106**, 467–82; reprinted in H.A. Simon, *The Sciences of the Artificial*, Cambridge, Mass.: MIT Press (1981).

Simon, H.A. (1981), 'The natural and the artificial world', in H.A. Simon, *The Sciences of the Artificial*, Cambridge, Mass.: MIT Press (originally published 1969).

Smith, A. (1982), *The Wealth of Nations*, Harmondsworth: Penguin Books, (originally published 1776).

Sober, E. (1984), 'Holism, individualism and the units of selection', in E. Sober (ed.), *Conceptual Issues in Evolutionary Biology: An Anthology*, Cambridge, Mass.: MIT Press.

Solow, R.M. (1956), 'A contribution to the theory of economic growth', *Quarterly Journal of Economics*, **70**, 65–94.

Solow, R.M. (1957), 'Technical change and the aggregate production function', *Review of Economics and Statistics*, **39**, 312–20.

Spencer, H. (1892), *Essays Scientific, Political and Speculative*, New York: Appleton.

Stigler, G.J. (1951), 'The division of labor is limited by the extent of the market', *Journal of Political Economy*, **49**, 185–93.

Stigler, G.J. (1961), 'The economics of information', *Journal of Political Economy*, **69**, 213–25; reprinted in D.M. Lamberton (ed.), *Economics of Information and Knowledge*, Harmondsworth: Penguin Books (1971).

Stiglitz, J. (1987), 'Learning to learn, localized learning and technological progress', in P. Dasgupta and P. Stoneman (eds), *Economic Policy and Technological Performance*, Cambridge: Cambridge University Press.

Stoneman, P. (1983), *The Economic Analysis of Technological Change*, Oxford: Oxford University Press.

Teece, D. (1981), 'The market for know-how and the efficient international transfer of technology', *Annals of the American Academy of Political and Social Science*, **458**, 81–96.

Teece, D. (1986), 'Profiting from technological innovation: implications for international collaboration, licensing and public policy', *Research Policy*, **15**, 285–305.

Teece, D. (1988), 'Technological change and the nature of the firm', in G. Dosi *et al.*, *Technical Change and Economic Theory*, London: Pinter.

Teece, D.J., Pisano, G. and Shuen, A. (1990), 'Firm capabilities, resources and the concept of strategy', CCC working paper no. 90–8, Center for Research in Management, University of California, Berkeley.

Teece, D., Rumelt, R., Dosi, G. and Winter, S. (1992), 'Understanding corporate coherence: theory and evidence', CCC working paper, Center for Research in Management, University of California, Berkeley.

Terreberry, S. (1968), 'The evolution of organizational environments', *Administrative Science Quarterly*, **12**, 590–613.

Tushman, M.L. and Anderson, P. (1986), 'Technological discontinuities and organizational environments', *Administrative Science Quarterly*, **31**, 439–65.

Tushman, M.L. and Anderson, P. (1990), 'Technological discontinuities and dominant designs: a cyclical model of technological change', *Administrative Science Quarterly*, **35**, 604–33.

Tylecote, A. (1993), *The Long Wave in the World Economy*, London: Routledge.

Veblen, T. (1898), 'Why is economics not an evolutionary science?', *Quarterly Journal of Economics*, **12**, 374–97.

Veblen T. (1919), *The Place of Science in Modern Civilization and Other Essays*, New York: Huebsch; reprintedwith a new introduction by W.J. Samuels, New Brunswick Transaction (1990).

Vernon, R. (1966), 'International development and international trade in the product cycle', *Quarterly Journal of Economics*, **80**, 190–207.

Von Bertalanffy, L. (1950), 'The theory of open systems in physics and biology', *Science*, 111, 23–9; reprinted in F.E. Emery (ed.), *Systems Thinking*, Harmondsworth: Penguin Books (1969).

Von Hippel, E. (1976), 'The dominant role of users in the scientific instrument innovation process', *Research Policy*, 5.

Walsh, V. (1984), 'Invention and innovation in the chemical industry: demand-pull or discovery push', *Research Policy*, **13**, 211–34.

Weitzman, M.L. (1992), 'On diversity', *Quarterly Journal of Economics*, **107**, 363–405.

Wilks, S. and Wright, M. (eds) (1987), *Comparative Government–Industry Relations*, Oxford: Oxford University Press.

Williamson, O.E. (1975), *Markets and Hierarchies: Analysis and Anti-trust Implications*, New York: Free Press.

Williamson, O.E. (1979), 'Transaction cost economics: the governance of contractual relations', *Journal of Law and Economics*, **22**, 233–61.

Williamson, O.E. (1981), 'The modern corporation: origins, evolution and attributes', *Journal of Economic Literature*, **19**, 1537–68.

Williamson, O.E. (1985), *The Economic Institutions of Capitalism*, New York: Free Press.

Woodward, J. (1965), *Industrial Organization: Theory and Practice*, Oxford: Oxford University Press.

Wright, M. (1988), 'Policy community, policy network and comparative industrial policies', *Political Studies*, **36**, 593–612.

Index